The Best of McSweeney's
Volume 2

The Best of McSweeney's Volume 2

EDITED BY DAVE EGGERS

HAMISH HAMILTON
an imprint of
PENGUIN BOOKS

HAMISH HAMILTON

Published by the Penguin Group
Penguin Books Ltd, 80 Strand, London WC2R 0RL, England
Penguin Group (USA) Inc., 375 Hudson Street, New York, New York 10014, USA
Penguin Group (Canada), 90 Eglinton Avenue East, Suite 700, Toronto, Ontario, Canada M4P 2Y3
(a division of Pearson Penguin Canada Inc.)
Penguin Ireland, 25 St Stephen's Green, Dublin 2, Ireland (a division of Penguin Books Ltd)
Penguin Group (Australia), 250 Camberwell Road, Camberwell, Victoria 3124, Australia
(a division of Pearson Australia Group Pty Ltd)
Penguin Books India Pvt Ltd, 11 Community Centre, Panchsheel Park, New Delhi – 110 017, India
Penguin Group (NZ), cnr Airborne and Rosedale Roads, Albany, Auckland 1310, New Zealand
(a division of Pearson New Zealand Ltd)
Penguin Books (South Africa) (Pty) Ltd, 24 Sturdee Avenue, Rosebank 2196, South Africa

Penguin Books Ltd, Registered Offices: 80 Strand, London WC2R 0RL, England

www.penguin.com

This collection first published 2005
1

Collection copyright © McSweeney's Publishing, 2005
Introduction copyright © Dave Eggers, 2005
pp. 366–70 constitute an extension of this copyright page

The moral right of the author has been asserted

Set in 12/14.75 pt Monotype Garamond 3
Typeset by Rowland Phototypesetting Ltd, Bury St Edmunds, Suffolk
Printed in Great Britain by Clays Ltd, St Ives plc

A CIP catalogue record for this book is available from the British Library

ISBN 0-241-14246-6

Contents

Contents

Introduction

The pieces in this collection were published in McSweeney's over the course of about five years, 1998–2003. They have almost nothing in common.

You, reader-man or reader-woman, will like only some of these stories; this is the nature of a collection of disparate works spanning many genres and styles. If you or your friends are surprised that you or they don't like every single thing in this collection, you are probably, in your life and travels, often surprised, and are perhaps disappointed more than the average person. I wish you well.

This introduction is being written long, long after it was requested by its British publisher. The delay is due to the fact that only four introductions, in the history of the written word, have had any merit. They are, most often, the perfect intersection of the boring and the bored, the long-winded and the impatient.

Thus, in lieu of further explaining what needs no explanation – a collection of pieces inclusive of fiction, satire, essay and bog-men-writing – I offer the following:

1. A drawing I did of a horse and a hose.

2. A brief discussion of the work of director Bill Forsyth, who is much beloved by many of us over here, and whose work is missed and wondered about.

3. A drawing of half a polar bear standing next to a ghost.

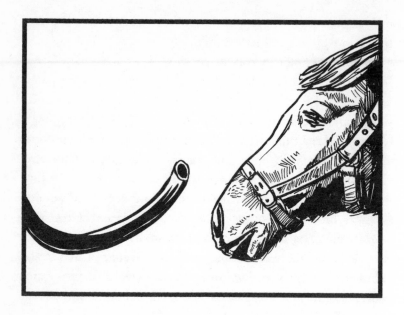

4. One salient point about literary magazines in the United States.

5. A drawing of a ghost talking to some wood.

Man, I miss Bill Forsyth. As I write this, I don't know if he's alive or dead, but I miss seeing new movies by that man. The first of his I saw was *Local Hero*, and I have no idea why I was originally attracted to it. I think, though I'm making this up, that I had been invited to the home of an attractive widow, and when I arrived, after she took off my shirt and gave me some lemonade, she asked me to sit with her and watch *Local Hero*.

The movie starred Peter Reigert, who had disappeared from most people's thoughts after playing one of the fraternity guys in *Animal House*. He was in *Local Hero*, as was Burt Lancaster, who was getting on in years at that point, and made few movies thereafter. The rest of the cast were unknown to people living in Chicago and its suburbs.

The movie's plot: a Porsche-driving oil executive (Reigert) from urban Texas is sent to the Scottish coast; his company wants to drill for oil there. He's supposed to buy the coastline, buy out the residents, and clear the land for a refinery and whatever else is required for oil-getting. But when Reigert arrives at this village, he falls in love with the coast, with the people, a barmaid, and the whole place generally. In the hands of less deft film-makers, this kind of movie would descend into that horrible Hollywood trope, wherein the hard-driving businessperson discovers what's really important, i.e. walks on the beach, trees, animals and high-fiber cereal. But Forsyth makes something lyrical and real from this. He had the touch of a short-story writer, one who knows how to

move a story along even while using only a poet's delicate tools.

Do I have any idea what I'm saying? Probably not. The point is I don't know what Mr Forsyth is up to, and if anyone knows, please write to: Search for Forsyth, c/o McSweeney's, 826 Valencia Street, San Francisco, CA 94110 USA. If he has passed on from this world, and his friends and relatives are reading this, please accept my condolences. He was a great man. He also made *Gregory's Girl*, which was perfect, as was *Comfort and Joy*, which was about a war between makers of ice-cream. Also very good.

If Forsyth is alive and working, I, representing all Americans alive and dead, salute him, and his friends and relatives. May none of you ever have to eat hummus.

Actually: There is something to be said, of a serious nature and involving literary magazines and short stories. I have recently been informed that there are very few literary journals in England. There are plenty of regular newsstand magazines, my source tells me, but there are deadly few non-commercial journals of the kind that include fiction and long-form non-fiction and poetry and the like. There is the great *Granta*, and then there are not so many more, my source says. In the United States, you may know, we have at least 1,250 such journals. They are all paperback-journal-looking books that try to appear on a quarterly schedule. They are published, for the most part, through the English or Creative Writing departments of the 24,000 or so colleges we have in America.

I was exaggerating about the number of journals over here. But I wasn't actually overreaching by much. We have enough of these journals that many people in the Appalachias line their homes with them, and in other parts of the country, they are used to create landmasses on which playgrounds and highways are built.

Each of these journals has a readership, and while this readership usually falls between 100 readers and 50,000 readers, the average readership of one of these journals is about 1,500. This is small by some standards, but either way is far more persons than you could fit in your home. And any number of readers who would not fit in your home constitutes, we at McSweeney's think, a good number of readers. So these journals continue, and, most believe, thrive. Each small magazine has its small-town feel, and a small town's worth of readers. And each of these becomes the perfect incubator for new voices; herein writers can experiment with style and voice and form, using the short-fiction form, which is forgiving of reader and writer alike.

But these journals start and end with a concentration on the short story, and of course few people in the world, outside our own country, give a rip about the short story. This is an endless source of fascination for us here in the United States: the seemingly unmitigated indifference the rest of the world feels for short fiction. Even in France, where they like their novels short, they do not like their stories that way. This seems a wilful contradiction meant to confuse us. Not that confusing us is particularly difficult, especially in these last five years.

How to get England and then Europe generally to love the short story, and thus foster many literary journals and new writers? Should we use some sort of threat of force? This is the main idea we export here in the United States, and we are thinking it will work in this instance as well as all others. Thus here it is: you must love the short story, and you must start your own many literary quarterlies, lest we bomb you and your people, and invade your shores, and send mercenaries to fight your insurgents. To our friends we will call it a crusade. To the rest of the world we will call it liberation.

THE BEST OF McSWEENEY'S
Volume 2

The Ceiling

KEVIN BROCKMEIER

There was a sky that day, sun-rich and open and blue. A raft of silver clouds was floating along the horizon, and robins and sparrows were calling from the trees. It was my son Joshua's seventh birthday and we were celebrating in our back yard. He and the children were playing on the swing set, and Melissa and I were sitting on the deck with the parents. Earlier that afternoon, a balloon and gondola had risen from the field at the end of our block, sailing past us with an exhalation of fire. Joshua told his friends that he knew the pilot. 'His name is Mister Clifton,' he said, as they tilted their heads back and slowly revolved in place. 'I met him at the park last year. He took me into the air with him and let me drop a soccer ball into a swimming pool. We almost hit a helicopter. He told me he'd come by on my birthday.' Joshua shielded his eyes against the sun. 'Did you see him wave?' he asked. 'He just waved at me.'

This was a story.

The balloon drifted lazily away, turning to expose each delta and crease of its fabric, and we listened to the children resuming their play. Mitch Nauman slipped his sunglasses into his shirt pocket. 'Ever notice how kids their age will handle a toy?' he said. Mitch was our next-door neighbor. He was the single father of Bobby Nauman, Joshua's strange best friend. His other best friend, Chris Boschetti, came from a family of

3

cosmetics executives. My wife had taken to calling them 'Rich and Strange.'

Mitch pinched the front of his shirt between his fingers and fanned himself with it. 'The actual function of the toy is like some sort of obstacle,' he said. 'They'll dream up a new use for everything in the world.'

I looked across the yard at the swing set: Joshua was trying to shinny up one of the A-poles; Taylor Tugwell and Sam Yoo were standing on the teeter swing; Adam Smithee was tossing fistfuls of pebbles onto the slide and watching them rattle to the ground.

My wife tipped one of her sandals onto the grass with the ball of her foot. 'Playing as you should isn't Fun,' she said: 'it's Design.' She parted her toes around the front leg of Mitch's lawn chair. He leaned back into the sunlight, and her calf muscles tautened.

My son was something of a disciple of flying things. On his bedroom wall were posters of fighter planes and wild birds. A model of a helicopter was chandeliered to his ceiling. His birthday cake, which sat before me on the picnic table, was decorated with a picture of a rocket ship – a silver white missile with discharging thrusters. I had been hoping that the baker would place a few stars in the frosting as well (the cake in the catalog was dotted with yellow candy sequins), but when I opened the box I found that they were missing. So this is what I did: as Joshua stood beneath the swing set, fishing for something in his pocket, I planted his birthday candles deep in the cake. I pushed them in until each wick was surrounded by only a shallow bracelet of wax. Then I called the children over from the swing set. They came tearing up divots in the grass.

We sang happy birthday as I held a match to the candles. Joshua closed his eyes.

'Blow out the stars,' I said, and his cheeks rounded with air.

That night, after the last of the children had gone home, my wife and I sat outside drinking, each of us wrapped in a separate silence. The city lights were burning, and Joshua was sleeping in his room. A nightjar gave one long trill after another from somewhere above us.

Melissa added an ice cube to her glass, shaking it against the others until it whistled and cracked. I watched a strand of cloud break apart in the sky. The moon that night was bright and full, but after a while it began to seem damaged to me, marked by some small inaccuracy. It took me a moment to realize why this was: against its blank white surface was a square of perfect darkness. The square was without blemish or flaw, no larger than a child's tooth, and I could not tell whether it rested on the moon itself or hovered above it like a cloud. It looked as if a window had been opened clean through the floor of the rock, presenting to view a stretch of empty space. I had never seen such a thing before.

'What is that?' I said.

Melissa made a sudden noise, a deep, defeated little oh.

'My life is a mess,' she said.

Within a week, the object in the night sky had grown perceptibly larger. It would appear at sunset, when the air was dimming to purple, as a faint granular blur, a certain filminess at the high point of the sky, and would remain there through the night. It blotted out the light of passing stars and seemed to travel across the face of the moon, but it did not move. The people of my town were uncertain as to whether the object was spreading or approaching – we could see only that it was getting bigger – and this matter gave rise to much speculation. Gleason the butcher insisted that it wasn't there at all, that it was only an illusion. 'It all has to do with the satellites,' he said. 'They're bending the light from that place like a lens. It just looks like something's there.' But though his manner was relaxed and he spoke with conviction, he would not look up from his cutting board.

The object was not yet visible during the day, but we could feel it above us as we woke to the sunlight each morning: there was a tension and strain to the air, a shift in its customary balance. When we stepped from our houses to go to work, it was as if we were walking through a new sort of gravity, harder and stronger, not so yielding.

As for Melissa, she spent several weeks pacing the house from room to room. I watched her fall into a deep abstraction. She had cried into her pillow the night of Joshua's birthday, shrinking away from me beneath the blankets. 'I just need to sleep,' she said, as I sat above her and rested my hand on her side. 'Please. Lie down. Stop hovering.' I soaked a washcloth for her in the cold water of the bathroom sink, folding it into quarters and leaving it on her night stand in a porcelain bowl.

The next morning, when I found her in the kitchen, she was gathering a coffee filter into a little wet sachet. 'Are you feeling better?' I asked.

'I'm fine.' She pressed the foot lever of the trash can, and its lid popped open with a rustle of plastic.

'Is it Joshua?'

Melissa stopped short, holding the pouch of coffee in her outstretched hand. 'What's wrong with Joshua?' she said. There was a note of concern in her voice.

'He's seven now,' I told her. When she didn't respond, I continued with, 'You don't look a day older than when we met, honey. You know that, don't you?'

She gave a puff of air through her nose – this was a laugh, but I couldn't tell what she meant to express by it, bitterness or judgment or some kind of easy cheer. 'It's not Joshua,' she said, and dumped the coffee into the trash can. 'But thanks all the same.'

It was the beginning of July before she began to ease back into the life of our family. By this time, the object in the sky was large enough to eclipse the full moon. Our friends insisted that they had never been able to see any change in my wife at all, that she had the same style of speaking, the same habits and twists and eccentricities as ever. This was, in a certain sense, true. I noticed the difference chiefly when we were alone together. After we had put Joshua to bed, we would sit with one another in the living room, and when I asked her a question, or when the telephone rang, there was always a certain brittleness to her, a hesitancy of manner that suggested she was hearing the world from across a divide. It was clear to me at such times that she had taken herself elsewhere, that she had constructed a shelter from the wood and clay and stone of her most intimate thoughts and stepped inside, shutting the door. The only question was whether the person I saw tinkering at the window was opening the latches or sealing the cracks.

One Saturday morning, Joshua asked me to take him to the library for a story reading. It was almost noon, and the sun was just beginning to darken at its zenith. Each day, the shadows of our bodies would shrink toward us from the west, vanish briefly in the midday soot, and stretch away into the east, falling off the edge of the world. I wondered sometimes if I would ever see my reflection pooled at my feet again. 'Can Bobby come, too?' Joshua asked as I tightened my shoes.

I nodded, pulling the laces up in a series of butterfly loops. 'Why don't you run over and get him?' I said, and he sprinted off down the hallway.

Melissa was sitting on the front porch steps, and I knelt down beside her as I left. 'I'm taking the boys into town,' I said. I kissed her cheek and rubbed the base of her neck, felt the cirrus curls of hair there moving back and forth through my fingers.

'Shh.' She held a hand out to silence me. 'Listen.'

The insects had begun to sing, the birds to fall quiet. The air gradually became filled with a peaceful chirring noise.

'What are we listening for?' I whispered.

Melissa bowed her head for a moment, as if she were trying to keep count of something. Then she looked up at me. In answer, and with a sort of weariness about her, she spread her arms open to the world.

Before I stood to leave, she asked me a question: 'We're not all that much alike, are we?' she said.

The plaza outside the library was paved with red brick. Dogwood trees were planted in hollows along the perimeter, and benches of distressed metal stood here and there on concrete pads. A member of a local guerrilla theater troupe was delivering a recitation from beneath a streetlamp; she sat behind a wooden desk, her hands folded one atop the other, and spoke as if into a camera. 'Where did this object come from?' she said. 'What is it, and when will it stop its descent? How did we find ourselves in this place? Where do we go from here? Scientists are baffled. In an interview with this station, Dr. Stephen Mandruzzato, head of the prestigious Horton

Institute of Astronomical Studies, had this to say: "We don't know. We don't know. We just don't know."' I led Joshua and Bobby Nauman through the heavy dark glass doors of the library, and we took our seats in the Children's Reading Room. The tables were set low to the ground so that my legs pressed flat against the underside, and the air carried that peculiar, sweetened-milk smell of public libraries and elementary schools. Bobby Nauman began to play the Where Am I? game with Joshua. 'Where am I?' he would ask, and then he'd warm-and-cold Joshua around the room until Joshua had found him. First he was in a potted plant, then on my shirt collar, then beneath the baffles of an air vent.

After a time, the man who was to read to us moved into place. He said hello to the children, coughed his throat clear, and opened his book to the title page: 'Chicken Little,' he began.

As he read, the sky grew bright with afternoon. The sun came through the windows in a sheet of fire.

Joshua started the second grade in September. His new teacher mailed us a list of necessary school supplies, which we purchased the week before classes began – pencils and a utility box, glue and facial tissues, a ruler and a notebook and a tray of watercolor paints. On his first day, Melissa shot a photograph of Joshua waving to her from the front door, his backpack wreathed over his shoulder and a lunch sack in his right hand. He stood in the flash of hard white light, then kissed her good-bye and joined Rich and Strange in the car pool.

Autumn passed in its slow, sheltering way, and toward the end of November, Joshua's teacher asked the class to write a short essay describing a community of local animals. The paragraph Joshua wrote was captioned 'What Happened to the Birds.' We fastened it to the refrigerator with magnets.

There were many birds here before, but now there gone. Nobody knows where they went. I used to see them in the trees. I fed one at the zoo when I was litle. It was big. The birds went away when no one was looking. The trees are quiet now. They do not move.

All of this was true. As the object in the sky became visible during the daylight – and as, in the tide of several months, it descended over our town – the birds and migrating insects disappeared. I did not notice they were gone, though, nor the muteness with which the sun rose in the morning, nor the stillness of the grass and trees, until I read Joshua's essay.

The world at this time was full of confusion and misgiving and unforeseen changes of heart. One incident that I recall clearly took place in the Main Street Barber Shop on a cold winter Tuesday. I was sitting in a pneumatic chair while Wesson the barber trimmed my hair. A nylon gown was draped over my body to catch the cuttings, and I could smell the peppermint of Wesson's chewing gum. 'So how 'bout this weather?' he chuckled, working away at my crown.

Weather gags had been circulating through our offices and barrooms ever since the object – which was as smooth and reflective as obsidian glass, and which the newspapers had designated 'the ceiling' – had descended to the level of the cloud base. I gave my usual response, 'A little overcast today, wouldn't you say?' and Wesson barked an appreciative laugh.

Wesson was one of those men who had passed his days waiting for the rest of his life to come about. He busied himself with his work, never marrying, and doted on the children of his customers. 'Something's bound to happen soon,' he would often say at the end of a conversation, and there was a quickness to his eyes that demonstrated his implicit faith in the proposition. When his mother died, this faith seemed to abandon him. He went home each evening to the small house that they had shared, shuffling cards or paging through a magazine until he fell asleep. Though he never failed to laugh when a customer was at hand, the eyes he wore became empty and white, as if some essential fire in them had been spent. His enthusiasm began to seem like desperation. It was only a matter of time.

'How's the pretty lady?' he asked me.

I was watching him in the mirror, which was both parallel to and coextensive with a mirror on the opposite wall. 'She hasn't been feeling too well,' I said. 'But I think she's coming out of it.'

'Glad to hear it. Glad to hear it,' he said. 'And business at the hardware store?'

I told him that business was fine. I was on my lunch break.

The bell on the door handle gave a tink, and a current of cold air sent a little eddy of cuttings across the floor. A man we had never seen before leaned into the room. 'Have you seen my umbrella?' he said. 'I can't find my umbrella, have you seen it?' His voice was too loud – high and sharp, fluttery with worry – and his hands shook with a distinct tremor.

'Can't say that I have,' said Wesson. He smiled emptily, showing his teeth, and his fingers tensed around the back of my chair.

There was a sudden feeling of weightlessness to the room.

'You wouldn't tell me anyway, would you?' said the man. 'Jesus,' he said. 'You people.'

Then he took up the ashtray stand and slammed it against the window.

A cloud of gray cinders shot out around him, but the window merely shuddered in its frame. He let the stand fall to the floor and it rolled into a magazine rack. Ash drizzled to the ground. The man brushed a cigarette butt from his jacket. 'You people,' he said again, and he left through the open glass door.

As I walked home later that afternoon, the scent of barber-shop talcum blew from my skin in the winter wind. The plane of the ceiling was stretched across the firmament, covering my town from end to end, and I could see the lights of a thousand streetlamps caught like constellations in its smooth black polish. It occurred to me that if nothing were to change, if the ceiling were simply to hover where it was forever, we might come to forget that it was even there, charting for ourselves a new map of the night sky.

Mitch Nauman was leaving my house when I arrived. We passed on the lawn, and he held up Bobby's knapsack. 'He leaves this thing everywhere,' he said. 'Buses. Your house. The schoolroom. Sometimes I think I should tie it to his belt.' Then he cleared his throat. 'New haircut? I like it.'

'Yeah, it was getting a bit shaggy.'

He nodded and made a clicking noise with his tongue. 'See you next time,' he said, and he vanished through his front door, calling to Bobby to climb down from something.

By the time the object had fallen as low as the tree spires, we had noticed the acceleration in the wind. In the thin strip of space between the ceiling and the pavement, it narrowed and kindled and collected speed. We could hear it buffeting the walls of our houses at night, and it produced a constant low sigh in the darkness of movie halls. People emerging from their doorways could be seen to brace themselves against the charge and pressure of it. It was as if our entire town were an alley between tall buildings.

I decided one Sunday morning to visit my parents' gravesite: the cemetery in which they were buried would spread with knotgrass every spring, and it was necessary to tend their plot before the weeds grew too thick. The house was still peaceful as I showered and dressed, and I stepped as quietly as I could across the bath mat and the tile floor. I watched the water in the toilet bowl rise and fall as gusts of wind channeled their way through the pipes. Joshua and Melissa were asleep, and the morning sun flashed at the horizon and disappeared.

At the graveyard, a small boy was tossing a tennis ball into the air as his mother swept the dirt from a memorial tablet. He was trying to touch the ceiling with it, and with each successive throw he drew a bit closer, until, at the height of its climb, the ball jarred to one side before it dropped. The cemetery was otherwise empty, its monuments and trees the only material presence.

My parents' graves were clean and spare. With such scarce sunlight, the knotgrass had failed to blossom, and there was little tending for me to do. I combed the plot for leaves and stones and pulled the rose stems from the flower wells. I kneeled at the headstone they shared and unfastened a zipper of moss from it. Sitting there, I imagined for a moment that my parents were living together atop the ceiling: they were walking through a field of high yellow grass, beneath the sun and the sky and the tousled white clouds, and she was bending in her dress to examine a flower, and he was bending beside her, his hand on her waist, and they were unaware that the world beneath them was settling to the ground.

When I got home, Joshua was watching television on the living room sofa, eating a plump yellow doughnut from a paper towel. A dollop of jelly had fallen onto the back of his hand. 'Mom left to run an errand,' he said.

The television picture fluttered and curved for a moment, sending spits of rain across the screen, then it recrystallized. An aerial transmission tower had collapsed earlier that week – the first of many such fallings in our town – and the quality of our reception had been diminishing ever since.

'I had a dream last night,' Joshua said. 'I dreamed that I dropped my bear through one of the grates on the sidewalk.' He owned a worn-down cotton teddy bear, its seams looped with clear plastic stitches, that he had been given as a toddler. 'I tried to catch him, but I missed. Then I lay down on the ground and stretched out my arm for him. I was reaching through the grate, and when I looked beneath the sidewalk, I could see another part of the city. There were people moving around down there. There were cars and streets and bushes and lights. The sidewalk was some sort of bridge, and in my dream I thought, "Oh yeah. Now why didn't I remember that?" Then I tried to climb through to get my bear, but I couldn't lift the grate up.'

The morning weather forecaster was weeping on the television.

'Do you remember where this place was?' I asked.

'Yeah.'

'Maybe down by the bakery?' I had noticed Melissa's car parked there a few times, and I remembered a kid tossing pebbles into the grate.

'That's probably it.'

'Want to see if we can find it?'

Joshua pulled at the lobe of his ear for a second, staring into the middle distance. Then he shrugged his shoulders. 'Okay,' he decided.

I don't know what we expected to discover there. Perhaps I was simply seized by a whim – the desire to be spoken to, the wish to be instructed by a dream. When I was Joshua's age, I dreamed one night that I found a new door in my house, one that opened from my cellar onto the bright, aseptic aisles of a drugstore: I walked through it, and saw a flash of light, and found myself sitting up in bed. For several days after, I felt a quickening of possibility, like the touch of some other geography, whenever I passed by the cellar door. It was as if I'd opened my eyes to the true inward map of the world, projected according to our own beliefs and understandings.

On our way through the town center, Joshua and I waded past a cluster of people squinting into the horizon. There was a place between the post office and the library where the view to the west was occluded by neither hills nor buildings, and crowds often gathered there to watch the distant blue belt of the sky. We shouldered our way through and continued into town.

Joshua stopped outside the Kornblum Bakery, beside a trash basket and a newspaper carrel, where the light from two street-lamps lensed together on the ground. 'This is it,' he said, and made a gesture indicating the iron grate at our feet. Beneath it we could see the shallow basin of a drainage culvert. It was even and dry, and a few brittle leaves rested inside it.

'Well,' I said. There was nothing there. 'That's disappointing.'

'Life's disappointing,' said Joshua.

He was borrowing a phrase of his mother's, one that she had taken to using these last few months. Then, as if on cue, he glanced up and a light came into his eyes. 'Hey,' he said. 'There's Mom.'

Melissa was sitting behind the plate glass window of a restaurant on the opposite side of the street. I could see Mitch Nauman talking to her from across the table, his face soft and casual. Their hands were cupped together beside the pepper crib, and his shoes stood empty on the carpet. He was stroking her left leg with his right foot, its pad and arch curved around her calf. The image was as clear and exact as a melody.

I took Joshua by the shoulders. 'What I want you to do,' I said, 'is knock on Mom's window. When she looks up, I want you to wave.'

And he did exactly that – trotting across the asphalt, tapping a few times on the glass, and waving when Melissa started in her chair. Mitch Nauman let his foot fall to the carpet. Melissa found Joshua through the window. She crooked her head and gave him a tentative little flutter of her fingers. Then she met my eyes. Her hand stilled in the air. Her face seemed to fill suddenly with movement, then just as suddenly to empty – it reminded me of nothing so much as a flock of birds scattering from a lawn. I felt a kick of pain in my chest and called to Joshua from across the street. 'Come on, sport,' I said. 'Let's go home.'

It was not long after – early the next morning, before we awoke – that the town water tower collapsed, blasting a river of fresh water down our empty streets. Hankins the grocer, who had witnessed the event, gathered an audience that day to his lunch booth in the coffee shop: 'I was driving past the tower when it happened,' he said. 'Heading in early to work. First I heard a creaking noise, and then I saw the leg posts buckling. Wham!' – he smacked the table with his palms – 'So much water! It surged into the side of my car, and I lost control of the wheel. The stream carried me right down the road. I felt like a tiny paper boat.' He smiled and held up a finger, then pressed it to the side of a half-empty soda can, tipping it gingerly onto its side. Coca-Cola washed across the table with a hiss of carbonation. We hopped from our seats to avoid the spill.

The rest of the town seemed to follow in a matter of days, falling to the ground beneath the weight of the ceiling. Billboards and streetlamps, chimneys and statues. Church steeples, derricks, and telephone poles. Klaxon rods and restaurant signs. Apartment buildings and energy pylons. Trees released a steady sprinkle of leaves and pine cones, then came timbering to the earth – those that were broad and healthy cleaving straight down the heartwood, those that were thin and pliant bending until they cracked. Maintenance workers installed panels of light along the sidewalk, routing the electricity through underground cables. The ceiling itself proved unassailable. It bruised fists and knuckles. It stripped the teeth from power saws. It broke drill bits. It extinguished flames. One afternoon the television antenna tumbled from my rooftop, landing on the hedges in a zigzag of wire. A chunk of plaster fell across the kitchen table as I was eating dinner that night. I heard a board split in the living room wall the next morning, and then another in the hallway, and then another in the bedroom. It sounded like gunshots detonating in a closed room. Melissa and Joshua were already waiting on the front lawn when I got there. A boy was standing on a heap of rubble across the street playing Atlas, his upraked shoulders supporting the world. A man on a stepladder was pasting a sign to the ceiling: Shop at Carson's. Melissa pulled her jacket tighter. Joshua took my sleeve. A trough spread open beneath the shingles of our roof, and we watched our house collapse into a mass of brick and mortar.

I was lying on the ground, a tree root pressing into the small of my back, and I shifted slightly to the side. Melissa was lying beside me, and Mitch Nauman beside her. Joshua and Bobby, who had spent much of the day crawling aimlessly about the yard, were asleep now at our feet. The ceiling was no higher than a coffee table, and I could see each pore of my skin reflected in its surface. Above the keening of the wind there was a tiny edge of sound – the hum of the sidewalk lights, steady, electric, and warm.

'Do you ever get the feeling that you're supposed to be someplace else?' said Melissa. She paused for a moment, perfectly still. 'It's a kind of sudden dread,' she said.

Her voice seemed to hover in the air for a moment.

I had been observing my breath for the last few hours on the polished undersurface of the ceiling: every time I exhaled, a mushroom-shaped fog would cover my reflection, and I found that I could control the size of this fog by adjusting the force and the speed of my breathing. When Melissa asked her question, the first I had heard from her in many days, I gave a sudden puff of air through my nose and two icicle-shaped blossoms appeared. Mitch Nauman whispered something into her ear, but his voice was no more than a murmur, and I could not make out the words. In a surge of emotion that I barely recognized, some strange combination of rivalry and adoration,

I took her hand in my own and squeezed it. When nothing happened, I squeezed it again. I brought it to my chest, and I brought it to my mouth, and I kissed it and kneaded it and held it tight.

I was waiting to feel her return my touch, and I felt at that moment, felt with all my heart, that I could wait the whole life of the world for such a thing, until the earth and the sky met and locked and the distance between them closed for ever.

Civilization

RYAN BOUDINOT

When I turned eighteen I was among the kids who received notice that it was time to make some sacrifices and fulfill our duties as Americans. My family had been receiving letters from the government since we'd registered as a nuclear unit. We had learned to discard the notes asking us to watch certain shows, skim the flyers with health and hygiene tips, and set aside the forms having to do with money or the variety of multiple-choice quizzes that gauge our happiness. I know that those of you living in less regulated earlier eras are probably raising your freedom-loving eyebrows at the idea of the government telling you what to do. But grant me the benefit of the doubt, because the time in which I reside is infinitely more complicated yet more peaceful than yours, as anyone like my grandparents, who straddled the ages, can confirm.

'Those were some hella shitty times,' my grandfather says from his vibrating barcalounger at The Home.

'Fer sure,' says my grandmother.

I'm a profiled procrastinator, and knew I had two months before I had to report to my Duty Manager to perform the terms of my duty. I tried to pretend that the remainder of my senior year was unburdened by what I had been asked to do. I imagined that the texture of my daily existence – hanging out with friends, eating bad-for-me food, petting heavy with a girl in the backseat of my dad's Buick – was the template from which everyone's life took cues. Yeah, but I had this 'thing' hanging over me, this immense, democratic responsibility. I tried to ignore my looming duty by pouring stolen porn-rock and Coca-Cola Classic Classic ('The cocaine is back!!!') into my head. But no matter which distraction technique I attempted, I could not escape the malformed, rotting mass of fear sitting on my chest every time I remembered that the USA had asked me to murder my parents.

Because I liked them well enough. They'd given me some great presents over the years, made me some fine meals. And while I didn't feel ready to perform what was expected of me, they none the less provided the same unwavering support they always had, like when I wrestled freestyle a whole season and never won a single match.

My dad, short, wearing a tie, by way of description, offered me a beer and made some noises about personal responsibility. My mom, who unlike my dad had been called to duty back in the day, said it was really a quick procedure, that I'd have my choice of instruments, and that she'd try not to make too much noise. Then we sat down as a family to watch the Homeless People Channel, and seeing those guys pushing their shopping carts around really made me feel like I had a lot of resources – natural and otherwise – to be thankful for.

My friends, of whom none had yet received duty papers, intensified my nervousness with stories of kids who'd only half-killed their folks, who'd had to chase them down stair-wells, hunt them in cornfields, even deal with their moms and dads fighting back. (Both my parents had assured me they wouldn't struggle.) Or the stories about brothers and sisters of duty-bound kids who'd strangled their siblings in the night to spare their folks. Luckily I was an only child, and one of the benefits of performing my duty was a paid-in-full scholarship to the college or university of my choice. I wasn't going to blow it like the stupid kids who signed up for Harvard and dropped out during the first semester, thereby losing their free ride.

I already had my eye on a little East Coast college no one had ever heard of that had a fantastic Egyptology program. Call me weird, but I've always had a thing for mummies and pyramids, I guess.

At school, my teachers let me slack that semester, aware of the enormous responsibility weighing so very hippo-like on my formative young mind.

I openly smoked the cheeb in the back of class and they didn't even make me drop Western Civ and take Rehab or Home Ec instead. You could get away with shit like that at my high school when you were assigned the task of preserving American democracy. After school one day I went to pick out caskets with my folks, and even though I would be tapping into my own grieving-stipend to foot the bill, I let them choose any style they wanted.

'Are you positive? We really shouldn't spend so much,' my mom said.

I could tell she had her eye on the 'Freedom through Strength' model, the curly maple one with the engraving of an American eagle clutching a bouquet of nuclear missiles in one talon and an Osama bin Laden head in the other. My dad picked the classic American flag model that plays the song of your choice when opened and 'Taps' when closed, even though he was never in the service. My dad told the casket coordinator that he wanted it to play the patriotic hit song written by the software band Mugwump 2.0. While I usually clashed with my dad over our music tastes, that song, 'Lightning Will Strike Our Enemies,' had been a real cross-generational hit and had even kicked the hypothetical Francis Scott Key's ass in the reality show National Anthem Smackdown. Afterward, we went out to dinner at this Italian-themed restaurant called Il Italiano and talked about my future plans, but really the only thing in my head was a loop of the following words: gun, knife, poison, blunt instrument, gun, knife, poison, blunt instrument. On top of that – Kee-rist! – I still hadn't taken the frickin SATs. Even though they were a formality at this point, I still had promised my parents to shoot for at least an 1100. To make myself feel better, I kept reminding myself they'd be dead when I got the results in the mail.

Our waitress, Pam, came by with the salad and breadsticks.

'Who wants pepper?' she said, bearing her mill. 'Just tell me when.'

None of us were stepping up to the responsibility of being the pepper when-sayer, so Pam kept cranking over the mound of iceberg, olives and pepperoncinis.

'Whoa. You folks must-a really like-a the peppa!'

'Enough,' my dad said, raising his hand. For a second I allowed myself to believe he was referring to this me-killing-them business.

'Fantastico,' Pam said. 'We have two specials tonight, a pesto radiatore with grilled salmon fillet and a raquetella with creamy Gorgonzola sauce and peas. Now, I don't expect you to know all these fancy Italian pasta names, so let me tell you that raquetella are little tennis racket shapes. The peas are supposed to be like the tennis balls. Can I get you started with some artichoke-spinach dip or ranch cheesy bread?'

'I don't care what we have,' I said.

My dad cleared his throat. 'Our son has been called upon to perform his duty for this great land of ours.'

'Oh shit,' I said, knowing what happened in these kinds of places when they learned you'd been served duty papers. And sure enough three minutes later the entire waitstaff of fifteen was crowded around our table clapping rhythmically and singing one of those dippy patriotic songs from the employee manual.

'This is bullshit!' I shouted, 'I don't want to kill you! I love you!'

'Please,' my mom said through lips stretched to the point of losing blood, 'We're in a restaurant.'

My father nodded to the restrooms and said, 'Go take a chill pill, Craig, and come back when you're ready to have a mature discussion about performing your duty.'

As I tearfully left the table I heard my father nervously chuckling, telling the assembled waitstaff that it was just some to-be-expected performance anxiety on my part. I was starting to see how seriously fucked my situation really was. My parents would never see things my way, because in their mind I was still just a kid. And if I didn't go through with the killings, the government would tax my family into poverty and I wouldn't get a chance to study Egyptology at the college of my choice.

The Il Italiano men's room had one of those urinals that played 'Flight of the Valkyries' when you peed into it, which I hated. Eating at Il Italiano over the years had conditioned me to race to the bathroom during one of my favorite scenes in that classic movie *Apocalypse Now Redux II*.

I popped one of my chill pills from its foil wrapper and

washed it down with warm water from the sink. After I fresh-
ened up I returned to the table, apologized, and had some
on-the-house house salad. My parents pretended my outburst
had never happened.

My parents had a lot of things to take care of before they died,
and their final weeks were crammed with meetings with the
title company, insurance agents, accountants, lawyers. In between all the meetings, though, they still managed to spend
quality time with me. One afternoon my mom was cool enough
to suggest that I skip fifth period and meet her for coffee. When
I arrived at the place, she was talking to two of her friends from
the State Lottery Commission, ladies who I suspected I could
have gotten in the sack had older chicks been my thing.

Catherine, the tall one whose nipples always showed through
her blouse and bra, ruffled my hair when I sat down at the
miniature table.

'Gloria, will you take a look at this young man?' Catherine
said. 'Just a couple–three years ago he was playing army men
in the conference room and now he's about to do the shit work
of making America proud.'

'Your mom and I were just talking about when we had to
perform the duty,' Gloria said. She was one of those cat-lady
types who is disappointed if visitors to her condo fail to com-
ment on the endearing wackyness of her Elvis shrine. 'I must
have bashed my pop over the head fifty times before the son
of a bitch gave up the ghost.'

'They gave you blunt instruments?' I said.

'Honey,' Gloria said, 'Back in the day we didn't have no
arsenic pills. We had to do things the hard way, isn't that
right, Sally?'

My mom looked down and smiled, as if she was embarrassed about how she'd shot my maternal grandparents. I got the sense she considered her duty easy compared to Gloria, and didn't want to appear too smug about it.

'Yeah, Mom, tell everyone how you offed Grandma and Grampa,' I said.

'It's not worth telling.'

'Oh sure it is,' Gloria said, 'Go on, Sally, your own son is old enough.'

'He sure is,' Catherine said, winking at me over her macchiato.

'It was easy,' my mom said. 'It's not that interesting. They gave me a choice of a Mach II machine pistol, a .44 Magnum, and a .38 Special. Since I was a girl they made all the plastic hardware pink with flowers on it.'

'Pathetic,' Catherine said.

'My duty officer told me the best bet was the .38, but I wanted to really do some damage, you know, just to show off. So I chose the .44.'

Chuckling, anticipating the punch line, Gloria said, 'Come on, that's not all.'

My mom sighed. 'Okay, sure, I was nervous. And in those days, let me just tell you, I know it's hard to believe, but I weighed a hundred pounds in the rain. Don't give me that look; I'm serious! So unfortunately I blanked out on all those shooting classes I'd taken to prepare for this very special day, because I must have locked my elbows and the thing just kicked and knocked me flat on my rear end.'

Catherine and Gloria howled, slapping the miniature table we were gathered around.

'So there I am, on my back, with a big bump on my head,

and it turns out I missed my dad by a mile. My mom is cussing up a storm, my duty officer is leaning over me asking how many fingers he's holding up, it was just a mess. In the end I went with the machine pistol and that was that.'

'Didn't you feel bad?' I asked.

'Well, sure, for a little while. But they gave me the pill.'

Gloria made a face. 'I heard in the early days they didn't give kids the pill. I can't imagine. Whatever you do, Craig, take the goddamn pill!'

'What's the pill?' I asked, worrying that I had missed mention of it in the brochure I'd been sent.

'The pill makes it all better,' Catherine said. 'It makes it impossible to feel like shit about what you just did. I feel funny saying this, but it's real Orwellian in a way.'

'You're thinking of Huxley,' Gloria said. '*Brave New World* was the one where they were always popping pills. Like that part when they all go to spring break and party with the Beatles.'

The three ladies laughed, and I felt as though I had stumbled into some foreign and primal feminine ritual. As they continued to talk, their voices faded away like they sometimes do on TV, when they want to indicate a character has just been slipped something in a drink.

Poison, shotgun, length of chain.

They abducted my parents while I slept, allowing them time to gather some personal effects and leave me a note on a Post-it on the kitchen island. 'Good luck, Craig! Don't let your nerves get to you!' read my father's blocky handwriting. I would have a day to contemplate my upcoming actions. I spent it like many teens who've been selected for duty, moping around the house, trying to chill out to the Sleeping Babies channel. My friends called to razz me because I'd been mentioned on the news and the anchorman had hilariously bungled the pronunciation of my last name. I attempted to will into being a series of events that would save my parents and me, a string of happenstance and luck that spiraled outward into a self-generating parallel reality. In my daydream my parents were rescued from their confinement by some kind of paramilitary freedom-fighter guys that in this reality only existed as contestants on reality shows. I left my house through the back door, jogged across the yard, climbed over the fence, and ran through the wheat field abutting our property, and this wheat field, instead of ending at Parkway Road with the Deli Mart that has the porno mags, extended uninterrupted across this grand continent, and while I ran, naked now in my imagination, a farmer on a tractor would occasionally tip his hat and call out, 'Way to go, son! You keep on a-runnin'!'

And it was maybe indicative of my own maturing process that I quickly pressed Pause on this fantasy and declared it stupid and infantile in my head.

The duty officer who arrived at my house in her midsized sedan looked not much older than me. Her name was Tisha and she smacked her gum as she wore a red, white, and blue tracksuit.

'All right,' Tisha said. 'Looks like we're ready. Are you totally psyched? I went through the procedure myself and can't tell you how much it has positively changed my life. Don't worry, you're going to do fine. I met your parents this morning at the center and can tell you they're really swell folks. They want you to do a good job. They'll be so proud of you up to the moment they die.'

As we pulled out of the driveway I declined Tisha's offer of Juicy Fruit.

'You read *1984*, right?' Tisha said, taking a free right. 'Ha! I know you did, I reviewed your school transcripts. Well anyway, I tell people who are maybe a little nervous just to think of that one part where Winston Smith kicks down the door of his neighbors and catches them smoking crack. Then the part when he turns to the hidden camera and says, "Time to unleash a lil' whoop-ass, don't you think, Big Bro?" and then he smokes those dirty hippies with his Glock! I know, you're going: like, what does this have to do with sending Mom and Pop to the boneyard? So what I'm saying is, you're going to have a real genuine American kind of moral authority real soon here, unleashing your own personal whoop-ass on your mom and dad for the sake of all our heterosexual liberties.'

The midsized sedan took a couple sharp turns and we passed the historic district with the office parks and brick-and-mortar schools, then the stadiums and the focus-group factories where people like my soon-to-be-retired parents worked. And the flaming sun was a chariot racing across the sky and I thought how incredible it would have been to be an Egyptian engineer shepherding gigantic blocks of limestone across the desert. How a guy with that kind of mindset would not be capable of comprehending such things as terrorists who hate us for having a movie-rating system that includes P for Penetration. We got to the Duty Center, which used to be a post office. They even had a faded poster for commemorative Marilyn Monroe and James Dean stamps in one of the windows. When I couldn't or maybe wouldn't get out of the sedan, two beefier-style duty officers named Mike and Otto extracted me. Inside, they handcuffed me to a waiting-room chair. There were three other kids sitting in the dusty semi-dark next to a table piled with old *Reader's Digests* with all the naughty parts censored with felt pen. We all looked nauseated and miserable, which struck me as ironic given that we were all recipients of free-ride scholarships. I read a little 'Humor in Uniform' to pass the time. After a few minutes a door opened and a kid appeared with his designated duty officer. The kid was my age, with blood spattered on his seriously grinning face. It was the kind of grin that looks fused in place, a grin accompanied by laughter generating in the back of the throat. As soon as the girl sitting beside me saw him she put her head between her knees and puked into a receptacle one of the duty officers had thoughtfully provided.

One by one the kids ahead of me were called back by their own personal duty officers, and one by one they returned about twenty minutes later clutching their college-admissions paperwork, weeping, shaking, or passed out in a wheelchair. I told myself I was just going to get it over with and keep thinking of the pyramids. Then my name was called and I followed Tisha, who now had a more serious demeanor, down a hall that seemed longer than the building we were in. At the end of the hall was a door that had been painted over many times, as if the room behind it had served many purposes over the years. Tisha opened the door on to a tiny, well-lit room where my parents sat back-to-back in foldout metal chairs, arms bound behind them. My mom's makeup was smeared down her cheeks and my dad's hair was ruffled. On a nearby table sat a fillet knife, a meat cleaver, and some kind of Oriental sword. Dammit. I'd been hoping I'd be one of those kids who lucked out and got a selection of poisons and a pair of syringes.

'You are about to perform an essential function of preserving

American democracy for generations to come,' Tisha said. 'I'll be out here in the hall if you need me. Just holler.'

Here we were, then, a family. My mom made a choking sound and her lips were quivering.

'Just get this over with, Craig,' my dad said.

'I don't want to do this,' I said.

'Do it!' my dad shouted, the same kind of shout he used when he was tired of reminding me to mow the lawn.

I approached the table and considered my weapons. 'The fillet knife is the sharpest,' my mom sobbed, 'but the blade looks flimsy.'

'If you want my honest opinion, I'd go with the sword,' my dad said.

'It's too heavy and dull,' my mom said.

'Craig can handle it. He'll just have to use both hands.'

'I think this is Craig's decision.'

'I'm not saying it isn't, honey. I do think, though, that the meat cleaver is out of the question.'

I selected the fillet knife and stood in front of my mother, and my admiration for her having performed this duty twenty-odd years ago grew.

'Just do it,' my mom whispered. I stabbed her in the chest. She gasped a deep, rattling breath. I took a step back and left the knife quivering, lodged between two ribs. She slowly looked down, her eyes ripped wide.

'Oh my God,' I said.

'You're not done . . .' my mom gasped.

'I can't!'

My mom scowled, blood sliding out the corners of her mouth. 'Craig, you pussy, finish the job.'

What followed, I guess, was just some sort of blacked-out

murderous rage. There was some missing footage and then I was sitting in a corner of the room, the three bloodied instruments lying on the floor, my folks slumped dead in their chairs.

After a while Tisha leaned down and offered me the pill and a glass of water. The pill was stamped with a picture of the president's face with a cartoon word-bubble containing the words 'Say No to Terror.'

'It'll make it impossible for you to feel remorse for this later on,' Tisha said. 'Trust me. Taking the pill is the most important part of the process. Not taking it will turn the rest of your life into a nightmare.'

Things turned out swell for me after fulfilling my duty, and I have to admit I'm a little embarrassed about how big a deal I made of it at the time. I write these recollections two years later in an encampment south of Cairo, where I am in charge of cleaning the equipment for a dig. The remains of a teeming city lie just beneath the shifting sands. The camels tonight are especially flatulent. An occasional fighter jet drags a contrail across the sky on its way to bomb countries that stubbornly refuse to let us help them achieve the American dream. I have watched a man lose his leg after falling off a train.

I have smoked hashish and found myself in bars speaking to German textile-plant owners trying to sell me their daughters. I have gazed upon the freaking Rosetta Stone. Digging through this barren landscape to uncover cities where real people once worked and raised families thrills me. I can't imagine going back to America. My life's true pleasures I have found in the remains of this lost, proud culture, in the solitude of their beautiful tombs.

The Kauders Case

ALEKSANDAR HEMON

1. Volens-Nolens

I met Isidora in college, at the University of Sarajevo, in 1985. We both transferred to the general literature department: she from philosophy, I from engineering. We met in the back of a Marxism class.. The Marxism professor had his hair dyed hell-black, and often spent time in mental institutions. He liked to pontificate about man's position in the universe: man was like an ant holding on to a straw in a Biblical flood, he said, and we were too young to even begin to comprehend it. Isidora and I, thus, bonded over tear-inducing boredom.

Isidora's father was a well-known chess analyst, good friends with Fischer, Kortchnoy, and Tal. He reported from world-championship matches, and wrote books about chess – the most famous one, an item in every chess-loving household, was a book for beginners. Sometimes when I visited Isidora, she would be helping her father with correcting the proofs. It was a tedious job of reading back transcripts of chess games to each other (K e-4, R d5; c8-b7; etc), so they would occasionally sing the games, as if performing in a chess musical. Isidora was a licensed chess judge, and she traveled the world with her father, attending chess tournaments. She would often come back with stories about the strange people she had met. Once, in London, she met a Russian immigrant named Vladimir, who told her that Kandinsky was merely a Red Army officer who ran a workshop of anonymous artists and then appropriated their paintings as his own, becoming the great Kandinsky. In any case, the world outside seemed to be a terribly interesting place.

We were bored in Sarajevo. It was hard not to be. We had ideas and plans and hopes that, we thought, would change the small-city staleness, and ultimately the world. We always had unfinished and unfinishable projects: once we started translating a book about Bauhaus, never finished the first paragraph; then a book on Hieronimus Bosch, never finished the first page – our English was not very good, and we had neither dictionaries nor patience. We read and talked about Russian futurism and constructivism, attracted to the revolutionary possibilities of art. Isidora was constantly thinking up performances, in which, for instance, we showed up at dawn somewhere with a hundred loaves of bread, and made crosses out of them. It had something to do with Hlebnikov, the poet, as the root of his name: *hleb* was the common word for bread in many Slavic languages. We never did it, of course – just showing up at dawn was a sufficient obstacle. Isidora did stage several performances, involving her friends (I never took part) who cared less about the hidden messages of the performance than the possibility of the random passer-by heckling them in a particularly menacing Sarajevo way.

Eventually, we found a socialist-youth institution and, with it, a way to act upon some of our revolutionary fantasies. The socialist-youth institution gave us a space, ensured that we had no interest in getting paid, and made clear that we were not to overstep the borders of decent public behavior and respect for socialist values. A few more friends joined us (Gusa, living in London now; Goga, in Philadelphia; Bucko, still in Sarajevo). We adorned the space with slogans hand-painted on bed sheets sewn together: 'The fifth dimension is being created!' was one of them, straight from a Russian futurist manifesto. There was an anarchy sign (and a peace sign, for which I am embarrassed now, but it was a concession to the socialist-youth people with hippie pasts), and Kasimir Malevich crosses. We had to repaint some of the crosses, as they alluded to religion in the blurry eyes of the socialist-youth hippies. This place of ours was called Club Volens-Nolens, a ludicrously pretentious name.

We hated pretentiousness, so the name was a form of self-hatred. Planning the opening night, we had fierce discussions whether to invite the Sarajevo cultural elite, idle people who attended the opening of boxes, and whose *cultureness* was conveyed by wearing cheap Italian clothes bought in Trieste or from smugglers working the streets. One proposal was to invite them, but to put barbed wire everywhere, so their clothes would be ripped. Even better, we could do the whole opening in complete darkness, except for a few stray dogs with flashlights attached to their heads. It would be nice, we agreed, if the dogs started biting the guests. But we realized that the socialist hippies would not go for that, as they would have to invite some socialist elite, to justify the whole project. We settled for inviting the elite, along with local thugs and people some of us grew up with, and generally people who had no interest in culture whatsoever. We hoped that at the very least a few fights might break out, bloodying an elite nose or two.

Alas, it was not to happen. No dogs, no bites, no fights –

the opening was attended by a lot of people, who all looked good and behaved nicely.

Thereafter we had programs every Friday. One Friday, there was a panel discussion on alcoholism and literature with all the panelists drunk, and the moderator the drunkest of all. Another Friday there were two comic-book artists, whose drawings we exhibited. One of them got terribly drunk and locked himself in the bathroom and would not come out, as the audience waited. After a couple of hours of our lobbying and outright begging, he left the bathroom and faced the audience, only to holler at them: 'People! What is wrong with you? Do not be fooled by this.' We loved it. Then there was the time when we showed a movie, called 'The Early Works,' which had been made in the sixties and banned almost every-where in Yugoslavia and never shown in Sarajevo, as it belonged to a group of movies, known as the Black Wave, which painted not so rosy a picture of socialism. It was one of those sixties movies, heavily influenced by Godard, in which young people walk around junkyards, discuss comic books and revolution, and then make love to mannequins. The projectionist – who was used to showing soft-core porn, where narrative logic didn't matter – switched the reels, showing them out of order, and nobody noticed except the director, who was present, but tipsy. We organized a performance of John Cage music, the only one ever in Sarajevo, by which I mean we played his records, including one with a composition performed by twelve simultaneously screeching radios and another with the infa-mous '4:33' – a stretch of silence on the record supposed to provide time for the audience to create its own inadvertent, incidental music. The audience, however, consisting by this time mainly of idle elite, was getting happily drunk – we heard that music many times before. When the performer, who came from Belgrade, forgoing a family vacation at the peril of divorce, stepped in front of the microphone, the audience was uninterested. Nobody had asked him to perform Cage in years, so he didn't care. The few audience members who glanced at the stage saw a hairy man eating an orange and a banana in front of the microphone, performing, unbeknownst to almost everybody, the John Cage composition appropriately titled, 'An Orange and a Banana.'

It was irritating not to be irritating to the elite, so even on the nights when we just spun records, the goal was to inflict pain: Gusa, the DJ, played Frank Zappa and Yoko Ono screaming plus Einsturzende Neubaten, the fine artists who used chainsaws and drill machines to produce music, all at the same time and at a high volume. The elite was undeterred, though their numbers declined. We wanted them all to be there and to be there in severe mental pain. This concept, needless to say, did not fly too well with the socialist hippies.

The demise of Club Volens-Nolens (which I might as well confess means 'willy-nilly' in Latin) was due to 'internal differences.' Some of us thought we had made too many compromises: the slide down the slippery slope of bourgeois mediocrity (the socialist version) clearly began when we gave up the stray dogs with flashlights. Before we called it all off, we contemplated having stray dogs, this time rabid, for the closing night. But Club Volens-Nolens went out with a whimper, rather than a mad bark.

We sank back into general ennui. I busily wrote self-pitying poetry, hundreds of dreadful poems, eventually amounting to one thousand, the subjects of which flip-flopped between boredom and meaninglessness, with a dash of generic hallucinatory images of death and suicide. I was a nihilist, living with my parents. I even started thinking up an Anthology of Irrelevant Poetry, calculating that it was my only hope of ever getting anthologized. Isidora wanted to assemble the anthology, but nothing came of it, although there was clearly irrelevant poetry everywhere around us. There was nothing to do, and we were quickly running out of ways to do it.

2. *The Birthday Party*

Isidora's twentieth birthday was coming up, and she – ever disinclined to do it the usual way – did not want it to be a booze-snacks-cake-somebody-fucking-in-the-bathroom thing. She thought that it should have a form of performance. She couldn't decide whether it should be modeled on a 'Fourrier-istic orgy' (the idea I liked), or a Nazi cocktail party, as frequently rendered in the proper movies of the socialist Yugoslavia: the Germans, all haughty, decadent bastards, throwing a lavish party, it being 1943 or so, while local whores and 'domestic traitors' licked their boots, except for a young Communist spy who infiltrated the inner circle, and who would make them pay in the end. For some unfortunate reason, the Nazi party won over the orgy.

The birthday party took place on December 13, 1986. Men donned black shirts and swastikas and had oil in their hair. Women wore dresses that reasonably approximated gowns, except for my teenaged sister, who was cast as a young Communist girl, so she wore a girly Communist dress. The party was supposed to be set in Belgrade, sometime in the early forties, with all the implicit decadence, as seen in the movies.

There were mayo swastikas on sandwiches; there was a sign on
the wall saying 'In Cock We Trust'; there was a ritual burning
of Nietzsche's *Ecce Homo* in the toilet; my sister – being a
young Communist – was detained in the bedroom, which was
a makeshift prison; Gusa and I fought over a bullwhip; Veba,
who lives in Montreal now, and I sang pretty, sad Communist
songs, about fallen strikers, which we did at every party; I
drank vodka out of a cup, as I was cast as a Ukrainian collabor-
ator. In the kitchen we discussed the abolishment of the Tito
cult, still running strong, and the related state rituals. We
entertained the idea of organizing demonstrations: I would be
looking forward, I said, to smashing some store windows, as
some of them were ugly, and, besides, I really liked broken
glass. There were people in the kitchen and at the party whom
I didn't know, and they listened carefully. The morning after,
I woke up with a sense of shame that always goes with getting
too drunk. I took a lot of citric acid and tried to sleep, but the
sense of shame wouldn't go away for a while, and, in fact, is
still around.

The following week I was cordially invited over the phone
to visit the State Security – a kind of invitation you cannot
decline. They interrogated me for thirteen hours straight, in
the course of which I learned that all other people who attended
the party visited or were going to visit the warm State Security
offices. Let me not bore you with the details – let's just say
that the good-cop-bad-cop routine is transcultural, that they
knew everything (the kitchen listeners listened well), and that
they had a big problem with the Nazi thing. I foolishly
assumed that if I explained to them that it was really just a
performance, a bad joke perhaps, and if I skipped the kitchen
demonstration-fantasies, they would just slap our wrists, tell

our parents to whup our asses and let us go home, to our comfy nihilistic quarters. The good cop solicited my opinion on the rise of fascism among the youth of Yugoslavia. I had no idea what he was talking about, but strenuously objected to the existence of such tendencies. He didn't seem too convinced. As I was sick with a flu, I frequently went to the State Security bathroom – no keys on the inside, bars on the window – while the good cop was waiting outside, lest I cut my wrist or bang my head on the toilet bowl. I looked at myself in the mirror and thought: 'Look at this dim, pimply face, the woozy eyes – who can possibly think I am a fascist?' They let us all go, eventually, our wrists swollen from slapping.

A few weeks later the Sarajevo correspondent of the Belgrade daily *Politika* – which was soon to become the voice of the Milosevic regime – received an anonymous letter describing a birthday party at the residence of a prominent Sarajevo family, where Nazi symbols were exhibited and values belonging to the darkest recesses of history were extolled. The rumor started spreading around Sarajevo, the world capital of gossip. The Bosnian Communist authorities, often jitterbugging to the tunes from Belgrade, confidentially briefed its members at closed Party meetings, one of which was attended by my mom, who nearly had a heart attack when she realized that her children were at the party. In no time letters started pouring in to Sarajevo media, letters from concerned citizens, some of whom were clearly part-time employees of the State Security, unanimously demanding that the names of the people involved in organizing a Nazi meeting in Sarajevo be released, and that the cancerous growth on the body of socialism be dealt with immediately and mercilessly.

Under the pressure of the obedient public, the names were

finally provided: there was a TV and radio broadcast roll-call in January 1987, and the papers published the list the next day, for those who missed it the night before. Citizens started organizing spontaneous meetings, which produced letters demanding severe punishment; university students had spontaneous meetings, recalling the decadent performances at Club Volens-Nolens, concluding with whither-our-youth questions; Liberation-War veterans had spontaneous meetings, whereby they expressed their firm belief that work had no value in our families, and they demanded more punishment. My neighbors turned their heads away, passing me by; my fellow students boycotted an English-language class because I attended it, while the teacher quietly wept in the corner. Some friends were banned by their parents from seeing us – the Nazi-party nineteen, as we were labeled. Even some who had attended the cursed party avoided meeting the others, including my girlfriend. I watched the whole thing, as if reading a novel in which one of the characters – an evil, nihilistic motherfucker – carried my name. His life and my life intersected, indeed overlapped. At some point I started doubting the truth of my being. What if, I thought, I was the only one not seeing what the world was really like? What if I was the dead-end of perception? What if my reality was someone else's fiction, rather than his reality being my fiction?

Isidora, whose apartment was searched, all her papers taken, fled to Belgrade and never came back, but some of us who stayed pooled our realities together. Goga had her appendix taken out, and was in the hospital, where nurses scoffed at her, and Gusa, Veba, and I became closer than ever. We attended the spontaneous meetings, all in the vain hope that somehow our presence there would provide some reality, explain that it was all a bad joke, and that, after all, it was nobody's business what we did at a private party. Various patriots and believers in socialist values played the same good-cop-bad-cop games at those meetings. At a Communist Party meeting that I crashed, as I was not invited, because I was never a member, a guy named Tihomir (which could be translated as Quietpeace) played the bad cop. He yelled at me: 'You spat at my grandfather's bones!' and then moaned in disbelief when I suggested that this was all just plain ridiculous, all while the Party secretary, a nice young woman, kept saying: 'Quiet, Tihomir.'

The Party, however, was watching how we behaved. Or so I was told by a man who came to our home, sent by the County Committee of the Party, to check up on us. 'Be careful,' he said in an avuncular voice, 'they are watching you very closely.' In a flash I understood Kafka. Years later, the same man came to buy some honey from my father (my father was, at the time, brazenly dealing honey out of our home). He didn't talk about the events regarding the birthday party, except to say, 'Such were the times.' He told me that his twelve-year-old daughter wanted to be a writer, and showed me a poem she had written, which he proudly carried in his wallet. The poem was really the first draft of a suicide note, as the first line read: 'I do not want to live, as nobody loves me.' He said that she was too shy to show him her poems – she would drop them, as if accidentally, so he could find them. I remember him walking away burdened with buckets of honey. I hope his daughter is still alive.

Eventually, the scandal fizzled out. When a lot of people realized that the level of the noise was inversely proportional to the true significance of the whole thing. We were scapegoated, as the Bosnian Communists wanted to show that they would nip in the bud any attempt at questioning socialist values. Besides, there were larger, far more serious scandals that were to beset the hapless Communist government. Within a few months, the government was unable to quell rumors about the collapse of the state company Agrokomerc, whose head, friends with Communist big-shots, created his mini-empire on non-existent securities, or the socialist version thereof. And there were people who were being arrested and publicly castigated for saying things that questioned Communist rule. Unlike ourselves, those people knew what they were talking about: they had ideas, rather than confused late-adolescent feelings. We had been our own stray dogs with flashlights, and then Animal Control arrived.

But for years after, I ran into people who were still convinced that the birthday party was a fascist event, and who were ready as ever to send us to the gallows. Understandably, I did not always volunteer information about my involvement. Once, up in the wilderness of a mountain near Sarajevo, while called up in Army Reserve, I shared the warmth of a campfire with drunken reservists who all thought that the birthday party people should have at least been severely beaten. I whole-heartedly agreed – indeed I claimed, perversely, that they should have been strung up, and got all excited about it. Such people, I said, should be publicly tortured. I became someone else, I inhabited my enemy for a short time, and it was a feeling both frightening and liberating. Let's drink to that, the reservists said.

Doubts about the reality of the party persisted. It did not help matters that Isidora did eventually become a downright, unabashed fascist. Belgrade in the nineties was probably the most fertile ground for the most blood-thirsty fascism. She had public performances that celebrated the tradition of Serbian fascism. She dated a guy who was a leader of a group of Serbian volunteers, cutthroats and rapists, known as the White Eagles, who operated in Croatia and Bosnia. She wrote a memoir entitled *The Fiancée of a War Criminal*. Our friendship ceased at the beginning of the nineties, and I keep doubting my sense of reality – maybe the fascist party was concocted by her fascist part, invisible to me. Maybe I didn't see what she saw, maybe I was a pawn in her chess musical. Maybe my life was like one of those images of the Virgin Mary that show up in the frozen food section of a supermarket in New Mexico or some such place – visible only to the believers, ridiculous to everyone else.

3. The Life and Work of Alphonse Kauders

In 1987, in the wake of the birthday party fiasco, I started working at a Sarajevo radio station, for a program geared toward younger urban people. It was called Omladinski Program (The Youth Program), and everyone there was very young, with little or no radio experience. I failed the first audition, in the spring, as the noise from the party still echoed in the station's studios, but was accepted in the fall, despite my mumbling, distinctly unradiophonic voice. I did this and that at the station, mainly writing dreadful film reviews and invectives against government idiocy and general stupidity, then reading them on the air. The radio heads gave the program considerable leeway, as the times had politically changed, but also because we could still easily take a fall, if need be, as we were all young nobodies.

What is important is that I was allotted three minutes a

week, on my friends' pretty popular show, which I used to air my stories. The timeslot was called, 'Sasha Hemon Tells You True and Untrue Stories' (SHTYTUS). Some of the stories I read on the air were shorter than the jingle for SHTYTUS. Some of them embarrassed my family – already thoroughly embarrassed by the birthday party – because I had a series of stories about my cousin, a Ukrainian, in which he, for example, somehow lost all his limbs and lived a miserable life, until he got a job in a circus, where elephants rolled him around the ring like a ball, night in, night out.

Around that time, I wrote the story, 'The Life and Work of Alphonse Kauders.' It was clear that it was unpublishable, as it made fun of Tito, contained a lot of lofty farts, and involved the characters of Hitler and Goebbels and such. At that time, most literary magazines in Yugoslavia were busily uncovering this or that national heritage, discovering writers whose poems would later become war songs. I broke up the story into seven installments, each of which could fit into the three allotted minutes of SHTYTUS, and then wrote an introduction for each – all suggesting that I was a historian and that Alphonse Kauders was a historical figure and the subject of my extensive and painstaking research. One of the introductory notes welcomed me upon my return from the archives of the USSR, where I had dug up revealing documents about Kauders. Another informed the listeners that I had just come back from Italy, where I was a guest at the convention of the Transnational Pornographic Party, whose party platform was, naturally, based on the teachings of the great Alphonse Kauders. A third introduction quoted letters from non-existent listeners who praised me for exhibiting the courage necessary for a historian, and proposed that I be appointed head of the radio station.

Most of the time, I had a sense that nobody knew what I was doing, as nobody listened to SHTYTUS, apart from my friends (Zoka and Neven, now in Atlanta and London, respectively) who generously gave me the time on the show, and the listeners who had no time to change the station as the whole thing was just too short. Which was okay with me, as I had no desire to upset the good cop or the bad cop again.

After all seven installments were broadcast individually, I decided to record the whole Kauders saga, reading it with my mumble-voice, still fondly remembered as one of the worst voices ever broadcast in Bosnia, and provided some historical sound effects: Hitler's and Stalin's speeches, Communist fighting songs, *Lili Marlen*. We broadcast the whole thing straight up, no breaks, for twenty-some minutes – a form of radio-suicide – on Zoka and Neven's show. I was their guest in the studio, still pretending that I was a historian. With straight faces and solemn voices, Zoka and Neven read the listeners' letters, all of which were phony. One demanded that I and people like me be strung up for defiling the sacred memories. Another demanded more respect for horses (as Alphonse Kauders hated horses). Another objected to the representation of Gavrilo Princip, the assassin of the Austro-Hungarian Archduke Franz Ferdinand, and asserted, contrary to my research, that Princip *absolutely did not* pee his pants while waiting at a Sarajevo street corner to shoot the Archduke.

With that, we opened the phone lines to listeners. I had thought that a) nobody really listened to the Kauders series, and b) those who listened found it stupid, and c) that those who believed it was true were potheads, simpletons and demented senior citizens, for whom the lines between history, fantasy, and radio programs were already pathologically blurred. Hence I did not prepare for questions or challenges or further manipulation of dubious facts. The phones, however, were on fire, for an hour or so, live on the air. The vast majority of people bought the story, and then had many a tricky question or observation. A physician called and claimed that one cannot take out one's own appendix, as I claimed Kauders had done, which obviously stands to reason. A man called and said that he had in his hand the *Encyclopedia of Forestry* – where Kauders was supposed to be covered extensively – and there was no trace of him in it. There were other questions, but I cannot remember them, as I had entered the trance of fantasy-making. I came up with plausible answers, never laughing for a moment. I inhabited the character completely, fearing all the while that my cover might be blown, fearing – as I suspect actors do – that the audience could see the real, phony me behind the mask, that my performance was completely transparent. I did manage to dismiss the fear of the good cop or the bad cop (probably the bad cop) calling in and ordering me to instantly come down to State Security headquarters. But the weirdest fear of all was that someone might call in and say: 'You know nothing about Kauders. I know far more than you do – here is the true story!' Kauders became real at that moment – he was my Virgin Mary, appearing in the sound-proof studio glass, behind which there was an uninterested sound engineer and a few people sparkling with the electricity of excitement. It was an exhilarating moment, when fiction ruptured reality and then overran it, much akin to the moment when the body rose from Dr Frankenstein's surgical table and started choking him.

For days, even years, after, people stopped me and asked: 'Did Kauders really exist?' To some of them I said yes, to some of them I said no. But the fact of the matter is that there is no way of really knowing, as Kauders really did exist for a flicker of a moment, like those subatomic particles in the nuclear accelerator in Switzerland, just not long enough for his existence to be recorded. The moment of his existence was too short for me to determine whether he was a mirage, a consequence of reaching the critical mass of collective delusion, or whether he had appeared to let me know that my life had been exposed to the radiation of his malevolent aura.

My Kauders project was an attempt to regain reality. I had blissfully persisted in believing I was a real person until I became a fictional character in someone else's story about the birthday party. I wanted Kauders – a fictional character – to enter someone else's reality and spoil the party by becoming real. After finding myself on the wrong side of the mirror, I threw Kauders back into it, hoping to break it, but he just flew right through and ran off, no longer under my control. I do not know where he might be now. Perhaps he is pulling the strings of fact and fiction, of untruth and truth, making me write stories that I foolishly believe I imagine and invent. Perhaps one of these days I am going to get a letter signed by A.K. (as he, of course, liked to sign his letters), telling me that the whole fucking charade is over, that my time of reckoning has come.

Notes From a Bunker Along Highway 8

GABE HUDSON

I know this is going to sound corny, at least to all the angry, cynical people in the world, but they can go to hell, because in the midst of everything that's happened with this screwy-ass war, yoga, and the deep concentration that I attain through yoga, has pretty much saved my life. I am probably a little addicted to it, but Dithers says that I am a complete fruitcake, and that yoga isn't going to save my butt from getting caught and thrown in the brig. Dithers says it's my queer dad that's the reason I like yoga so much. Just recently Dithers shouted, 'G.D., you know they're going to find us. You know Captain has men on us right now. It's just a matter of time. And when they find us, I'm going to be laughing my ass off at you.'

I was crouched in the Wide Galaxy pose with my eyes closed, and pretended not to hear him.

'I know you hear me, G.D.'

The Wide Galaxy is my favorite pose. It is the pose I like to finish with at the end of a sequence. I raise my palms to the sky, which is really just the concrete ceiling of this bunker, allowing 'my hands to become my eyes,' and victoriously breathe in 1–2–3–hold, and exhale 1–2–3–4–hold, and after fifteen minutes in the Wide Galaxy, my mind is right up into the void, and I feel truly shocked with bliss, grateful for the existence of every single atom in the universe.

'Hey, G. D. Hey, Zen Master. If you're looking for love, I'm your man. Come and get me.'

I opened my eyes, blinked, and strolled over to the far end of the bunker, and, with my e-tool, banged on the wood slats of Dithers's cage very hard. The chimps erupted into a chorus of screeches and started shaking the slats of their cages, which pretty much sealed the deal for me: getting my head up into the void was obviously out of the question now. So, choosing to ignore Dithers's laughter, I ambled down the hall and flung back the hatch and hoisted myself out of the bunker. I went for a walk in the cool desert night, where I mentally reprimanded myself for letting Dithers get the best of me.

But I should explain: I am not by nature a violent man, not anymore anyway. I believe in the sanctity of all people. And now my only allegiance is to Life, that Golden Kaleidoscope which turns always in circles, riddled as it is with its patchworked bits of magic and beauty. Here in my underground bunker, which is where I'm writing this from, and which was abandoned by Iraqi soldiers well before I ever arrived on the scene, I salute Life every day to the fullest, and beyond the steel hatch of the bunker, and moving thirty yards south, lies Highway 8, which is the main road that runs from Basra to Baghdad. And it's on this highway that the starving, the depraved, the war-weary Iraqi civilians, mothers carrying their dead babies, one-legged orphans, whole caravans of families with shattered faces from witnessing the catastrophic demolition of their homes and villages, the fleeing Iraqi soldiers, not the demonic Republican Guard, but the scared boys and old men forced into service by their vicious dictator, where hundreds of charred tanks and scorched cars line the highway and the ditches alongside the highway, still even tongues of flame reach out to lick the sky, and the noxious odor of burning human flesh chokes the air – like some kind of permanent backyard barbecue smell – this apocalyptic highway, are making their pilgrimage on foot to the supposed safety of Baghdad, where they will probably be blocked from the city's gates anyway.

Now some people might call me a criminal, a traitor, or worse even, because I deserted my Green Beret brothers and my country, but they are fools, because I know now that the heart is the highest law there is. And I find that if I turn an ear inward and pay very close attention, then my heart speaks to me louder and louder each day.

So there I was, strolling along that night and chewing myself out for the Dithers thing, when I stumbled upon a kindly old Iraqi woman crawling in the ditch along the highway. This was my first patient of the night and my heart quickened. I slid my ruck off and dug out my medical kit. I got down on my knees and set this woman's mangled leg in a splint. She started to speak, but I gestured shhhh. I cleaned the infected area on her calf, and picked maggots out with tweezers. I rubbed the wound down with salve, which I knew must have burned. And it was then, as I was cleaning her leg and I saw the hot tears of gratitude in her eyes, it was then that I found the peace of mind that had eluded me back in the bunker.

Hunting for Scuds, and how I helped prevent a nuclear war

It doesn't matter who you are, at some point something will happen to you out of the blue and your life will instantly be changed dramatically and forever. There's the crackle of lightning, the clouds part, and you see a muscular arm reach down and the Big Guy in the Sky deals you The Card. Well, I got The Joker. And it's funny, because once you realize the joke's on you, the last thing you want to do is laugh. And so it was for me, though even looking back on it all now there still doesn't seem to have been any sign of what that night had in store. This is how it started: Our team was on patrol up near Al Haqlaniya, right along the banks of the Euphrates River. I was behind the wheel of the Land Rover and Marty was scoping the landscape with his thermal sight. Our mission was to hunt and destroy Scuds deep inside Iraq, and a Scud is almost as dangerous as a beebee gun, and definitely less accurate. They have no guidance system, and so the Iraqis just point them in a general direction and presto: off goes a deadly Scud. Of course, our gazillion-dollar Patriots, courtesy of that genius Reagan, are just as ridiculous, because when a Scud starts to drop it shatters into a thousand little parts of scrap metal, and when we fire a Patriot it just locks in on one of those little pieces, and those jerkoffs claim they shot down a Scud. CNN runs the story, then everyone back home waves their flag, and the whole thing starts to remind you of a professional wrestling match.

'Hey,' said Marty, 'what's up with this shit detail?'

'You're stopping a nuclear war,' said Dithers, 'so quit your bitching. You're going to be able to tell your grandchildren about this.'

That was our little joke. The thing about the nuclear war. On January 14, some dozen Scuds smashed into Tel Aviv and Haifa. Next thing you knew Israeli prime minister Shamir aims mobile missiles armed with nuclear warheads at Iraq. The Saudis stated in no uncertain terms that if Israel got involved in Desert Storm, then they'd yank their ally status. Bush convinced Shamir to hold off starting a nuclear war by sending his best men, Green Beret, behind Iraqi lines for the sole purpose of Scud busting.

'Yo,' said Marty, 'what's that?' pointing. 'I think those might be Scuds.'

We turned and saw a stoic shepherd surrounded by teeming sheep. The shepherd angrily waved his cane at us. He was Bedouin, and these guys hated us. They were the black magic gypsies of the desert.

Everyone started whooping back at the shepherd. 'Yeah,' said Dithers, 'those are some deadly looking Scuds. We'd better call it in.'

Cynicism was at an all-time high. We'd been inserted by Pave Lows three weeks ago and other than a couple skirmishes with some weak-ass Iraqi soldiers, there'd been no real action to speak of. And no Scuds. Every couple days an MH-60 Blackhawk would shoot out to deliver fuel supplies and drop off our mail. It was freezing up there, with these wicked sandstorms, shamals, I think they're called, and we'd cruise all night in our Rover, and then hide out and catch some Z's during the day.

I jerked the wheel and said, 'Hold on, gents.' I started cutting sharp circles around the sheep. They panicked, bleating, scrambling every which way, some tumbling on their faces and others trampling them. The next thing I knew, I heard the crack of a rifle shot, and Marty says, 'Damn.' I glanced over and there's a blotch of blood on Marty's shoulder. But there was no time, another shot, and our right front tire exploded, and in a blur I wrestled with the wheel as the Rover swerved and rolled up on its side. I tumbled out and aimed my Beretta at the shepherd, who was sighting in on us with a rifle. Then, and this is like nothing I'd ever seen, seven or eight of the sheep stood up on their hind legs and cast off their wool coats, and I saw that underneath were Iraqi soldiers brandishing AK-47s. A volley of machine-gun fire cut the dirt around our position, tink-tink-tink in the Rover, and I lunged and radioed our SAS counterparts for backup.

Some of us scurried through the smoke and dove and set in on the backside of a little dune. Diaz was calling in our coordinates to air support. I heard a buzzing sound and saw a team of SAS on motorcycles burning up in the rear. I was laying on heavy fire with my Heckler, and next to me Dithers was blasting rapid-fire bursts with his SAW. A feather of smoke curled up off the tip of Dithers's SAW. 'Your barrel!' I shouted. 'You're melting.' And that's when I saw the moonlit shadow fall in the sand in front of me, and that's when Dithers let out an earsplitting scream. I rolled over just in time to see the Iraqi soldier lunging at me, driving his WWII-style bayonet glittering with Dithers's blood right at my chest. Dithers's arm had been sliced off, and was lying in the sand off by itself, and the hand of the arm was still clutching the barrel he'd been trying to change out.

There was a chainsaw buzz and an SAS dude in a black jumpsuit plowed into the Iraqi with his motorcycle, planting him in the sand next to me. The Iraqi was doing the funky chicken, flopping around like something neural had been severely damaged. I looked at Dithers and a red flower of blood had begun to bloom at his armless shoulder socket. 'Oh Jesus! Oh Jesus!' he cried out. 'I can't feel my legs! Oh Jesus! I'm so cold! I'm so cold!' Now there was blood everywhere. Blood on Dithers, blood in the sand.

'Hang in there, buddy! You're okay! Just relax, Dithers!'

My vision of George Washington, and the ensuing epiphany

Then, and I don't know why I did this, I glanced up for a split second, and I saw George Washington right out there in the middle of all the smoke and chaos. He was shirtless, sitting in a wooden hot tub with his arms draped around two blonde Bud Girls in bikinis. There was a patch of fuzzy, white pubic hair on his chest. I saw a half-eaten burrito perched on the edge of the tub. George had his head tilted back in open-mouth laughter, with the moon light winking in his giant ivory teeth, but suddenly he stopped and looked at me and his face lit up, and he said, *'There* you are. I've been looking all over for you, G.D.' He smiled. 'Come,' he said, and lifted one hand and nonchalantly waved me over, mafioso style. 'You must be tired. Come reap some of the rewards of all your toil on the battle-field, son. This is Carrie and Belinda.' The girls giggled. Washington held up an apple. 'We're going to bob for apples. How does that sound? You want to bob for apples? I sure could use your help, son, because I don't think I can handle it alone, if you know what I mean?' he said with a wink, and gestured expansively, spreading his arms wide behind the girls' shoulders. Just then a young African American man strolled up behind George carrying a tray on which were three silver goblets, and said, 'Yous ready fo ya'lls drinks, mastah?'

Dithers yelled. I glanced down at Dithers, and when I looked back up George Washington was gone. And that's when the weight of it all: the senselessness of war, the absurdity of America and ideals, its bloody history of oppression, its macho Christian religious certainty, finally came flooding into my mind like a great white ray of liquid light. What the hell am I doing here? I asked myself. How can you defend a country that slaughtered the entire Native American race, a majestic civilization which patented the mocassin and controlled the weather through a primitive, wireless form of breakdancing? Why should We The People be exhalted for having obliterated the peace pipe in favor of irony and the crack pipe? A country whose publicity-starved flag is a prophylactic against compassion, and is synonymous with a heat-seeking penis (God), waving its ignorant seed of disregard and enititlement in every beleagured face it can find. A country whose secret service conspired to shoot its premiere motivational speaker, Martin Luther King. A country which steamrolls across the planet like an obese golf ball, contaminating innocent indigenous peoples with its tech-based White Virus, while knighting murderous dictators as CEOs in the so-called new global economy. A country where women are deported to a cell (kitchen) and held captive in the shackles of an apron, handcuffed with spatulas and cake-making devices, and where in the currency of human dignity a vagina relegates its owner to the status of a greenstamp. Why doesn't America's Power Elite recognize that a person who can issue milk from their nipples is clearly superior to a person who can not. A woman president would be able to feed America's hungry babies with her nipples. And where does the word love fit into all this? Then I gave myself the answer: You are a goddamn fool.

So right then and there, with the unshakeable resolve of a man who has had the blinders ripped from his eyes after wandering for so long in complete darkness, I scooped up Dithers, who'd passed out by then, and started to walk off. Marty, firing his pistol desperately, glanced at me and shouted, 'G.D. what're you doing?!' There were maybe twenty Iraqis now, firing and advancing on our position, rushing up and hitting the sand on the fly. Dead sheep littered the landscape like fallen clouds. I could hear screams, weapons cooking off, motorcycles, sheep bleating, but in a sense, it already seemed far away. I kept walking, picking up my pace, and glanced over my shoulder. Marty shouted again. 'Hey, G. D., get your ass over here, motherfucker. What're you doing?' Marty was on his feet now, still firing his pistol. I slung Dithers over my shoulder and started to jog, looking back at Marty. As Marty was glaring at me, a flying Iraqi bum-rushed him and they were instantly grappling in a sandy commotion till death did they part. And then, with Dithers slung across my shoulders in the fireman's carry, I fled for my life, south, my heart in my throat, away from the fighting and chaos, leaving Dithers's arm and Green Beret behind me for ever.

My *dad the Vietnam hero, who now reads Chomsky, plus* Dad's *vigilant anti-war protest*

Everybody in Green Beret knows about my dad. He's a distinguished Green Beret alum, with a Medal of Honor from Vietnam, and you can find his name on the Wall of Fame at the Special Forces Training Center in Fayetteville. Like a lot of veterans, Dad never talked about The Nam. Whenever I asked him about it he'd tell me to shut up. And when Desert Storm started and we were called up, my dad wrote a letter to my commanding officer, Captain Larthrop, telling him that as a former Green Beret he vehemently opposed America's participation in Desert Storm. He quoted Noam Chomsky's famous essay, 'The Invisible Flag,' which apparently states among other things that the Invisible Flag 'waves for all of humanity.' My dad wrote Larthrop that he couldn't sit by and watch American boys get bogged down in another Vietnam quagmire, another 'intervention,' and so as an act of protest – he has a twisted sense of humor – he was coming out of the closet, was turning gay. He wrote me a letter explaining the whole thing. He informed me that he'd taken a lover, a forty-six year old criminal lawyer named Rob who he'd met at his yoga class at the Y. The same Y we used to do yoga together at when I was growing up. I felt betrayed. He said Rob had been openly gay for his entire life and that Rob was being a great support during the transition period. The whole letter was Rob this and Rob that, like I was supposed to be grateful or something.

I wrote my dad back. Lots of times. I begged him to reconsider his position. I used whatever logic suited my argument. I told him first and foremost that what he was doing was an affront to the gay community, and that he should be careful about what his method of protest inferred. I sent him articles clipped from *Science* magazine explaining how gay people had no more choice over their sexual preference than heterosexual people did, that it was all genetics. He wrote me back to inform me that he'd just sent a letter to Jesse Helms's office, suggesting that North Carolina make a motion to legalize gay marriages. He said, maybe I'm jumping the gun here, but this is the happiest I've been in years. I sent him a *Times* article about the vicious underground militia of the gay organization BPC, Better Population Control, and that he should watch out because they'd be pissed if they heard about the mockery he was making of their sexual orientation. He sent me back a full-color photograph of a naked blue-eyed man sitting on a porous rock on a beach in Jamaica that had been clipped from a magazine called *Out*, and scrawled at the bottom of it in my dad's handwriting was: 'This is still a free country, right?' And he'd drawn a little smiley face.

That last letter took the wind out of my sails, and I didn't write him back. I guess I thought it would blow over, but my dad called the *Raleigh News* and *Observer* and they broke the story. The story spun, and it suddenly got a ton of media play. A highly decorated Vietnam soldier, former Special Forces with a Medal of Honor, as an act of protest, announces that he will be gay until every single American boy is home safely. My dad was a guest on all the TV and talk-radio shows, liberal, right wing, it didn't matter to him, he was just looking to get his message out. Rush Limbaugh had a field day with it, brought him and Rob on his TV show for an interview. I didn't watch it, but Dithers did. Dithers said the title of the show was American Hero Bends Over for Peace.

My dad's got a pretty good sense of humor, so he wore a wry grin the whole time and busted jokes and kept the aggressive audience in stitches, is what Dithers said. When it comes to being a wise-ass, you really cannot mess with my dad.

Dithers's dangerous coma, and the inadvertant discovery of bunker

With Dithers slung across my back in a fireman's carry, I fled south along the foamy bank of the Euphrates. I ran for hours and hours, not stopping to think about the magnitude of what I'd just done, afraid that if I did I might lose my nerve and turn back around. The cold night wind bounced off the water and blew through my bones, and in the chaos of my mind I hoped maybe it would sweep me up like a kite and carry me to a land far, far away from there. Dithers had slipped into a dangerous coma, and I kept stopping to douse his wound with water, and then patched it up as best I could with a T-shirt. Then it was more shuffling, guided by the North Star. I recall a rock I camped under at the bank of the river, and I remember Dithers, coming to at one point and shouting, 'Help,' and then passing back out. It was well into the second night that I saw from a distance the great paved highway with the fires blazing alongside it. I was gasping for air as I came up to the edge of the highway. I heard someone shout something in Arabic, and the flash of a muzzle lit up next to the skeleton of a bombed-out car. 'Stop,' I shouted. '*Salam alaikum!*' Which is the only Arabic I know, and it means peace be with you. A whole slew of orange flashes erupted, and the sand around my feet was jumping in the air, making it difficult to see. I didn't have any fight left in me, and I resigned myself to whatever happened, and in a way, that desperation was what gave me courage, I knew nothing could hurt me now, as I scrambled to the other side of the six-lane highway in a flurry of enemy fire, nothing, that is, except for an errant round that shaved off a quarter inch of my kneecap. The pain exploded up my spine, and my brain went wet with shock and fear. Even now I've got a slight limp. I collapsed face first into the sand, using Dithers to break my fall. I got to one knee and dragged Dithers behind the cover of two huge boulders, and that's when I spotted the steel in the sand. One of the Iraqis was blowing a whistle, and there were shouts, and I heard a pack of men scrambling in my direction. I yanked back the steel hatch, and threw Dithers in first, and then I jumped down in, pulling the hatch to. The fall was about ten feet, and Dithers and I landed in a heap on the ground. It would only be later that I found the steel ladder fastened to the wall. I heard the soldiers shouting in Arabic up above. I held my breath in fear and my heart knocked on the door of my ribcage. I saw the milk white of my kneecap where the bullet had shaved off the skin and felt woozy. Finally the soldiers up above us moved on. It was only then that I noticed the horrible stench of the place. Screeching sounds erupted from what sounded like the center of the earth. With Dithers in my arms like a newlywed, I ventured cautiously down the hall, casting the beam of my flashlight over the concrete walls.

The chimpanzees who were here before us

Something furry crashed on my head as I crossed the threshold, and a cacophony of screeches erupted, reverberating off the inside of my skull, threatening to split it down the middle. I envisioned the dust that my brain had become spilling out. Dithers fumbled out of my arms and I felt leather hands pounding and tugging at me. In the commotion I managed to light a flare from my cargo pocket and then I sprang to my feet and shrugged off my attackers, and in the fiery shadows I saw several chimpanzees screeching at me and waving their fists over their heads. Their yellow eyes were filled with hate. Like everyone else I'd seen the psyops pamphlets Iraq had dropped with a picture of King Kong eating the heads of terrified American soldiers, but I never thought there was anything to it. I spotted Dithers motionless on the floor in a heap. His forehead was pale and slick with sweat. His shoulder was a gory red flesh mess, and I realized he could be dead for all I knew. I shouted, 'Getoutahere!' and waved the flare around in my hand like a sparkler and then franticly chased the chimpanzees into the back of the bunker with it.

The bunker looked like it had been abandoned in a hurry. Later, once I'd found the light switch, I also discovered the pinewood cages and figured out that the chimps must have escaped from them after the Iraqis deserted the bunker. There was a giant metal table against the south wall, which was strewn with papers and booklets I couldn't read, but, judging by the pictures and illustrations, I guessed they were booklets describing how to make chemical weapons. Then there's the hand-to-hand combat stuff, and an English dictionary from

1964. In the closet I found a big box of MREs. There was also a giant cache of weapons, but with no ammo. RPGs, AK-47s, M-16s, the works. On the north wall was a little bathroom area complete with toilet and sink. And a couple lightbulbs dangled from the ceiling. And like I said, the wooden cages, eight total, stacked up on one another, pushed up against the east wall.

How I came to be known as G.D.

This was at Fort Bragg, North Carolina. We were rehearsing hostage rescue. My team crashed through the third-story window, and I hit the deck, lying on cover fire with my 9 mm, while Dithers scurried forward with Marty to search the bedrooms and bathroom and laundry room. A robot, The Dad, came rushing in from the kitchen, crying out, 'Help help, they've got my son.' A three-dimensional hologram of a German shepherd appeared on the wall. The dog started barking at me and baring its teeth, threatening to compromise our mission, so I blew its head off with my 9 mm, and synthetic blood splattered everywhere. The graphics were amazing. I leapt up and moved swiftly to The Dad, reciting my lines, 'We're here to help, sir. Please lie down on the floor under a table until further instructed. You are safe now.' I was in mid-speech, on the word table, when Dithers dove back into the room, squeaking, 'Hit the deck, hit the deck!' as he sprayed The Dad with his Koch MP-5 series machine gun, so that the robot's chest ripped open and a fuse shorted and blazed momentarily, and then the machine's lights went out. I turned to Dithers, and shouted, 'What the hell?' But he was already beside The Dad, and he yanked off The Dad's face, revealing the grinning, pockmarked mannequin face of the Middle Eastern Terrorist (MET) we'd been instructed to terminate. A baby in diapers waddled out from the kitchen, and I said, 'Here's number one. Got'em,' and scooped him up, then sprinted into the kitchen, where the baby's dad was lying, apparently bludgeoned by the MET with a toaster. The father gasped, 'You took too long, and now I will die because of you. If I were a real person you would now have to live with the burden of my death for the rest of your life, soldier.' Marty came bursting through the kitchen door and I jumped and the baby dropped from my arms, landing on its head. 'You moron,' he said. The baby started howling like a fire engine, and Captain Larthrop's voice crackled on the intercom. 'Christ Almighty, son, where the fuck is your head? Good job, Dithers, but it looks like the real terrorist here is you-know-who.' You-know-who was me. 'Grab your gear and get in the frigging Debriefing Room, you knuckleheads.'

On the way to the Debriefing Room, Marty turned to me and spit, 'Nice job, Mr Gay Dad. Next time why don't you just hug the MET to death.' Dithers started laughing, and said, 'Yeah, G.D. Why don't you give him a big kiss next time,' and it was with that laughter that my new name was born.

Dithers's near-death experience, and my spiritual conversion to the art of healing, not hurting

It was touch and go for a week or so there, but then I finally got Dithers to regain consciousness. Snatched him right out of the jaws of death. Those first couple days I tended to him around the clock. He was shaking and his teeth were chattering and not once did he open his eyes. I gingerly pulled back his eyelids with my thumbs and saw nothing but white. I thought maybe hypothermia and shock. I squeezed perfect droplets of water into his mouth with a wet rag. Endlessly wiped his damp forehead with leaves. Changed his soiled skivvies. He'd lost a ton of blood. I patched up his shoulder with gauze dressing from my medical kit. When the gauze was saturated red I would change it out. I changed and I changed and I changed. On the third day the bleeding stopped. Just like that. And throughout all this I would talk to Dithers in his fevered state, words of consolation.

'Hang in there,' I'd whisper into his ear. 'You're in for a little shock, buddy. You've lost your right arm. But you shouldn't worry about it, even though some people are going to think you're a one-armed freak, screw them. Do you know why, my friend? Because that missing arm is a symbol of something very important. It's a symbol of the sickness you left behind when you quit the war.' Then I would pause to let all this sink in, before going on. 'You don't know yet that you've quit the war. But Dithers, you can rest easy now, buddy. Because all that stuff is behind us now.'

When Dithers finally came to, his eyes fluttered, and then they opened very wide as if for good. He smiled. 'Hey,' he said.

'It's good to see you.' He reached for my hand and squeezed it. 'God, it's good to see you, G.D.' Then he asked me where the rest of the team was. 'Where are we? Hey,' he said, looking around. 'You're not going to try and make a move on me now, are you G.D.? G.D.? Hey, what's wrong?' he said with a cocksure grin.

My dad's propaganda campaign, in the form of letters sent to me since I've been in the Middle East

Dear Son,

You amuse me. When you say I have dishonored my country, and the uniform I served in, and the proud Tradition of American Warfare, just because I prefer to make love to men rather than women, you drive home my point even further, that the biggest mistake I ever made was putting my dick inside your mother. That was truly a 'dishonorable discharge.' You are emblematic of everything that is wrong with your pansy, self-conscious, haven't-worked-for-anything and have-no-sense-of-history generation. Let me tell you something about honor. I fought the mighty Vietcong, and here you are in the Persian Gulf war, sitting in the desert, making sand castles. I piss on your war, and it has no more bearing on history than an ant's testicle. I can't wait to see the great stories your generation writes about their war. Oh boy. That's going to be fascinating. What do you know of honor, of sacrifice, of death anyway? And what are you fighting for? Oil. How digni-fied, how noble, how principled. What is the battle cry over there, 'Filler up?'

So I could care less if your team is making fun of you for having a gay dad. I broke dink necks with my bare hands because I could, danced with a dead gook in my arms for an entire night while smashed out on opium. I saw a boy from Georgia keep himself alive by holding his guts in his hands. You tell Marty or Dithers or anyone else from your team that if they were here with me right now, I would bend them over and 'break them off something.'

Now listen, son, let me give you a piece of advice. It sounds like you are all wound up over there, and that you are focused on all the wrong things. What I recommend is the next time you find yourself in a foxhole with Dithers, you get him to give you a blowjob. I cannot recommend this highly enough, and I think you will instantly recognize the sagacity of my advice. Who else would know best how to give a blowjob but a man? That is my one real regret. When I think back to The Nam, and consider how many lonely nights I spent, I feel the bitter taste in my mouth of lost opportunity. Of dark regret.

As ever,

Dad

Establishing alliances, the first step toward the projected coalition

It has not been easy getting used to these chimpanzees. What kind of disgusting creature has a carpet of pubic hair all over its body? A chimpanzee. They are dirty and they stink. I can smell them right now, which is why I tend to stay on this side of the bunker. But they are my friends, or at least they will be soon. I am training them to be my friends.

After setting up shop here, I went ahead and named the chimpanzees, respectively: Ingrid, Ronald, Beverly, Lorraine, and Dennis. Ingrid is gentle, and the first thing she tried to do after that first bit of unpleasantness was pet my cheek. Her favorite song is 'Happy Birthday.' When you sing 'Happy

Birthday' she tries to bounce up and down on her head. Ronald likes to make kissing noises and then look around as if he didn't know where they were coming from. Beverly is deaf. It took me a while to figure out she was deaf until finally I snuck up behind her and clapped my hands. Lorraine. Well, Lorraine is the brooding poet type, she just sits around and stares with a superior look on her face. And Dennis is a gigantic male with big biceps. I've seen Dennis amble up and mount each of the other chimps at will, girls and boys. I keep a close eye on him. So you might wonder how I could be sure which are the girl chimps and which are the boys. Well this would tell me that you've never seen a chimpanzee in person before, because a chimp's penis is something that can't be ignored.

It wasn't until later that I put them back in their cages. Of course there wasn't any way for me to know if I was putting them back in their original cages, but I didn't care. A cage is a cage is a cage. And at first the chimps didn't take to the idea, and Dennis and Lorraine tried to gallop down the hall to the bunker hatch, but I've always had a quick first step and even with this bum knee I was able to get the jump on them. In fact, and I don't want to step on anyone's toes here and presume to speak on behalf of the chimps, but I'd be willing to bet that if these chimps could speak English they'd say they prefer this arrangement to the one that they had before. If for no other reason at least they're safe from Dennis now.

I make my case to Dithers, who has some trouble seeing the light, but eventually comes around

The penalty for desertion is the brig. Pure and simple. The brig's where they can, because it's Military Law, strip you naked and throw you in solitary 'think tanks' all in the name of Justice. If you make too much noise they'll break your jaw and then wire it shut. Standard cuisine is bread and water. I met a blind Marine once at the V.A. hospital, a young private who'd spent three months in the brig, he had a white bandage over the top of his head, and apparently a guard had conked him in the nose with a club and those things that hold your eyeballs in place had come detached. 'They float every which way now,' he said. 'Every which way but loose,' and then started cracking up. 'Because check it out. They're sending me home with a medical discharge as long as I don't make a stink about it. Full benefits.'

And because my heart tells me that I don't deserve to spend the rest of my life in the brig, I have now, metaphorically speaking, changed my identity, and so I've renamed myself Help People. Help People's my name because help people is what I do. Every night, following a long yoga session, after getting my mind up into the void, running through the routine of Peaceful Rainbow, Fierce Cricket, Sun Salutation, and then finishing off with Wide Galaxy, I slip out into the night with my medical kit and tend to the wounded Iraqi pilgrims littered along the sides of the highway.

I'm a quick study. And I've learned the Ways of the Desert, so fueled on by the victorious breathing that I feel all the way down to the soles of my feet, when I go out on my nightly forays for the Good of Mankind I'm basically an untouchable phantom. The secret is to move with the land not against it. One night I might filter myself out amongst the stars, and on another I might blend into the billions of grains of sand that line the desert floor. I become and do whatever's needed when I let my heart steer me through the madness. I always wear my NVGs, night vision goggles. I've still got all my gear: rifle, rucksack, e-tool, flak jacket, Gore-Tex, helmet, gasmask, poncho, poncho liner, maps, and of course the most important item of all, my medical kit.

So, when Dithers came out of his coma, lying there holding my hand, and started hammering me with all those questions, I told him the truth. 'G.D. is dead,' I said. 'My name's Help People now, Dithers.'

One of his eyebrows arched.

'Help People?!' he said with a half grin, his voice raised.

I tried to figure out what else he needed to know. Then I spoke. 'Yes. Help People. And I move with the Ways of the Desert.'

His smile grew wider. 'Come on man. What are you up to? We've got to get back and blast those Scuds, right? What about the nuclear war?' he said, smiling.

I told him about seeing George Washington. I told him how America had no real culture of its own and how that burrito was a symbol for what we'd done to our downtrodden neighbor, Mexico, how America raped other countries of their cultural artifacts and then filtered them through its sadistic and glamorous lens of ultra-consumerism. 'We put everything in neon letters,' I said. I told him how America was the home of the gun-toting white supremacists, and that Charlton Heston was really the Grand Wizard of the KKK. The more

I talked the more pissed I got. I told him that the Native Americans were living works of art and we'd murdered them, that even the term Native American was an oxymoron. I said, how can we fight for a country where only forty years ago it was no big deal to lynch an African American. My mouth ran on and on. I redressed his shoulder with gauze bandages as I talked, and I watched as the smile slid right off Dithers's face. I could see the wheels churning in his head as I talked. Finally, breathless, I stopped, and the second I stopped talking he spoke right up. What he said popped right out of his mouth as if it had been on the tip of his tongue the entire time.

'So when do we leave here, G.D., and get back to the guys?'

'We're not leaving,' I said. 'That's the whole point. Haven't you been listening to a word I've said?'

'I could be ready in a couple days,' he said, and tentatively stretched one of his legs out. 'Of course it's gonna be difficult with this,' he said, and nodded to his bandaged shoulder. 'But I'm willing to give it a shot.' And as he said this his head slowly turned and his eyes met mine and held them.

I think the look on my face said it all. My eyes were stone that burned fire in the middle. I waited for the idiocy of what he'd just said to sink into his head. Finally he turned away and stared at the table with all the papers and books spread over it. I watched his brow furrow. His brain appeared to be chewing something over.

Then his face broke into a smile and he turned to me and said, 'Well, it seems like you've been doing a lot of thinking. And I'm glad you're doing what you're doing. Help People, huh? I like that.' He glanced at his armless shoulder. 'Because let's face it. If it weren't for you I probably wouldn't be alive right now.' Then he looked back up at me, the smile widening.

'So how about that, Help People? Say. You got any chow around here? What do we eat anyway? I'm starving.'

Propaganda letter #2

Dear Son,

Everyone's saying Desert Storm looks like a video game on the TV, but from where I'm sitting you couldn't get me to pay a quarter to play it. Hell, I'd rather play Pong – remember how I used to kick your butt at Pong – or pinball. I have one question for you. Is that war as boring to fight as it is to watch on TV? I sure hope not, for your sake. Because too bad for you, you can't just click the remote and flip to another channel. Rob said he wondered if the ratings sink low enough on Desert Storm, they'll yank your prime-time spot and put it on late night with all the infomercials. Have you even got to fire your weapon yet? I heard on NPR where American soldiers in Saudi Arabia had to conserve ammunition over there, so when they practiced drills they had to make sounds that approximated the sounds of rounds being fired. I heard one grunt going, 'Bata-tat-tat-tat.' What kind of war is that, where you have to pretend to fire your weapon? Shit. There's more killing in the American inner cities everyday then there is in your entire Desert Storm so far. Compton, California, is more dangerous than Kuwait! Maybe if you want to prove your manhood by shooting people, Mr Bigshot, you should start dealing crack over there, then you might see some action.

Get your head out of your ass and come home, son. Have you ever thought about why you're over there in the first place? Did you know that the American government used to consider Saddam an ally in the fight against the Russians and Iran, and that we funded him and gave him weapons? That we supported him when he pulled a Hitler

*and gassed the Kurdish town of Halabja in 1988? America beds
down with any country that will do its dirty work. American foreign
policy amounts to being a slut. Can't you see how the government is
playing you for a fool? They're setting you up, son, you've inherited
that myth. So don't believe it for a second.*

*But listen, if you do insist on fighting over there, let me give you
another lesson in history. Did you know that almost all the men in
Rome were gay, and did you know that the Romans were some of the
mightiest warriors who ever walked the face of the earth? The reason
for this is the young gay couples in love would be sent out together into
the battlefield. This way, when a man took up arms, he wasn't just
merely fighting for his empire, or even for his own survival, he was
fighting to protect his gay lover, who was right next to him in battle
– now that's what I call esprit de corps. And this ingenious mixture
of love on the battlefield elicited a fierceness and aggression in the
Roman soldier that could not be matched by his enemies. So, if you're
still not sure, consider this: Wouldn't you be more inclined to fight to
the death if Dithers were by your side, he being the man whom you
had made passionate love to the night before? Just wanted to plant
that thought in your head.*

As ever,
Dad

Dithers's gratitude, and his sense of wonder and naiveté, which seemed to mask ulterior motives

At first Dithers was grateful as hell to me for saving his life.
And I have to admit it felt nice to be appreciated like that. Of
course hiding out in this bunker took some getting used to,
for both of us. But we stuck it out together, making do with

what we had. It was difficult for both of us, scary even, but we toughed it out together. It's a pretty gruesome scene up there on the highway. Packs of roving dingoes that feed off the dead. Sometimes a car will pass through, weaving around the demolished cars spilled in the lanes, rubbernecking to stop and stare at the accident. And buzzards wheeling in the sky. And that stench is sometimes too much. I have no idea what battle took place up there, but it was definitely huge. Yesterday I stumbled across a busload of civilians, lying on its side, just fully charred, and when I opened the door, I couldn't help it: I puked. I hadn't said anything to Dithers yet, but I was hoping eventually, when he was well enough, that we could start going out on these missions together. Of course that was a ways off.

We had some good talks during that first week or so. I told Dithers more about my recent revelation, and he seemed to listen to me with much interest. I really couldn't have asked for a more attentive audience. Sometimes I'd talk to him as I cleaned the chimps' cages, making sure he watched closely, so that when he was well enough he'd know how to do it. He'd say, 'Roger that, Help People,' and, 'I couldn't have said it any better myself,' as he munched on a chicken a la king MRE. Dithers sure had worked up a huge appetite during his time in never-never land. I didn't care though, we had more than enough chow.

But at some point I sensed Dithers wanting to get back to the killing, to the mayhem. I also got the feeling he wanted to go back and see if he could find his other arm. This was just a hunch on my part, and there was no concrete evidence that that's what was on his mind. 'You know they can sew these things back on,' he'd say, holding his right arm out in front of him. 'I'm not complaining or anything. So don't take this the wrong way. But it sure would've been nice if you'd grabbed my arm when you split like that.' And then after some really loud bang, one of those explosions that comes every few days where the bunker rattles and little pieces of plaster flake from the ceiling and twirl to the ground, Dithers would raise up off the sleeping mat I'd set up for him and say, 'What the heck do you think's going on out there? Huh? What do you think that was, Help People?'

His curiosity seemed to have an ulterior motive. In the mornings when I came back I'd climb down the ladder, flushed from the night's rescues, and almost land on Dithers. He'd be standing right at the base of the steel ladder, staring, I guess, up at the hatch. I knew he couldn't get out. Because whenever I left, I shoved a big boulder on top of the hatch so it couldn't swing open. I also did this to ensure that nobody on the outside would discover the bunker if they happened to be wandering around. It was a perfect, simple system. Then one morning I came back and found that Dithers had rooted through my stuff and found the maps. 'Look what I found,' he said. I didn't say anything. I figured he was just bored and that he'd lose interest. But then he started spending all his time looking at the maps. Too much time, as far as I was concerned. I'd come in and he'd have the maps spread out on the table, and he'd be making notations on them with his one arm. He'd look up from a map and say, 'Now where exactly are we? What are the coordinates, Help People?' I hoped I wasn't being paranoid.

Eventually I had to take the maps away from him. 'We're here to celebrate Life,' I said, folding up the maps and putting them in my cargo pocket. Then I made a tube with my fingers and held it up to my right eye to indicate the Kaleidoscope of Life. 'Who cares where we are.'

His eyes glazed over, and he said, 'Life, right. Sure. Definitely Life.' But I could tell I was losing Dithers. And I knew I was going to have to do something to help him see things my way. I had to make him love his newfound life here, as I did. I knew we needed to get closer, to become friends. That this was going to take some personal investment on my part. You can't just expect someone to care about what matters to you, if he doesn't see that you care about him too.

Propaganda letter #3

Dear Son,

I mean what business does America have in the Kuwait? If it's really defending certain ideals, then why don't they go to all the other places in the world where there's oppression? I'll tell you why. Because they don't have oil. The US government is no better and no worse than any other government. The only difference is we've currently got the most original and innovative story in the world to guide our ship by – the Constitution. Throughout history the most successful populations have always been the best storytellers, because they know how to redress reality with a great story that justifies their cruel instincts and desire to survive. Our forefathers, those liars, those storytellers, have given America a way to feel morally justified when we do the same thing as every other country: murder, conquer, breed our population, and generate income and luxury. America the so-called big kingpin for freedom came to this land and murdered the Native Americans who were here before us. America the so-called big kingpin for freedom bought Africans from the Dutch and then kept them in chains. Don't even get me started, the contradictions are too numerous for me to note. But we're not alone in our hypocritical ways, every government is just

as guilty, and so it seems like man is doomed the instant he starts to
live in organized groups, but in this late stage of history, with
overpopulation, man is doomed if he doesn't. That's why I've got Rob.
At night, the soft moon outside the window, and with Rob's hard dick
in my hand, all the worries of the world just seem to melt away.

   As ever,

   Dad

My campaign to restore honor and heterosexuality to my dad

I was subjected to all kinds of humiliation because of my dad. The guys would be like, 'Hey, G. D., were you scared when your dad tucked you into bed at night? If he read you a story at night, what was that, like foreplay?' I was deeply ashamed, so much so that I didn't even point out that they were buying into the stupid myths that surrounded gay people, that they were more inclined to be promiscuous, that they were somehow a greater sexual threat to children. It was idiotic, but then so was my dad. Gay people were fine, in theory. But not so fine in reality, if they were your dad, who was your absolute hero. My dad had dishonored not only his service to our country but mine too. He'd made us a laughingstock. You always assume your dad won't do something to make you the butt of every joke you hear. And I didn't have the will to fight back when the guys ganged up on me, because in a sense, I knew they were right. I wanted to kill my dad for this.

Of course I'd known for a while that after Vietnam my dad had flirted with Communism. I'd seen the red flags up in the attic. I knew my dad went though the disillusionment that many Vietnam soldiers felt. Plus my dad had been through some hard stuff. Enter my mom. He'd met my mom in China Beach and he'd fallen in love with her, and brought her back to the States. But things went awry after that, my mom embraced Americana one hundred percent, and starting spending her days in the mall and at beauty salons, much to my dad's distress. They drifted apart and when I look at the pictures of her in Vietnam standing next to a moped in a mini-skirt with no makeup I can't believe it's the same person. And then the day my mom came home from the salon with three inch tape-on leopard-striped fingernails, my dad went through the roof, and started shouting that's why he fell in love with her because she wasn't like the women over here, but she didn't understand. Mom didn't speak English. Finally she took it one step too far and tried to get breast implants on the sly from a doctor she'd seen on a late night paid advertisement on TV, but there was a complication (the doctor claimed afterward that he'd warned her that 36Ds were too much for her little body frame, and then showed us the release forms she'd signed absolving him of any responsibility – the signature was the familiar X), and her heart stopped forever under the weight of all that silicone. I was devastated but because of the language thing we weren't super close. And plus I was only eight when all this happened. I do remember some things though, like how at night she'd hum pretty Vietnamese songs to me in bed and stroke my hair. So yes, my dad had definitely gone through some hard times, but that didn't do squat for my shame.

A couple days before we shipped out for Saudi, I hopped on my motorcycle, a Kawasaki Ninja, and shot up to Raleigh, North Carolina, to put an end to all this. On the way, my hopeful thoughts muffled inside my helmet, I envisioned myself sitting down at the table and hashing everything out reasonably. I thought maybe if I let my dad know how important he was to me that would help. Maybe the whole gay thing was from low self-esteem, I thought. So I roared into the driveway and barged through the back door and spotted a man with a brown mustache seated at the dining room table, and my dad swept into the room wearing an apron and his customary rope sandals and said, 'Son, what a nice surprise. I had no idea. Hey,' and he opened his palms toward the mustache man, 'ta-da! Here's Rob. You two have heard a lot about each other. Wow. This is a special moment.' This was even worse than I thought, my dad was the femme of the relationship.

I've never liked men who wear mustaches. All my life this is something I've felt deeply. It's a gut instinct and you've got to trust those. My fourth-grade gym teacher Mr Jenkins, who used to come in the locker room and watch us boys change, had a mustache. My dad's brother, Uncle Ray, who was always borrowing money for his get-rich-quick schemes had a mustache. Hitler had a mustache. In my experience a man with a mustache is someone who doesn't play fair. And this Rob character was no exception.

Rob stood up and put his arm around my father's waist, drawing him in close, and said, 'Nice to meet you. We were just about to have some pancakes. Would you care for some? They're blueberry.'

'In your dreams!' I shouted. 'Pancakes?! Are you fucking crazy?!' I knew my face was bright red.

'Listen, you,' I said, and I took a menacing step toward Rob. Then I told Rob in no uncertain terms that I'd be back tomorrow and that if I found him in my house I'd kick his ass from here to kingdom come. I told him that he was sick, ruining my family like this and that I'd cut off his head and stick it up his ass.

Rob sneered. 'Which one is it? Are you going to kick my ass? Or are you going to stick my head up my ass? Because I don't know how my head would fit up my ass if you're busy kicking it.'

My dad laughed. 'Ha!' I noticed a red barn stitched on the apron he was wearing. There was a girl skipping rope in front of the barn. A friendly cow smiled from behind a wood fence. Then my dad put his hand over Rob's hand, and said, 'Take it easy, Robby. I told you he'd be like that. Don't pay attention to him. He's a good boy with a good heart, just a little misdirected.' I knew why my dad was laughing, and he knew I knew why he was laughing. My dad was all fun and games until he got mad, and then he was the scariest thing I'd ever seen and there's no question that he could kick the living crap out of me if he wanted to. I couldn't believe it. My dad was taking sides. So I did the most hurtful thing I could do: I announced to my dad that from this day on, I had no dad. I said, 'You're dead to me, Mr Fag-man. I sure hope he's worth it. Because from now on you don't have a son.' I instantly saw the hurt in his blue eyes, and even though part of me wanted to run to him and say, 'I'm sorry,' my principles wouldn't allow it. I stood my ground. He'd always been my hero, and now what he was doing was sick.

That was 107 days ago, and we haven't talked since.

The cages, and why they are necessary to insure personal safety and to maintain order

How I got the idea for using the cages was from Dithers. It wasn't Dithers's idea, it was my idea, but it came about because of Dithers. Because when I had to leave him to go out on my nightly missions, I realized he was still too weak to fend off the chimps. After one of my first missions for the Good of Mankind I came back and the chimps had dragged Dithers to the rear of the bunker. They were punching him and jumping up and down on him. He was shouting, 'Help People! Help People! Help People!' When I came bounding back there, the first thing I saw was that Ingrid had Dithers's big toe in her mouth. So I put Dithers in one of the cages in the back of the main room. And it worked. I'd return in the mornings and the chimps would be screeching and banging on Dithers's cage with the empty ammo cans that were strewn around on the ground, but they couldn't get in. Then when I appeared at the base of the ladder, the chimps would scatter to the very back of the bunker. Especially since I always came in with a handful of rocks. No chimp likes to be pelted with a rock.

Eventually I just stopped letting Dithers out of the cage. It seemed like I was always coming and going, and it became too much of a hassle to be putting him in there and taking him out again and putting him in there and taking him out again. At first Dithers didn't even seem to mind, he even claimed to see the logic in it, but when his stump was almost fully healed, he started begging me to let him out.

'Look, Help People, I want to stretch my legs. I can keep things clean around here, straighten up. I'll clean the cages.

I'm strong again. I can hold down the fort while you're out running your Missions for the Good of Mankind. It'll make things easier on you.'

'Dithers. To be perfectly honest with you. I've just grown accustomed to you being in there. I mean what if I came back and accidentally mistook you for a chimp and pelted you in the head with a rock?'

'That won't happen. How could that happen. The chimps are in their cages now. So why would you be throwing rocks?'

'Good point,' I said.

Finally I relented. I didn't know for sure if I trusted Dithers. He was still acting funny, but my heart told me I had to be big and give him the benefit of the doubt. I truly believe that if you want to make progress, you have to learn to trust people. To take risks and put your faith in them. Plus Dithers did make a lot of sense. He was a lot more useful to me free than he was stuck in that cage. I was sick to death of cleaning those foul cages. And I was rewarded for my trust. Because even though Dithers only had his one arm, it turned out that he was a really good worker. It was like he used his missing arm to his advantage, as an inspiration. He got to where he could do one-armed push-ups. It was pretty damn impressive. It was like he would do something just because he knew technically he wasn't supposed to be able to, with his disability. I respected this quality in him. Dithers even fashioned this little broom out of a board and a stick. He hummed while he swept. One time I heard him humming 'Amazing Grace,' which is my favorite song now, because of the lyrics. 'I once was lost but now I'm found.' So I started humming along with Dithers. And he looked up at me and we grinned together.

It warmed my heart. I could feel what I considered to be a real bond beginning to form between the two of us.

A *brief summary of my missions for the good of mankind so far*

I don't mean to pat myself on the back here, but this is what it's all about. Straight up. This is the justification for my very existence. And so I think it's important to keep track of all that I've done for other people. All total, I've administered medical aid to twenty-seven Iraqis, and most of them have been civilians. I put little notches into the wall of the bunker for each person I've helped.

It can be heartbreaking work, and you never know what you're going to find. A little over a week ago I came up over a dune and found a young Iraqi man gasping for air by the side of the highway. He had a nasty sucking chest wound. He had a bushy head of hair and a big nose and a mustache. He had sensitive eyes, and they were bulging, as his head rocked back and forth. When I knelt down over him, I saw all the pores in his face.

He was ugly.

His chest rattled each time he gasped for air and it sounded like somebody shaking a tin can with a rock in it. The lung had already collapsed, so there wasn't much I could do. It was pretty clear he was about to make the journey to the Great Beyond. Through the gaping hole in his chest, you could see his insides. His liver was a shiny white in the moonlight. It didn't seem like he even knew I was there. But I never give up hope, so I pushed down on him, getting him to exhale, and then stretched a piece of plastic over the chest. Then I slicked on the first-aid dressing over the plastic. His breathing smoothed out a little, but he also closed his eyes, which wasn't a good sign. Then I held his hand for a moment and whispered, 'Go ahead, friend. There's another world out there somewhere. A world where there's no pain. A world where you can be young forever. Hurry, my brother.' I shed a quick tear, which twinkled on my cheek in the moonlight, and then let go of his hand and took his rifle and went further on into the darkness.

Dithers's rehabilitation

I knew I had to go out of my way to make sure Dithers enjoyed his life here. And I knew I'd made real progress over the past couple weeks. It got to where we were talking all the time. He'd tell me about his dreams, and I'd tell him what I'd done the night before on my mission. He still wasn't, in my opinion, well enough to leave the bunker, and so of course he was really curious about what it was like up there. I'd tell him about the carnage. The innocent civilians. And he'd say, 'That is seriously screwed up. I wonder if those people have any idea how lucky they are that you're around to tend to them.' It was a question I'd asked myself plenty of times. I knew we were making real progress if Dithers could see things like that. I thought the day was fast approaching when we could go out together. I looked forward to it, because sometimes those nights got lonely. The fires by the highway burned constantly, and the sight of it all could definitely get a person down.

So I did what I could to speed up Dithers's recovery. And

once while Dithers was sweeping up, I said, 'Hey Dithers, have you ever tried yoga?' The chimps were fast asleep, and the peaceful atmosphere made me feel generous. Having personally benefited from the extreme results of regular yoga, I was anxious for him to reap the rewards too.

Dithers rolled his eyes. 'You mean that stuff that you're always doing. The bending down and the breathing. Tying yourself up in knots stuff.'

I chuckled. I hadn't thought to consider what my yoga looked like on the outside. Since for me it was such a spiritual thing. The whole point was to burrow so deep down into my body that I'd forget I even had a body. I know a lot of people say it's about self-realization, connecting the mind, body, and soul, but that's not my take on it. 'Yeah,' I laughed. 'The knot stuff.'

Then Dithers nodded his head and stated unequivocally that he hadn't ever done yoga, and that yoga was for fags. I opted to ignore the dig, because I knew he didn't mean it like that, that he wasn't thinking of my dad when he said it, and I asked him if he'd like me to show him some moves.

'Thanks but no thanks. Maybe in my next lifetime, Help People,' said Dithers. 'You just do your thing. I'll keep cleaning,' and he moved into the corner, away from me, energetically whisking the broom around.

I took his response as a yes. 'Here,' I said, taking the broom from his hand and setting it against the wall, 'this'll take just a couple of minutes. You'll thank me for it later, I promise. If you don't like it, you'll never have to do it again.'

Dithers got this numb look in his eye, his arm slumped by his side, and he said, 'Okay.'

I moved in close and put my hand on his hip. I was suddenly

conscious that this was the first time we'd touched since I nursed his wound. 'Let's try this first,' I said. I showed him how to get into position for the Downward Facing Tree pose. 'Now envision the roots of your feet slowly growing down into the ground, anchoring you to this spot,' I said. I reached down and adjusted the back of his leg, and he laughed. A short, quick, 'Ha!'

I looked at him like what the hell was that.

'Sorry,' he said. 'That just felt kind of funny.'

We spent the rest of that afternoon going from pose to pose. I showed him how to flow from one to the next. We got all sweaty. There were some obviously embarrassing moments, like when I told him to raise his hands to the sky, but the mood was light, and he forgave my blunders. It was suddenly late. We were having so much fun I decided to skip my Mission for the Good of Mankind that night, and instead we just hung out in between the yoga stuff, and rapped about things. Dithers told me that his dad was an albino. And an alcoholic. He said, 'It was kind of sad. But I think my dad used to drink to try and forget.' Then he told me that when his dad started getting rough with his mother, shoving her around and yelling at her, he'd always step in the way and let his dad beat him instead of his mom. I said that I'd always known he had a good heart, and that story was proof positive. There was a moment of silence.

'I've never told anyone that,' said Dithers, looking over at me. I turned and saw the steam coming up off him from all the sweat.

'You're all steamy,' I said. I looked over at the chimps in their cages. They were staring back at me, patiently, expectantly. Dennis cooed, 'Hoo-hoo-ha.' I realized I hadn't fed them dinner yet.

'Hey, Help People.' Dithers slid over a little closer. 'I'm sorry, man.'

Everything was very quiet. I was getting this weird vibe I couldn't explain.

'For what?'

'For calling you Gay Dad. That G.D. stuff. Back at the base. For giving you such a hard time about all that. That wasn't cool.' He said it was probably his insecurity, because of who his own dad was. I tried to envision Dithers as an albino.

Then I told him, don't worry about it, that my dad was a fucking queer, and that I hated his guts for it. 'So don't sweat it,' I said. 'No biggie. Trust me.' Then I rolled away from Dithers and grabbed some MREs and started to feed the chimps their dinner.

Propaganda letter #4

Dear Son,

War sure has changed, and frankly I think whatever dignity used to be in it has been bled out of it by the stupid technology. Last night on Nightline they were showing how a little remote-control airplane with a live video feed, an Unmanned Vehicle or something like that, was flying over Saudi Arabia and a bunch of Iraqi soldiers ran up to it waving white flags. The Nightline guy kept saying it was a historic moment in warfare, the first time humans surrendered to a machine. And I was thinking, wow, this is the fourth most powerful army in the world? How do they grade these things, on a bell curve, because I'd sure hate to see the fifth most powerful army in the world. Do you realize that the citizens of Iraq don't even want to be in a war, and that Saddam has forced them into military service, so that when you are killing Iraqi soldiers you are killing innocent people who don't want to be there anyway. I've read in the news that most of the Iraqi soldiers are little boys and old men, what does that tell you? And why is it that our government won't let any journalists in the war theater? Why the censorship? They're denying us the liberty that they claim you're over there defending.

Rob's been asking me a bunch of question about my time in Vietnam, and recently I haven't been able to sleep because all these memories keep flooding back. Sometimes I feel like I'm back in the shit all over again, and I can smell the rice paddies and the water buffalo in the bedroom with me. Rob suggested maybe I was being too hard on you. He said how do you expect your son to understand where you're coming from when you've never even talked about your own war experiences. When Rob said this he was holding my Medal of Honor because he'd asked to see it. I know you think I'm a hero but I want you to know that I'm not. There was nothing heroic about what we did over there. I was a sick young man back then. Sometime I think Nam is the hangover that Bush is trying to cure by a silly victory over there in Iraq. Because you know in the big picture we got our asses kicked over there, right? Don't let anyone tell you different, the NVA and the Vietcong were the toughest and mightiest warriors that America has ever seen. The government tricked us into fighting that war with all their bullshit about the heroics of WWII. They used words like evil and honor and dangled our fathers in front of us so that we wanted to go over there and be heroes too. We walked into a war that had been going on for twenty years before us and got our asses trounced.

And the things I saw. You'd be out on patrol and come up on a mine site, where some gooks had been blown apart. There'd be pieces of bodies strewn everywhere, arms, legs, half a skull, a torso with the ribs poking out, a kneecap, and the thing is I stopped looking, I didn't even care. What happens to a person when he stops caring? You forgot

that the Vietnamese were even people. One time I was crawling though this underground tunnel, because we'd been told there were some NVA officers in there. I heard these voices, all this chattering, and I was thinking, hot damn. So I crawled up to the opening where the voices were coming from and chucked a grenade in there and then bam. When I went to inspect the damage you know what it was, it was a room full of women. They had on some kind of religious costumes. They were all dead. I've got a hundred more stories like that. The things you do in war you have to live with for the rest of your life. How am I supposed to live with something like that? You tell me. How am I?
   Dad

Finally the day came for Dithers to leave the bunker

Finally the day came for Dithers to leave the bunker. We'd been getting along great for the past couple weeks, and I knew he needed to get his endurance up, if he was going to accompany me on my missions. So I suggested we go out and play some catch. To help that arm of his get stronger. We exited the bunker and went about thirty clicks off the highway so that we were out of sight.

'Oh my God,' said Dithers when he saw the highway from a distance. Plumes of smoke were trailing up off the smoldering cars.

'See,' I said. 'Can you smell it?' The barbecue smell was especially strong that day. And then we threw a detonated grenade back and forth. It made me feel like a kid again, and we both laughed, especially because Dithers was having to learn how to throw with his left arm. He looked positively goofy.

'Try to get your hips into it,' I shouted at Dithers, after retrieving yet another dud throw from the sand. I looked at Dithers and he was grinning. The sunlight was catching in his hair. I decided right then and there that we'd make an effort to get out more. I reared back, signaling to Dithers that I was going to really hum this one.

I played all the sports as a kid, but baseball was my favorite. In Little League I played third base for the Fancy Death Life Insurance Bombers. My dad never missed a practice. He'd stand out there in his rope sandals with a couple of the other die-hard parents. And my whole thing was I would pretend as if I didn't know Dad was there. I'd make a flying leap to stop the ball and whip it to first like a cannon. I'd skin my hip to a pulp sliding into home. Then when I stepped up to the plate I would blow my arms out trying to knock the ball out of the park. I knew a lot of the kids thought I was a jerk. For trying so hard. But I didn't care. This didn't have anything to do with them.

I threw the ball and Dithers dove to catch it, and ended up doing a face plant in the sand. He came up laughing. 'Hoo! I don't think I'm going to the big leagues any time soon,' he shouted. A breeze picked up and the barbecue smell came up off the highway. I tried not to think about all the rotting corpses out there.

'Here,' I said. 'Throw me.a fly ball. Make me work.'

Dithers got to his feet, and then did this little hop-skip, and chucked the grenade way, way up in the air, so that I thought it was going to knock the sun out of the sky.

I remember one game we were getting routed by the fourth inning. Coach moved me from third base to pitcher because he'd used up the other pitchers' eligibility the week before, and because I guess he figured he had nothing to lose. Dad and I always secretly suspected that I'd make a great pitcher, I had a strong arm, and this was my big chance to save the day and show the coach what Dad and I secretly knew: that I should be the starting pitcher. I could almost hear Dad tighten up in the bleachers with excitement as I trotted out to the mound and threw some warm-up pitches. I was really humming them, and I could feel the world smiling at me, claiming me for one of its marvelous creatures. I touched the bill of my cap. I wet the tip of my fingers with my tongue. I blazed a couple more fastballs across the plate for good measure. Then the umpire shouted, 'Play ball.' And for the rest of that inning, until we had to forfeit, I've never felt more shame in my life. I threw wild ball after wild ball. I walked six batters straight. And when I wasn't throwing wild, the other team was connecting with everything I threw. Even their benchwarmers were getting a piece of me.

I sprinted after Dithers's fly ball and leapt and stretched out, my body soaring parallel to the ground, and there was the smack of the grenade as it landed in my palm. I crashed into the sand, victorious.

'Damn,' shouted Dithers. 'Awesome.'

I stood up and waved the grenade like a trophy. I took a bow.

'I'd give you a standing ovation but,' and he nodded at his shoulder, 'you know the whole sound-of-one-hand-clapping thing.'

My face was flushed, and I felt the thrill of the catch rush through my body. I felt like running into the highway and picking up a tank and throwing it.

'Hey,' said Dithers, trotting up to me. 'That was really fucking amazing. Did you used to play ball or what?!'

All the blood rushed out of my face. I felt the crushing reality of our situation set back in. I wanted to puke because of that smoky smell. All those dead people. If I ran out into the highway, I'd probably just get run over. I thought about my dad, who was dead to me now. I thought about how it was probably his fault that I was stuck in this mess. Suddenly Rob's mustached face was hovering there in front of me. 'Which one is it? Are you going to kick my ass? Or are you going to stick my head up my ass? Because I don't know how my head would fit up my ass if you are busy kicking it.' Then I heard my faggot dad's laugh.

'Naw,' I said, to Dithers, turning to head back to the bunker. That life was buried and gone. 'I never did get to play. I always wanted to, though.'

After my humiliating pitching experience, I couldn't stop crying on the drive home. There was a purple can of grape pop in my lap that I hadn't even bothered to open. I was crying because I was so embarrassed that I was crying. Dad had this tight look on his face and he didn't say a word the whole time. I could tell he wasn't upset, he just felt my pain and knew there was nothing he could say to make it better. When we pulled into the driveway and the car came to a stop, he squeezed me on the shoulder and said, 'We don't have to try and explain this to your mom. You go in and get washed up. But I don't care what happened out there. I'm proud of you. Do you hear me? You are my son. Don't ever forget that.'

The days began to blur

The days began to blur, and it got so I couldn't remember life any other way. There were more and more Iraqis on the highway at night, trying to make it back to Baghdad. Some nights I'd tend to as many as three people. My only concern was the MREs. We still had plenty, but between me and Dithers, and the chimps, we'd already run through half the box. Dithers and I fell into a routine of doing yoga together in the evening, right before I'd head out for the night. He was a natural. Sometimes I'd inadvertently come out of the void because I lost my concentration, and I'd look over and Dithers would be crouched down, holding the Half Moon pose, with this very serene look on his face. I have to admit I was a little jealous.

But one time I opened my eyes, and Dithers was standing right in front of me with a big smile on his face. I tried to hide my surprise.

'Dithers,' I said. I didn't know what else to say. 'Hi.'

'Hey,' he said. 'I want you to show me that one pose you do.'

I said I didn't know what he was talking about. He was right up in my face.

'You know the one. Where you lay down like this.' He got down on the ground face first. He looked idiotic.

'You mean the Half Locust?' I lay down in the Half Locust.

'Yeah,' he said, smiling even wider. So I showed him. I put my arms around him, guiding his limbs into the correct posture. I knelt beside him as he lay there.

'But what about this part here?' he said. 'This doesn't feel right,' pointing to his hip.

'Looks right to me,' I said. I reached down under him and before I knew what was happening, Dithers had adjusted himself so that my hand was cupping his groin area. I got a very strange feeling in my stomach. An odd sensation. His hand came up around my neck and pulled me to him, very hard. It felt aggressive. 'Help me, Help People,' he murmured, but there was some menace in his voice and my hand was pinned between his groin and the ground. I felt things spinning out of control, and that weird feeling had bloomed so that it was running through my entire body. The closest I could describe it is electricity.

'Help me, Help People,' only this time louder, meaner. Like a growl.

I swung my elbow around and clipped his jaw and then leapt to my feet.

'What the fuck,' I shouted. The chimps joined in, barring their teeth and hooting.

Dithers looked genuinely surprised to see me on my feet. He was rolling his jaw around. I noticed he had an ammo can in his hand, which he tossed away.

'I'm sorry,' he said, getting to his feet. 'I don't know what that was. I think it's the stress. Maybe being cooped up down here is starting to get to me. My bad. Okay. I'm sorry. No problema, right?'

I was confused. I didn't want to know what any of this meant. I couldn't quite get my mind around what had just happened, and the confusion turned to anger. I looked at the chimps and wanted to chop their heads off. They started hooting and screeching, as if they could read my thoughts.

I threw the broom at Dithers and said, 'Here. This place is a fucking mess.'

A *quick clarification, before we go any further*

No matter what I may be accused of, I am definitely not gay. I want to put that right out there. The closest I have ever come to being gay was in the fourth grade, and that was a long time ago. I mean, to be perfectly honest with you, my fourth grade year was probably the gayest year of my life. That was the year that I spent each recess out on the corner of the playground playing Truth or Dare. And on that fateful day in late spring, Freddie Slacknit produced a carrot he'd smuggled from the cafeteria, and double-dog dared me to stick it up his 'pooper.' At first I didn't know what to do. The other kids looked at me expectantly, and Freddie already had his pants down around his ankles. I almost walked away. But in the end Freddie had to go to the school nurse to get the carrot out, and by the next day word of what had happened spread through the Parent Majority Coalition. And somehow I was being pegged as 'the ringleader.' The kids at school started calling me Rabbit Butt. They'd spank themselves and start howling when I walked by. Secret PMC meetings were held. Teenagers from the high school drove by and hummed carrots and lettuce heads at our house. Four months later it was so bad we had to move to a house on the other side of Raleigh, and I transferred schools. That was a long time ago. So obviously I didn't feel compelled to mention any of this to my recruiter when he asked me if I was gay.

Propaganda letter #5

Dear Son,

This is going to be hard for me to talk about, but I am doing it for you, so that you recognize how empty the pursuit of killing other human beings is. I hope that by the time you're done reading this you will realize what a hollow word bravery is in the context of war. I wore the craziness of the war like a cheap suit and sealed the lock from the inside so I couldn't get out even when I wanted to. One day we were on patrol, near the town Dak Tho in the province of Quang Mgai. We'd gotten word there might be some NVA in the area, and so we were roving through the banyan trees and bamboo thickets. Suddenly Charlie caught us in an ambush. My buddy Kitrick falls into a tiger pit. He yelled, 'Fuck,' and then the light went out of his eyes. We're suddenly taking a lot of fire, and I'm scared and confused. We scrambled for cover, and Gordon got his leg shot to shit. I bent over to check the wound, and Gordon moved and something blew up in my face and I was blind. I hear screams and I know the VC are moving in on us. I wiped my eyes and there was blood on my hands but I could see, and then I ran out into this little clearing and started blasting with my pistol. There were five dinks total, and there was a split second where we all looked at one another and the colors were ultra-vivid and it was if we were on stage and this was the scene we'd all been waiting for, and then the pistol is guiding my hand, jerking it around, dropping them out. When I was done I started calling out for our guys to come up but it's quiet. The wind was coming through the banyan trees and it was almost pretty. Everyone dead except for me.

That's how I got my 'Medal of Honor.' Two more tours and my mind just shut off and I didn't even think about the killing and I

wondered about that later. My mind was a blank slate. When I
rotated back to the world, I had to pick up a piece of chalk and start
writing my new life story on it. I'm sorry to be having to tell you this
and for you to know it about me.

I'm not the same person I was back then, son. Read Chomsky.
As ever,
Dad

How our cover was almost blown

A couple days after that strange yoga incident, I was returning
to the bunker when I spotted a lone figure in the distance. A
human dot on the landscape. There'd been a lot of Republican
Guards in the area recently, making my night missions more
difficult. The sun was just starting to dawn, a blood-red
symphony of light, playing its chorus of hope over the horizon.
I was worried this figure was some Iraqi soldier snooping
around the hatch to my bunker. Maybe he'd sat on the boulder
and saw the shine of the metal underneath. I didn't know what
I'd do if that were the case. Should I sneak up behind the Iraqi
and club him with a rock? What would I do with him then,
drag him down into the bunker for questioning? But I
wouldn't be able to question him because I don't speak Arabic,
so then what? Just keep him in the extra cage? What would
Dithers think. Plus surely he'd be missed. How long would I
keep him in the cage, because it's not as if we had all the food
in the world? We were already starting to run out of MREs.
And it didn't seem right for me to hurt someone who was
sneaking around. But then again, it didn't seem right for me
to be discovered and captured. Because who would care for

the wounded pilgrims then? So I got down in the sand and speed-crawled up very quietly on the Iraqi in a roundabout fashion, until he was about thirty yards away.

I raised my binoculars to my eyes and I was relieved to see that it was only Dithers. In the binoculars he was suddenly close, and I could see a drop of sweat dangling from the tip of his nose. By now he was walking very fast alongside the high-way and kept checking over his shoulder. He was headed north. I wondered if maybe one of the chimps had escaped and he was trying to catch it. I knew Dennis had been acting funny recently. Then a very strange thought came into my mind. I realized that Dithers was not in the underground bunker, which is where he said he would stay, and I realized that if Dithers were in the underground bunker, there was no way Dennis could get out.

I stood up. 'Dithers,' I called. 'What are you doing?'

I guess he couldn't hear me because he didn't turn around. So I called out again.

'Dithers!'

He turned and saw me.

I waved.

Now this is the part that left me stunned and heartbroken. When Dithers saw me he started running in the opposite direction from where I was. I realized right then and there that if Dithers made it back he'd rat me out. All of his previous questions suddenly came flooding back. 'What exactly are our coordinates? Is there a landmark you use to know where the underground bunker is? Do you ever get lost?' And there was no way I was going to the brig. My only crime was my compassion. It was easy to catch him. Even with my limp. I tackled him.

Propaganda letter #6

Dear Son,

I have a confession to make. I didn't want to tell you this, but Rob encouraged me to come completely clean with you. He said if I was being all high and mighty with you, then I had to lead by example, so I am going to come clean. I want you to know the truth about your mom. Now I know you were never close to your mom, because of the language thing, and because she tragically passed away when you were eight and it's true I often expressed my disappointment in her to you. I shouldn't have done that. And sometimes you may wonder why I stayed with her all that time? Especially if I was so unhappy. The answer is because of the guilt. When I met your mom she was a green-eyed ten-dollar whore in China Beach. My team was on a twenty-four hour R&R. We didn't have any language to share, your mother and I, so we communicated through clumsy, passionate hand signals, under the sheets. And when the weekend was over, your mom stood at the edge of town in a red white and blue straw shawl and waved goodbye to me as our Jeep pulled out, her head full of my empty promises that I passed on to her through a translator. That I would return soon in a giant yacht named O Powerful One to marry her and bring her back with me to America, where we would live in a gold mansion. But as you well know, I did come back for her. And though her life was sad and strange, I am always grateful to her for having given me you. I didn't mean what I said earlier, about you being the worst mistake I ever made. Sometimes I get angry and loose my cool.

As you can probably tell, Rob's a pretty good influence on me and keeps me walking a straight line, and what once started as an ironic gesture, with this protest, which I still stand by, has become very serious and sincere. I think I am in love. Did I mention that Rob isn't circumcised? I'll admit that that freaked me out at first. It looked so silly to me, but now I've grown used to it and sometimes when I look down at my own unit I wish it wasn't circumcised, because Rob says he gets more pleasure that way, and based on the noises he makes I believe him. But all that aside, I'm ashamed of the way you acted when you came over here and started yelling right before you shipped out. Now I realize this can't be easy for you, but you're going to have to trust me on this one. Homophobia is one of the ugliest things on earth, and it stems from ignorance and fear. All I am trying to say is I hope you will give Rob another chance. He's a really good man. And he's got an interesting past, can you believe he grew up in London? And he said he has forgiven you for your rudeness and looks forward to really getting to know you. I know if you would just give him a chance the two of you could maybe become friends. I hope you will consider this while you are over there, and realize that I am finally happy after all these years and that should stand for something. Happiness is not easily come by in this world.

Love,
Dad

Dithers was back in the cage full-time now

Dithers was back in the cage full-time now. And I began to see him for what he truly was, a liar, a conniver, a coward. He started having these mood swings and shouting a lot. 'Let me out of here. I won't tell anyone you're here. I promise. I just have to get back to the guys. My mom will be worried about me. Can't you understand what that's like? Please.' Then he'd start crying. Other times he'd turn angry and violent. 'Help People, I'm going to kill you. Your days are numbered, Help

People. See this bare hand?' And here he held up his one arm. 'I'm going to kill you with my bare hand.'

Wrestling as a form of connection, and as a preventative measure against possible future attacks

The only time I let the chimps out of their cages is when we wrestle. This was my idea too. Not Dithers's. I thought it was good for the chimps to have physical contact. Dithers didn't seem to care for the chimps one way or another. He wouldn't even acknowledge they were there. Like he was better than them or something. Lots of times I'd see that they were lonely and go over and talk to the chimps and make funny faces. But not Dithers. And beating a chimpanzee in a wrestling match gave me confidence, and I knew if I could take a chimp then Dithers wouldn't have a chance against me if he ever did try anything. Dithers's one arm was a trunk, and I'd seen him doing all those push-ups. But you go five rounds with Dennis and a little guy like Dithers becomes a joke. Even with the trunk. That's why I always wrestled the chimps right in front of Dithers's cage, where he couldn't miss any of the action. Every fight is 80 percent intimidation. So I made it my business to psyche Dithers out before he made his move.

A couple days ago, while wrestling with Ronald, I got myself in a pinch. I was crouched down low, circling around with my arms spread kung-fu style, when suddenly I slipped on an ammo can and fell over backward. The bunker has gotten real messy with Dithers in the cage all the time. Ronald leapt on me and started punching me everywhere at once. I was surprised. There'd always been a playful undertone about the wrestling matches but Ronald wasn't holding back. He knocked the wind out of me. He stomped on my bad knee, and I saw a hairy fist in front of my face. Blood came spurting out of my nose. I heard, as if from very far away, the chimpanzees start screeching. Then there was the unmistakable sound of Dithers's cackling. My vision went foggy under Ronald's little concrete fists. Boom boom boom boom boom. I decided I needed to do something fast because this situation was about to turn very bad for me, and then I blacked out.

When I came to I saw Ronald poised with an empty ammo can raised over my head. I quickly slid out from under him and flipped Ronald over on his back and then pinned his shoulders to the ground with my knees. I punched Ronald hard in the face and he went limp. Then I looked up at Dithers and shouted, 'You want some of this?! You want some of this?! Come on then! Come and get some, Dithers motherfucker!' But as soon as I said it I knew I'd crossed a line and I felt pretty bad about the whole thing, and I tried to apologize to him later.

Beverly's the best wrestler. She's got a headlock that could crush a shark. Chimpanzees are five times stronger than human beings. So when I beat one of the chimpanzees like that, I have to wonder if I'm something better than a human being. Some sort of super human being.

The debilitating conundrum of food as an energy source

Despite my impressive defeat over Ronald, this situation with Dithers only got worse over the next couple days. It was highly unpleasant. And it worried me too. Because when I left the underground bunker at night I wondered if Dithers would be able to get out. I always checked the lock on his cage before I left, but you never knew. I wasn't free to be my new self anymore. My identity as Help People was being compromised by Dithers. I didn't understand how he could do this to me considering how I'd saved his life and helped him rehabilitate his arm. And how could I devote myself to giving medical attention to the innocent victims of war when I was worried that this maniac Dithers was going to be there waiting to crush my skull when I came back to the bunker in the morning?

To make matters worse, it was about this time that our food rations started to run out. Even though I'd carefully rationed out our MREs they were dwindling fast, and then one day they were gone. There were no more. I felt bad about this, because I knew how hungry the chimpanzees and Dithers were getting. And that didn't seem fair. But I've always been resourceful, and soon after that I started catching lizards for food. There are these little pink lizards that skate around on the concrete walls of the bunker and disappear in the cracks. The lizards are translucent, and you can see their tiny skeletons under their skin. Their eyes are almost half as big as their bodies and look like Tic-Tacs. About the only thing you can't see is their thoughts.

My effort to eliminate anything that posed a threat to my newfound mission

Catching enough lizards to feed two men and five chimpanzees takes a lot of time, and I found that I was sleeping less and less. I tried to catch catnaps here and there. But I was starting to see lizards in my dreams. Then I started to dream that I was a lizard. I would scurry around on all four legs and people would laugh at me because they could see my insides. Until finally I just quit sleeping altogether. I found that I didn't need to sleep. Now I haven't slept in weeks, and it seems strange to me that this was something that I ever did.

Incarceration as a form of rehabilitation, because I remained hopeful and optimistic

And I still didn't know what to do about Dithers, but I hadn't given up hope on him yet. I was confused but optimistic. Sometimes it's hard to make someone see the light. I was crushed because I felt like all my hard work was down the tubes. I tried my best to come up with ways for him to like our new life here. I told him to look inside his heart. I told him I wanted him to be able to come out with me at night on the missions. I was getting tired of witnessing all the atrocities of war alone. I begged and pleaded with him to consider my position in all this. He'd yell at me. But still I didn't give up. I even offered to let him do some yoga with me. I told him I'd let him out of the cage if he wanted to do some yoga. He kept yelling. I told him how he was becoming just like his alcoholic dad. I told him, Don't be that way.

'You're not an albino. You're not an albino,' I said.

But Dithers began to show the true darkness in his heart. He was talking all the time. Nonstop. Every time I tried to do some yoga. Shouting at me. Yoga was out of the question, and I started to lose my internal balance. It was a racket. I couldn't think straight. The void was slipping further and further away. It was like garbage can lids banging in my head. Taunting me. Heckling me. Calling me Gay Dad. Gay Dad. I'd come back to the bunker and lie down with my hands over my ears. Gay Dad. Gay Dad. Gay Dad. Gay Dad.

What happened when the lizards ran out, and the pursuit of alternative energy sources

The lizards ran out. At some point I realized there weren't any lizards left. Dithers saw me scrabbling around for lizards and realized what had happened and started laughing. 'Great, what are you going to do now, Gay Dad? I'm hungry!' he shouted. But then Dithers said a curious thing.

He whispered ever so softly, 'Eat me.'

I turned on him. 'What did you just say?'

'Eat me. I'm delicious. I taste good.'

That time I knew exactly what I'd heard. I said, 'Why did you just tell me to eat you, Dithers?'

He got this funny look on his face.

'Shut the hell up. I didn't say anything. I haven't said a word since you got back. I'm being good for once. What the hell are you talking about?'

But then he followed that up with his whisper again, 'Eat me. Eat me. Eat me. I'm yummy. Look at this arm of mine. This arm looks delicious.'

I turned and looked at his arm.

'What the hell are you looking at?' he said.

'Don't worry yourself about it. No need to play games. I heard you the first time, Dithers.'

I went back to scrounging around in my rucksack, but then

in an instant I knew exactly what I was going to do. I went to the back of the bunker. The chimps were hissing and screeching. Dithers was shouting. Then I picked up an empty ammo can and started for Dithers's cage.

My dad's final propaganda letter, which I received the day before I scooped up Dithers and quit the war

Dear Son,

The idea that I have fathered a son who wants to kill other human beings in the name of his country breaks my heart. I am begging you, please don't do the things I did you will regret them for the rest of your life, I promise you. Man is not made to relish pain in others and it is the sickness of war that propagates this belief, and we have to hold on to what makes us human, and not revert back to the life of animals. I butchered human beings and killing became a pleasure I do not want for you to suffer the black scars on your soul that I have on my mine because of Vietnam please listen to me I am not joking anymore this is the most serious thing I have ever said to you you are my son and don't forget that.

    Dad

The inevitable liberation of Dithers

I flung open Dithers's cage and swung the ammo can at his head and missed. The chimps were banging on the slats of their cage and screeching, and in the chaos I closed my eyes and focused and swung again, this time it was different though, this time I swung with the confidence and ease of a man who knows it's going to be a homerun. I opened my eyes. Dithers's cage was empty. In that split second I was shoved from behind and heard the ominous click of the lock as the cage door slammed to. I whirled and crashed into the slats and fell over. Dithers was beaming. For the next half hour as I calmly stared out through the slats while seething with outrage, Dithers went around the bunker packing my ruck with stuff for his journey, informing me as to how he was going to grab Marty and the guys and that they'd be back to beat the living shit out me and then flexcuff me and ship my ass to the brig. 'The game's up, Mr Fucking Asshole Freak. I sure hope you like those bars, cuz you're gonna be seeing a lot more of them from here on out,' said Dithers, and then he breezed out of sight, and I heard the hatch swing open and then slam to. A half-hour later I finally jimmied open the lock with a paper clip from my pocket, and sprinted out of the bunker and out into the night, scanning the horizon desperately for Dithers. I searched all up and down the highway for the next several hours until the sun came up, ignoring the wounded Iraqi boy who called out to me as I raced past. But Dithers was gone.

And then today I came back and paced around the bunker, consumed with bitterness and rage and a deep sense of betrayal, but I finally caught my snap and moved past that, realizing that these emotions were of no use to me. I found forgiveness in my heart. I realized that Dithers did what he did not because he's a hateful person, but because he's simply misguided. And, most importantly, I found confirmation that I was a good person. And then tonight, exhausted but with a renewed sense of resolve, I started to go out on my Mission for the Good of Mankind, with hardly any of my stuff because Dithers had stolen it all, and I reached for the handle on the hatch but it was stuck. I shook it harder, but it wouldn't budge. Then I heard Marty's snickering voice call out, 'Hey, what's going on down there, Help People.' A chorus of laughter erupted, and I could tell there was a bunch of them up there. I heard Dithers's distinctive cackle, 'Hoo! What's amatter, can't get outta there! Hey, whadya know, there's a boulder up here! Ha-ha!' Then Diaz called out in a low voice that rose as he went on, 'Hey, help help. Help me, Help People! Help Help!,' and then they all chimed in and were roaring it together, over and over, 'Hey, help help. Help me, Help People! Help! Help!'

And it hurts, because they don't know this but I really would, I'd rescue each and every one of them if they needed it. There's no ocean or stretch of land I would not cross to save their lives, and here they are, just fifteen feet away, doing everything they can to keep me from it.

The Tears of Squonk, and What Happened Thereafter

GLEN DAVID GOLD

In late March, 1916, a week before the Nash Family Circus came to Tennessee, their spotty poster advertisements clung to the sides of buildings throughout the railroad town of Olson. Olson was best described as sleepy, save for the constant rattle of the railroad yards; it was not at all a place for murder. And the Nash Family and their hired performers seemed anything but evil.

The posters, stock images dated and fading already, promised tame acts. A horseback rider here, a clown there, a roaring lion, and finally a pair of juggling clowns pasted next to each other to lend some small company. Taken together, they looked as forlorn as the orphans who sometimes stood outside the tent and imagined far greater attractions than those that ever actually wheezed through their paces under the single, patched canvas big top.

The talents of the Nash family clowns were generally tepid. Some of the horses had been remarkable in their youth, true, but they were tired – granted, only half as tired as the acrobats, who mostly daydreamed of returning to Germany when the war was over. No, what the Nash Family Circus had to offer was the moral backbone of its patriarch, Ridley Nash.

Nash had been in the circus business since 1893, when the traveling carnival had been born. A cook in Chicago, and a splendid mimic of the world's cuisines, he had made the daily meals at the international pavilions at the Colombian Exposition. He had been so impressed by the clean family entertainment, he purchased his first wagon then and there, on credit, from a dealer in the dry goods pavilion.

By 1916, he was referred to as 'Colonel' Nash, which dismayed him privately, as he had never served in the army, and he felt the term disrespected those who had. Still, it was the custom among traveling circuses to have a faux colonel at the helm, and so he bore it manfully.

Among the Nash Family Circus posters was a broadside of printed text which Nash had set himself. He insisted that every word be true, beginning with 'A Moral Entertainment,' and ending with '23 Years of Dealing Squarely with the American Public.' In between were other promises, such as '8 funny clowns,' and if the eighth clown was under the bottle that night, to keep the count honest, Colonel Nash donned the red nose and let himself be hit with the slapstick.

At the center of the broadsheet was a woodcut of an elephant, Mary, billed as the third-largest elephant in captivity. She was seen in a headdress and cape, with an indication by her side that she stood twelve feet at the shoulder.

The elephant was indeed the third-largest in captivity, and she stood exactly as high as the Colonel claimed, and one morning had been measured three inches taller, but the Colonel kept the smaller number, as he could count on it being verified.

The posters he'd designed to showcase the elephant were for many years treasured, not for their moral authority, but simply for how Mary was shown both head-on and from the side. Nash felt this presented her headdress and cape *squarely*, to use his preferred term, but more than one spectactor to her final performance commented – be-fore spiriting away a copy of the broadsheet – how prescient the Colonel had been in showing her as if she were posed for a police blotter's mug book.

The morning of Mary's last day, roustabouts swung sledge-hammers along the stake line, and ring-makers were leveling the field exactly forty-two feet in all directions from the center pole, which was erected by a line of ten men chanting as they had since the days of Dan Rice, 'easy, easy, easy, PULL.'

The sky was iron grey with clouds, and the humidity brought an odd smell, something rusted and cruel, from the train yards, which surrounded and dwarfed the town. Tiny Olson sat in the shadow of Wildwood Hill, the top of which was a graveyard for freight cars. In the town, the parade band attempted in vain to tune their ratty instruments, and beyond and above them was the hulking, distant silhouette of Ol' 1400, the McKennon Railway's 100-ton train derrick, which was used to snatch trains off the track and then drop them, helpless as baby turtles, onto the scrapheap.

The parade was a chance to show the town just a little for free, to build anticipation for that evening's show. At eleven a.m. the brass band was fully engaged and marching: the scruffy and heartbroken Nash children, plus two pony boys and a mule skinner who had some legitimate use for the slide trombone. Next were the three acrobats who normally did handsprings in the street, but because of the mud, they rode on the back of a flatbed cart pulled by goats, and made a human pyramid at one end, tumbled down, then reassembled at the other end. Next came the eight funny clowns, most of whom seemed, at eleven a.m., not so much funny as wrestling with philosophical discontents.

The sole clown of merit was Squonk. When he and Mary had joined the Nash Family early in the season, the Colonel billed Squonk in the programs as 'Joseph Bales, portraying Squonk the Clown,' in the spirit of full disclosure, but Bales, a trained artist who had studied in Europe, was furious. 'Nash,' he said, folding his arms, 'I'm a trained artist and when I studied in Europe, we didn't give away our names, not for the world.' Bales argued that pantomime, make-up, false nose and floppy Bibleback shoes were all poetics, in the Aristotelian sense, intended to preserve mystery. Grudgingly, mostly to keep the temperamental Bales at ease, Nash – who wasn't quite sure about the Aristotelian reference, though it sounded impressive – billed him from then on, in entirety, as 'Squonk.'

That morning, Squonk – in his dunce's cap and bloated single-piece checked suit with three yellow pom-poms down the front – seemed to be everywhere at once, miming the trombonist's slide and puffed-out cheeks, then threatening to topple the human pyramid. In what warmed the crowd as a rib-tickling lampoon (though it lacked the same effect on his peers, who glared daggers at him), Squonk became stern with the other clowns, tutting their performances. He showed them the proper way to toss a child into the sky, lofting and catching a small girl and handing her a daisy all in one motion as smooth and delicate and transparent as glass.

But this was just the warm-up for the big finish. At the head of the parade, two front door men began to wave their arms, standing as if to block the side streets. They cried out, 'Hold your horses! Here comes the elephant!'

The crowd fell to a respectful hush, as there was something glorious and humbling about seeing, once a year at most, such an impossible beast. Some regarded the bizarre mix of parts –

trunk, tusks, huge ears – as evidence of the existence of a bounteous and clever God. Nash, who was swayed by the God argument, also spent stray moments here and there staring Mary in the eye, sensing within her a wonderful intelligence. Squonk wrote out a quotation for him to use during his pitch: 'Comte Georges Leclerc de Buffon, famed naturalist from France, tells us the elephant "by his intelligence makes as near an approach to man, as matter can approach spirit."'

Hence the warning about horses. Elephants would tolerate being chained to a freight car and stuck with a hooked pole, and forced to stand on their hind legs and trumpet. But they would not tolerate horses. The mere fact of horses drove them into an atavistic frenzy. The eye clouded over, almost as if *musth*, the elephant madness, had invaded the brain.

When the street was thought to be secure, Squonk loped forward, dropping all of his humorous antics. His years of European training rushed to the forefront. His rigid posture, his head tilted upward, arms flourishing gracefully, indicated that behind him stood a magnificent work of art known as an elephant. The crowd produced a kind of applause that was at once awed and hesitant.

Mary walked slowly, trunk held forth in a question mark that tilted left and right as she marched through the muck. She wore a sequined headdress, and a long cape with a Shake-spearean ruff. There was a kind of knife-scarring on her ear, an M, made to indicate her name (elephant theft was rare, but costly). The more educated patrons of the circus, upon seeing the outfit, and the M, understood at once how fitting her name was. They would murmur, *Queen Mary*, as the ground trembled with each step.

Bales had trained Mary in a unique manner – she was never

humiliated into squirting water at the crowd, or balancing a ball with her trunk. He was more demanding, more of a martinet than that. Mary performed ballet.

Thus the Nash broadside included mention of Mary's dynamic performances for the crowned heads of Europe (citing, as per Bales's resume, Carlos II of Spain and Sophia of Greece, since Nash was aware that 'crowned heads' was an unacceptably vague term that invited suspicion). The crowd at the parade was there to see ballet, and, had the show at Olson gone as had every other performance that season, Mary would have indulged them with one simple motion, a curtsy, that would have guaranteed a full house that night. It was such an indescribable gesture that most members of every previous crowd were driven to sputter to friends, 'You have to see it – you just have to see it.'

Alas, at 11:15, as the town clock was striking the quarter-hour, Mr. Timothy Phelps, senior director of the McKennon Railway, arrived at the parade via the narrow alley between the Second National Bank and Tannenbaum's hardware store. He appeared mounted, with exquisite form, on his English saddle-backed horse, Jasper.

What happened next was so terrible, so simple, so unbelievable, that townspeople's memories could never have been trusted to relay it accurately. In fact, the story would surely have been demoted to the realm of folklore were it not for a single motion picture camera.

The Pathé Prevost Camera, the camera of choice for professionals, had but one drawback: If the camera fell over and struck a hard object, the film stock tended to explode into flames. An amateur filmmaker named Alexander Victor was experimenting that morning with acetate 'safety' film. He'd ridden the rails of the American South, tinkering with improvements in the optical range finder, and shooting endless locomotives in transit, train-crew razorbacks waving at the camera. Today, he had alighted on the circus parade, which was ideal to him for its interesting motion.

He hand-cranked his camera on the sidewalk, directly across from the alleyway. And so local memories, hazy in other details, are precise in this regard, all of them, no matter where they were that day, recalling it from the same vantage point. Their memories took on the scratched negative, the variable speed and mysterious lighting of amateur film. Mary broke from the parade route, trotting left with an almost magnetic attraction to Jasper and his rider, scattering to the four winds the townspeople between her and her quarry. Standing next to the brick wall of the bank, Phelps and his horse – rather a greyish smear in the frame-by-frame dissection of the scene – nervously paced back and forth, but couldn't make up their collective mind, and then Mary, headdress and cape buffeting with each step, was upon them. It was as if she needed to scratch an itch against the rough bricks, one quick flex of her shoulder, forward, then one slower, luxurious kind of return back, and horse and rider were no more.

This was horror enough. But next, camera still rolling, citizens of Olson sepia blurs crossing the foreground, Mary lowered one front foot to Phelps's back, as if holding the corpse steady, and then she wrapped her trunk around his neck. The next motion was fluid, like drawing a reluctant cork out of a champagne bottle.

There was pandemonium in the streets, people unsure of exactly which direction constituted proper fleeing, and

Alexander Victor's film ends with a man in bowler hat running his way, his vest and watch fob suddenly filling up the screen, and then, blackness.

Nash, rooted in the mud, hadn't seen exactly what happened, but tried to calm the situation, his clear showman's bellow ineffective. He saw the village blacksmith run forward and withdraw a pistol from his apron, which he proceded to empty at Mary's flank. The bullets made small pockmarks in Mary's hide, and she flapped her ears in concern, but she continued walking and there was no further outcome.

Squonk stood paralyzed, his jaw wavering, in the middle of the street. He removed his pointed, conical hat, and lowered his head. He put his palm over his eyes as Mary, his friend and companion, approached him and gingerly reached out her trunk for the apple she always received at the end of every parade.

The rumor that the show must go on was one started by patrons and furthered by newspaper men who liked how it sounded. Many a circus folds without a second thought, and Nash knew, at noon, and at one o'clock and at two o'clock, that there would be no performance that night. He had returned Mary to her freight car, and put most of his men around it to guard her. When a group of townspeople approached, excited as boys invited to their first dance, and armed with rifles, pistols, and sticks of dynamite, Nash stopped them himself. Nash had expected them, and had been girding himself all afternoon to tell a lie. It was the first lie he knowingly told the public.

'You can't kill an elephant that way,' he announced.

His tone was so authoritative, so dismissive, he wondered

where his voice was coming from. He sounded as if he were reciting Leviticus. 'A gun, even a stick of dynamite, that will in no way pierce this beast's hide.'

The men of Olson exchanged glances. There was a problem at hand, but some of them were known to be clever, and it was only a matter of time until someone yelled, 'Electricity!'

Nash shook his head. 'Edison himself attempted that once and failed. It just made the elephant angry.' His second lie.

This caused murmurs, and Nash knew where this would go, a building kind of frustration and impatience. As soon as one man was telling the rest he could call his cousin in Frazer, who had a cannon from the War Between the States that might still work, Nash stopped them. He found himself saying, more of a circus man than he'd ever been, 'We will settle it tonight, gentlemen. We will not leave this town without settling it, publicly, fully, and demonstrably.' He wasn't sure why he added that last word, but it seemed to hold promise to the men, who, upon being assured that Mary would die somehow, turned, and walked away, holding their pistols or their rifles forlornly.

So the Colonel sat in his wagon, which was parked atop its brass brake shoes in a swampy depression nearest Mary's freight car. He was unsure of what to do. His elephant had killed someone – apparently done so with vigor, though he hadn't seen it, and continued to have his doubts. There was a very reasonable demand for vengeance. The idea of having a murderous animal in his charge made him feel ill. But what made him feel worse was the deeper source of his lie to the townspeople: if Mary were killed, he could never pay off his loan.

The finances of a circus were as arcane and toxic as the combinations of Ural Mountain herbs the property men used to jazz up the Sterno squeezings they swilled on long winter evenings. There were loan-outs, buy-backs, reverse repurchase agreements for contracts based on projected earnings. In short, Nash only owned Squonk and Mary's contract because he had guaranteed a bank in Chicago $8000, payable in installments through the end of the summer season. He had paid off $1500 so far. There was no way he could now make up the balance, and for him, financial responsibility was the basis of modern civilization. He had never pitted that belief against his belief in animals' basic nobility, and when the two forces rubbed together like this, the friction upset him.

At three o'clock he called Joseph Bales into his wagon to see how best to proceed. Bales entered with his head hung low, and when Nash began to speak – he began with an overall statement of how he still believed in the intelligence of the elephant, and was about to discuss whether female elephants perhaps fell under the sway of *musth* – Bales interrupted him. 'Hanging,' he said.

'Pardon?'

It was a conversation Nash would recall, helplessly, without conscious effort, many times for the rest of his life. The specifics were worn away, but the general feeling of dread was quite solid.

'Mary committed a crime,' Bales said. 'She should pay. By hanging. It would be poetic.'

Usually Bales spoke in sentences forged from many dependent clauses welded together by sarcasm. Tonight he sounded like a different person. Determined, a man who has made the right choice quickly, begging for no time to reconsider it. He leaned forward and pointed with one articulated, bony finger, out the window. And there, on the hilltop, was the 100-ton railroad derrick, looming just like a gallows.

Nash shook his head, but said nothing. Bales stood, put his hand on the door handle, and as a way of departing, jammed his hat down upon his head. His back was shaking, shoulders quivering. Then, determined, he whispered, 'And it would be more poetic, still, in the deepest sense – poetic justice – when we charge admission.'

When the door closed, Nash stared after it, his own eyes welling up. A terrible taste came into his mouth, a vile copper flavor, exactly like that of a penny.

That night, the whole town of Olson turned out on Wildwood Hill. Also present were the whole towns of Softon, Burroughs, Myers and Carmel, over two thousand people, each of whom had paid the exorbitant sum of two dollars for the privilege of standing among the train wreckage to see an elephant hanged.

Nash himself elected not to attend. That an animal would be done such violence broke his heart. Just before dusk, he returned to Mary, who stood chained in her freight car, and looked her one last time in the eye. He saw within the same intelligence and kindness he had always seen. The longer he stood, the less he could forgive himself for taking the financially responsible way out of this. He retreated to his bed for the rest of the sleepless night.

Alexander Victor set up his camera, to no great effect. Even by the kerosene-fueled pan lights, with their reflectors and occasional flashes, there was not enough light, through the silt and smoke drifting over the excited crowd, to see anything more than vague shapes, suggestions of some tribal ritual.

Wildwood Hill was a gentle slope of about two hundred feet, with spiraling rails and a footpath, terminating in the antediluvian detritus of trains gone extinct. There were men and women and children walking gaily up the path, finding good vantage points surrounding the final length of railway track. The derrick's wheelhouse, belching diesel smoke, sat atop a powerplant the size of a locomotive. And extending from the wheelhouse, at the midpoint of its iron belly, was a kind of mechanical trunk: a muscular crane with a superstructure of steel girders, and at the end of it, a dull steel hook.

At seven o'clock, the doors to Mary's freight car were thrown open and she was led by torchlight along the pathway to the hill. The crowd, upon seeing her at a great distance, cheered for a while, but as her stride was stiff and slow, and the circular pathway uphill quite long, they soon lost their appetite for cheers, and fell instead into muted conversations.

When she finally appeared, it looked at first as if Mary would pass toward the derrick without trouble, but when she came upon the crowd, she froze solid. Some swore that she seemed to eye the steel hook, but perhaps her psychology was more simple than that. She was usually led to perform at this time of night, and yes, she was wearing her headdress and cape, and yes, there was a cheering crowd. But no tent. And the tenor of the crowd, for a creature that lived on emotion over reason, must have frightened her.

She shied away from the path, and it took several quick pokes of the elephant stick to keep her from retreating. Still, no power in the world could get her to go forward to her fate. Long minutes passed this way, with the crowd yelling out its disappointments, until resolution came from an unlikely source. A figure fought his way through the shoulder-to-shoulder overalls. It was Joseph Bales, out of his uniform. No make-up. Woolen jacket, beaten work trousers, a derby. From his occasional missteps and slurred speech, it was apparent he had ladled out applejack for himself from the canned heat wagon. If you looked closely, you could see a fine tapestry of broken capillaries around his eyes, which he wiped at with the back of his sleeve.

Mary immediately reached out her trunk for her friend, who patted her gently. 'This way,' he said, and walked several steps toward the derrick. She followed, but then stopped, and nothing, not all the pats and praise and reassurances in the world, could get her closer to the hook.

Bales tried to smile at her, but failed. Just as the crowd began again to grow unruly, he held out his hands to his sides, palms out, as if trying to stop a fight. He put his head down, and let out a sigh of awful resignation.

When he next raised his head – plainface or not – it was Squonk the Clown who looked up, light and limber as a dishrag. He did a mild leap, from foot to foot, and then back again, then once forward, once back, and then he pointed back at Mary. Understanding passed through her, and she, too, put her feet outward, then back. Then she stepped to the left, then the right, then turned around in a full circle. The audience let out a lusty cheer – Mary was doing her ballet!

The pas de deux was based on Plastikoff's *La Chauve-Souris Dorée*, a rare work in that it celebrated not courtship, but daily love, the often-pale and unnoticed emotions that pass between a man and wife. When Squonk performed a *saut de l'ange*, Mary, who could not of course jump with all four feet in the air, nevertheless responded by extending one leg behind her, and her opposite forward leg straight ahead, in a perfect arabesque.

She did not notice that, far overhead, the crane was swinging into position.

Finally, Squonk performed a series of *assemblés sur lé point*, jumping with his legs together, turning in midair, going up on his toes, springing again, with a kind of grace that would seem unrepeatable until Mary followed him, shuffling in a circle like a trolly on a turntable. For her big finish, she did exactly what she'd done a thousand times before – rear legs slightly crossed, lowering herself until she was almost belly to the ground, and dropping her head as if in supplication: a perfect curtsey.

And that was when Squonk stepped forward and slipped the hook into the chain around her neck.

She startled backwards, but it was too late. Gears far away, deep in the power plant, began to grind. Mary stood up herself, shaking her head like a dog shedding water. And then her forelegs were lifted off the dusty ground. She walked on her two legs, balancing, and the turbine whined awfully as something seemed to slip, and she started to return to the earth – briefly, though – as the crane applied inexorable force, she was pulled upward again, and her rear legs were removed from the earth, too.

All around, on the tops of dead scrap, of passenger cars stripped bare, of tankers gone to rust, the men and women and children lost their ability to cheer. An elephant is not meant to leave the ground, and the sight is sickening, a kind of rebuke to the natural order – fossils found in a churchyard, a rainfall of salt cod in the desert. There was a hush under the smoldering pan lights. Mary's stubby legs kicked in the air, and then, just once, after long moments, the eye startled wide in recognition of what was happening. The trunk sprung straight, a quick and disappointed half-strangling trumpet, and then she went limp.

No one knows for certain how long the elephant hung over Wildwood Hill. A man schooled in night photography offered to let people pose with the corpse, but there were no takers. There was a general call toward Squonk, and then confusion, then realization: He was gone. He had probably turned away the moment the crane began its work. He was never seen again.

A year passed. Then another. The Nash Family soldiered on, barely, sending in cash to cover a good portion of Mary and Squonk's contract, and then making small monthly payments. There was no longer a big finish to the Colonel's circus. Instead, Nash added a trained chimpanzee, who, dressed in a toga, rode in a chariot pulled by two basset hounds. He also added a castaway from the Sparks circus, Captain Tiebor, who had a team of sea lions he claimed were college graduates. Nash dutifully wrote that into his new broadsides, and if that absurdity troubled him, he said nothing about it. He still claimed to offer a moral entertainment, though there was no longer a chronological measure of his dealing squarely with the American public.

In winter, 1918, the family went off the road for a season. Nash went alone to a rented ranch-style hacienda in an unincorporated valley not far from Los Angeles, California. His idea, expressed vaguely to the family he left behind, was to find new talent associated with the motion picture industry – perhaps some tumblers or wild animal acts were dissatisfied with the life behind the camera, and perhaps they truly wanted to see the world.

But the words seemed hollow to him, and in their letters, no one asked him how the quest was going. Since Mary's hanging, Nash had been directionless. He knew no one in Los Angeles or its environs, which he found lonely and strange – acres of olive groves and citrus trees somehow mysteriously kept alive in the desert climate. He half-heartedly visited Famous Players once, but was turned away at the secretarial pool when he couldn't remember the name of the man he was supposed to meet. He spent the rest of the afternoon riding the trolley cars home.

When he cared to think about it in culinary terms, a habit he retained from his previous career, Nash believed there were two types of circus attractions: the sweet and the sour. The sweet consisted of wholesome entertainments that were exactly as presented: the trapeze, the animals, the clowns. The sour were those that relied on fooling people. The India rubber pickled punks in jars, talked up as two-headed babies. The pink lemonade they sold that was actually water the clowns had washed their tights in. They had seemed too easy to keep apart, those worlds, but at some point Nash had crossed a line, and gone sour himself.

One February afternoon, Nash was interrupted in his morning ritual of shaving by a knock at his door. He peered out the keyhole, worried that it might be an associate come to take him back early to the circus; but no, the man on the other side of the door was no one he knew. Wiping away the foam, Nash let him in.

The stranger's face was broken and scorched, with patches of red skin among wrinkles, the expression a perpetual wince, as if he'd spent every moment of his life in hostile weather. His age was impossible to guess. He wore the familiar black cape and hat of a railway detective, which was the main reason Nash had so readily let him in.

Unaccustomed to company, Nash fumbled to offer him coffee, which the stranger accepted, announcing at the same time his name, 'Leonard Pelkin.' Pelkin had once been a railway detective, he continued, but he had retired and was now working privately.

They sat on either side of a galley that had been built into Nash's small kitchen, cramped but breezy, with a good view of the valley over Nash's shoulder. Pelkin took the opportunity to admire it while digging a portfolio out of his knapsack.

'Might I ask you some questions?'

'Certainly.'

Pelkin carefully removed a stack of four-by-five photographs. As if dealing a hand of poker, he placed them face down in a field of five. 'It's about a murder,' Pelkin said. He cleared his throat, as if he had more to say. Nash nodded, to indicate he was being helpful. Pelkin nodded back, and then took a sip of coffee. He gestured with the coffee cup, toward the photographs. 'Suspects,' he continued.

Then he turned over the photographs, each making a confident snap as they went face up.

For a moment, Nash was silent.

'These are murder suspects?' he finally asked.

Pelkin nodded. 'Do you recognize any of them?'

'They're elephants,' Nash said.

'Look again.'

Nash didn't need to look. He was upset, as he felt this was a problem that had been handled long ago, destroying a good part of himself in the bargain.

'I'm sure they're elephants. If you're here, talking to me, then you know why I'd know that.'

Pelkin put up a finger. 'One elephant,' he said. 'Just one.'

The five photographs had been taken years apart, the earliest ones streaked and bubbling with emulsion. Each of them showed an elephant in the midst of carnivals or circuses – Nash recognized a wagon from the Sells organization, and a Ringling banner, and, finally, his own sagging big top, whose patches were as identifiable as surgical scars. It was like the sun breaking over a mountaintop.

'Mary,' he said.

'Can you indicate where you see her?' Pelkin asked.

'Are you serious? She's the elephant standing before my tent.'

'Is that her in the other photographs?'

It was hard to tell. In one, she wore a kind of tiara, in the rest, she was unadorned. 'It could be.'

'Did she have any identifying marks?'

'Well. Well. She was exactly twelve foot tall. Is that what you mean?'

Pelkin's eyes narrowed. 'Twelve foot? Or twelve-foot, three-inches?'

'No, exactly twelve-foot, as per the broadsides.' He blew out his cheeks. 'Of course, that one morning in Denver, she seemed to be twelve-foot-three.'

Pelkin brought his hand down on the table hard enough to make the spoons jump.

'Yes!'

He leaned forward, and said, as if trying to be calm, 'Is it possible she was, all those other times you measured her, slouching?'

'I don't understand.'

Pelkin eased away. He looked over Nash's shoulder, at the elm trees beyond the window. 'Any other marks you remember?' he asked, faintly.

'She had an M on her ear.'

'Like this?' Pelkin thumbed through some photographs until he found what he was looking for, and snap, it went down on the table: It was a close-up of an elephant's ear.

Nash nodded. 'Yes, except Mary had an M and this elephant has an N.'

Weighing that statement with a frown, Pelkin brought out a fountain pen, shook it, then added a single down-stroke. 'An M like this, is what Mary had?'

'I'm sorry, how many elephants have letters on their ears? Perhaps all of them. I've only examined one up close.'

And at once there came forth the bitterness Nash had been trying so hard not to taste. The glimpses he'd had into Mary's eye, the raw mind he'd seen there, how she had been betrayed.

'One elephant, I'm thinking,' Pelkin said. 'There was an elephant named Nommi, with Ringling, and four years ago she killed a man. I think they just hustled her out the back way in the middle of the night, changed her name, and sold her to you.'

'That's impossible,' Nash said, but as he did, he brought up the photographs one by one and stared at them. 'These are Nommi?'

'One of them is. One is of a Sells elephant, name of Veronica. She was a killer too, six years ago. And the name, see, if you—' Pelkin awkwardly put up two fingers to make a V, and then joined with them a finger from the other hand, which made a backwards N. He moved his fingers around, trying to get it right, and then gave up. 'Before that, Ionia. That's the one with the tiara.'

Nash wanted to tell Pelkin that he was insane, but could somehow not move his mouth to form the words. He had a sickly feeling, one tinged with guilt, as if he himself were being accused.

'The man Mary trampled in Olson, he was on a horse,' he said, meaning by this to begin a conversation that would end with Mary being, if not blameless or excusable, than at least understandable: an animal pushed beyond her natural limit.

'Mary didn't exactly trample Phelps, did she?' Pelkin said.

'Well . . .'

Pelkin started packing up his photographs, and Nash hoped this meant it was over. But instead, there was a new photograph to study. It was about eight inches tall, and of such length that it came in a roll which Pelkin unwrapped. He smoothed it out, then weighted it down at either end with coffee cups.

It was a safari shot. Five men at the center, in white pith helmets, Springfields cracked open across their laps. Native bearers of a tribe Nash did not recognize were to the left and to the right. Some of them covered their faces before the camera, but left the rest of themselves exposed, including the women, a detail Nash dwelt on for a shameful amount of time before realizing what, exactly, he was being shown.

The five hunters were all posing with their trophies: one man atop them, two on either side, two kneeling before them – a half-dozen dead African elephants.

'Oh, my lord,' Nash cried.

There were pencil marks around the men's faces, which were half-crinkled in the photograph, hardly recognizable to begin with. Pelkin tapped on the image of one man to the right, whose rifle was jauntily slung over his shoulder. 'Timothy Phelps,' he said, 'when he was a much younger man. The Southern Crescent Railroad, in 1889, took its senior-most managers on safari to the dark continent. Five of them are now dead. Killed by elephants.' He picked up his coffee cup; the photo rolled shut. 'An elephant.'

Nash smoothed out the photo, holding it open himself. He stared until full understanding settled in on him. He felt buoyed by it; he could make sense of this. Almost giddily, he whispered, 'Mary's family, then?'

'What?'

'The elephants who were killed here on the hunt. They're Mary's family, aren't they? She's been having her revenge.'

There was a rotten silence in the room as Pelkin sized him up, astonished. Not in a pleasant way. At once, the sourness of the circus returned to Nash. Pelkin's look was the kind reserved for the lowest hick, the kind who buys the Fiji Mermaid, the he/she dancer blow-off, the pickled punks and the lemonade, all of it, hook, line and lead-heavy sinker.

'You think . . .' Pelkin grinned. 'You think Mary, an elephant, is the mastermind, or something?'

'Well.'

'Look.' Pointing again into the group of hunters. Toward the left, isolated from his comrades, arms folded, wearing no gun himself, was Joseph Bales.

'Oh! How? How?' Nash paused, helplessly.

'You know him as Bales, right? That's not his name. His name is Bowles. The clever ones, when they change their names, make them similar enough they'll answer to them in their sleep. Bowles was supposed to be promoted, and he wasn't. I hear he was a terrible safari member, made a big fuss about everything, spent hours telling his fellow men around the campfire how uneducated they were. After the safari, he was fired. He went bitter, Nash. How bitter, no one knew. Some bitter guys, they scheme but they don't have any follow-through. They fade. Not Bowles. He went out and became a circus clown, the way some of the really bitter ones do. For the last dozen years, he has been luring these men to their deaths. The day before your circus arrived in Olson, Phelps received a telegram telling him to ride his horse to the parade, as a wonderful surprise was waiting.' Pelkin shook his head. 'Wasn't so wonderful, in my opinion.'

For a great deal of time, Nash said nothing. He felt he should say something, but the specifics eluded him. Pieces of this macabre plot surfaced: Bowles scheming revenge, Bowles becoming a circus clown, alighting on the poetic justice of death-by-elephant. Finally, he said, 'Aristotle.'

'What?'

'He liked Aristotle,' he said, blushing a bit.

Pelkin shrugged, and then wrote Aristotle on the back of one of the photographs. 'Any ideas where Bowles might have gone?'

'Why did he kill her?'

'Pardon?'

With no difficulty, Nash was back in the circus wagon, with Bales opposite him, Bales holding back tears – or was he actually crying them? – and determined to have Mary hanged. 'He said killing her would serve justice.'

'Oh. Yeah, the justice expert. Sure. He was done, Nash. He'd managed to get her out of trouble four times before that. Slipped away in the dead of night four times, changing her name, changing his name. This time, he didn't need her any-more. He'd killed everyone he wanted to, and this way he wasn't going to leave any evidence behind.'

'Hmmph.' Nash nodded. 'So he betrayed her.'

'Sure,' Pelkin said. Like most railway detectives, he was

terse, but when revealing secrets he took a shameless delight in relaying the horrors behind them. 'They were partners. She didn't know the game was rigged until the blow-off.'

'I see.'

He now wanted Pelkin to depart, as he was beginning to feel a strange and restless feeling, as if impatient for a loved one returning from a long trip. He wanted to throw open the door, look down the drive, and see, bags in hand, himself. He hardly listened as Pelkin snapped out another pair of photographs.

'These men, though, it seems Mary – or whatever her name was at first – she killed them in 1902. That was two years, as far as I can tell, before she met Bowles. It was a pretty fair partnership, I'd say. A good match.'

'Yes, yes, I see,' Nash said, impatiently. He was beginning to listen not to Pelkin but to a story unfolding in his brain. Mary, an animal, whose impulses were harnessed by a bad man. The tragedy of her life, coupled with the sheer evil of Bowles, made him hurry through the remainder of the interview with Pelkin. He was unsure of all things in the world, save one: He needed to be alone.

The conversation continued for less than five minutes. Pelkin had confirmed the trail was cold here. Abruptly, he shook Nash's hand, and he left.

When Nash was quite alone, he dug out a wax pencil and a sheet of butcher paper, and began to write down all he remembered about Mary, trying to balance the good (her intelligence and, generally speaking, kindness) with the bad – her having murdered people, for instance. He remembered then the salty tracks on Squonk's cheeks – if they had been there at all – and as he thought of them glistening, they enraged him.

False, awful, sour, heedless crocodile tears, the worst kind of carny, the lowest of men, working Nash like a sucker.

He wrote long into the afternoon, had a snack, and then began to re-write everything into a short and morally instructive playlet, which could be performed by a small circus. It was about a wicked clown and the elephant he tricked. When he was done, Nash realized he was about to shop for another elephant, and he made a note to send out wires to Sarasota, where the circus exchange kept track of such requests.

From 1919 to 1924, the Nash Family presented their circus as ever, sometimes lucky enough to adhere to a strict schedule when times were good, other times blowing the route and wildcatting it until business caught on again. The lynchpin of their show was Nash's playlet, a melodrama that featured the impish and terrible antics of Moxie, a clown, and Regina, a luckless and sad elephant suffering fits during which she accidentally murdered people. Finally, she was taken outside, and, as seen in a silhouette projected against the raw canvas tent, hanged until dead.

In his broadsides, and his talking before the performance, Nash explained that every word was the truth, including the hanging, though he had changed the names. It was said that the finale was done in shadow because of its graphic and disturbing nature, which was true, but actually secondary to its function as a special effect. Nash would never really harm the elephant, whom he loved: a second love, the cautious kind. This one was named Emily, and she had credentials so spotless her owner liked to say she could run for the Senate.

The crowds were entertained and disturbed by the spectacle, which was never quite the success Nash hoped. When the flaps to the tent opened after each performance, the crowds were hesitant to leave, and some audience member stayed behind to talk to Nash. There had been rumors, promulgated in whispers by other Nash Family performers, that Mary had killed even before she'd met Squonk. He was an awful man, to be sure, but wasn't Mary herself also guilty? Wasn't the execution, even if facilitated by Squonk, somewhat just? And Bales, did he escape, just like that? Did he kill again? Why wasn't he brought to justice in the end? And though Nash tried to answer the questions, he always grew flustered, as if the audience were missing the point, and he would retire to his wagon for the night.

There is no record of the last performance; it was never truly historical or important. It was unusual, a sort of passion play on a pachydermic scale, but though generous in spirit, it was too small a venue – melodrama – to incorporate a serious truth: Just as there are intelligent, wicked men, there are intelligent, wicked elephants. A thing of pure nature is not by necessity a good thing.

Just before the turn of the new century, the story of Mary was determined to be folklore, a confused truncation of the truth, something contradicted by old-time Olsonites, rerouted by oral historians: all a lie, it was now said. There were rumors of an amateur film (long-since disintegrated 'safety' film that was no more stable than nitrate in the end) – exactly the kind of red herring 'evidence' that indicated an urban legend at play. There had indeed been posters featuring an elephant named Mary, and several years later an odd play about hanging an elephant. But this was a play put on nowhere better than a circus, and it was apparent people had confused this with the truth. An elephant hanged? Papers were composed in the anthropology department of the University of Tennessee about the conflation of lynching narratives with that of an elephant. It was explained that the story evolved from a need to de-humanize the victims, or, in a contradictory interpretation, to enrage the very people who would never lift a finger to protect a fellow human being.

When facing the past, and attempting to do so squarely, it's difficult to understand what is marvelous, what is real, what is terrible, and what points overlap.

But there has been a recent development: Wildwood Hill, long ago surrounded by the blue fencing and tarpaulins of a Superfund site, has been purchased by the petrochemical com-bine that inherited the land in a deal with the vanished McKennon Railroad. There is a move to cap the area in advance of a toxic waste cleanup, and the first gesture is to dig wells into the hill's core, to test the soil for penetration of leeching chemicals.

Ten yards from the end of the tracks, under debris from six generations of abandoned railroad technology, is an excavation site twenty feet wide and twenty feet deep, scratched out of the clay almost a hundred years ago, and filled in again almost immediately. At the center, among the roots and weeds, the tiny stones and shards of broken glass and metal, lie elephant bones.

Caked with dirt, dark with dried tissues, they also gleam with a necklace of stainless steel chain, and there is a shroud, once probably red, once likely ruffled and imperial, now as decayed and colorless as the dirt.

Note: This story could only have been written with the aid of *The Day They Hung the Elephant* by Charles Edwin Price.

No Justice, No Foul

JIM STALLARD

Whenever I hear some historian on PBS prattling about the Supreme Court, I have to step outside for air. I know it's a matter of seconds before the stock phrases – judicial review, legal precedent, activist court – will start rolling out, and I'll feel my blood coming to a boil as I hear the scamming of yet another generation

Are you sitting down? Everything you were taught about the Supreme Court and its decisions is bunk. For most of the nineteenth century and all of the twentieth, our biggest, most far-reaching legal decisions have been decided not by careful examination of facts and reference to precedent but by contests of game and sport between the justices. The games varied through the years – cribbage, chess, horseshoes, darts – even a brief, disasterous flirtation with polo. (Now do you understand *Plessy* v. *Ferguson?*) But ever since 1923, basketball has been the only game, and as the years rolled by and the decisions came down, the whole thing has settled nicely into place. Basketball has shaped the way our society is today, every contour, every legality, every way that one person relates to another in an official, sanctioned sense.

I know, I know – you're thinking I got this stuff from radio signals in my head. Actually, the reason I'm privy to this info is really quite mundane. My father was a Supreme Court maintenance worker from 1925 until he retired 40 years later. He started sneaking me in to see games when I was 8. I saw my share (though none of the landmarks) and heard from many sources about countless others.

Oliver Wendell Holmes hit on the basketball idea after attending a collegiate game in New York during the Court's Christmas recess in 1922. He thought he had finally identified the type of contest that could involve all the justices, could be played indoors when the Court was in 'session,' and, most important of all, did not involve horses.

Holmes brought the idea back to Washington and pitched it to Chief Justice Taft. The corpulent chief had been lobbying for Greco-Roman wrestling, but he was starting to realize none of his colleagues would go for a sport in which they might be killed. (The Fatty Arbuckle incident was fresh on everyone's minds.) Taft finally agreed that basketball offered a superior form of jurisprudence.

After a little tinkering, the procedure came down to this: whenever the justices were evenly split over a judgment (4–4 with one judge abstaining) and the deadlock persisted for more than a week, the issue would move to the hardwood. In general, the 'teams' could be described as liberal vs. conservative, although as court watchers know, legal philosophies cannot be reduced to such simplistic terms. The justice voted most valuable player in the game was allowed the choice of writing the opinion or – in the case of a political hot potato – making someone else do it.

For the first twelve years, the justices scrapped in a dreary gymnasium tucked in the basement of the Capitol Building. The floor was cement and the baskets were mounted flush on the walls so that every fast break or lay-up carried the threat of a concussion. (Owen Roberts became notorious for his short-term memory and was constantly being carried off the floor.)

When the new Court building went up across the street in 1935, the justices insisted that the fourth floor remain mostly vacant to house the real highest court in the land. Because of a mix-up in the architectual plans, the room had a ceiling that was far too low – a fact that made Chief Justice Charles Evans Hughes livid and which has left its imprint on American history: Many landmark decisions might have gone differently if the room could have accommodated justices with a high arch on their shot – Stanley Reed, Robert Jackson, and most tragically, Abe Fortas.

Mind you, everything leading up to the actual decision was, and is, legitimate. The Court still accepted petitions on merit, they still read the briefs, listened (or dozed) during oral argument and then went into conference prepared to vote one way or another. When the deadlock came, however, the bifocals came off and the hightops went on.

Let's look at some of the landmark games, with impressions gleaned from those lucky few who witnessed them:

Near v. Minnesota (1931)

A First Amendment ruling that came down in favor of a sleazy Minnesota newspaper being sued for libel after using ethnic slurs. Charles Evans Hughes (28 points, 13 rebounds, 7 steals) thought some of the newspaper's comments were pretty funny, so he set out to win the MVP and the opinion that followed. 'He was good, and he loved to talk out there,' said one observer. 'I'm no choirboy, but some of the things he was saying had my face turning red. The ref finally gave him a technical to quiet him down.' Hughes's mouth finally got him in trouble in the waning moments. After hitting nothing but net, he pointed at Justice Pierce Butler – a bookish sort who had been the subject of persistent rumors – waited a few beats . . . and then yelled 'Swish!' The observer recalled, 'It was the only time I've ever seen a referee give two technicals at once to the same guy: One, two, gone.'

Hirabayashi v. United States (1943) (see fig. 1)

The case involved the rights of a Japanese-American citizen as the wartime government was herding his kind around California, but it turned out to be about so much more. Harlon Stone lured Robert Jackson into committing three charging fouls and turned the game around with a steal, a blocked shot, and a wicked bounce pass to Felix Frankfurter that left Owen Roberts and Stanley Reed glued to the floor, their mouths agape. Stone is credited by more than one as the person who remade the legal landscape in this century. 'That was the start of a new kind of law,' says one observer who was privy to the Court's biggest cases over decades. 'No longer were people standing and taking two-handed set shots. No law is going to survive without being innovative and flexible.'

FIG. I. Pivotal play in *Hirabayashi* v. *United States* occurred with 1:23 left in the game, when Harlan Stone (1) dribbled to his left toward the top of the key (2) and then threw a behind-the-back bounce pass to Felix Frankfurter (3), who had faked outside and then cut back into the lane. Reed was busy trying to deny Rutledge the ball and so did not react in time to stop the pass.

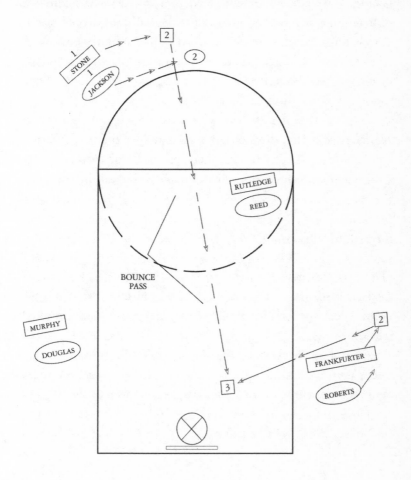

Jim Stallard

Brown v. Board of Education (1954)

Those who watched remembered Earl Warren, 'The Aircraft Carrier,' posting up and calling for the ball four, five times in a row and kicking it back out until he saw a hairline crack in the defense or a teammate left completely undefended for a jump shot. 'So agile for a big man,' said one clerk. 'They underestimated him at first, then they learned to play him tough. Not that it did them any good.' (Interesting side note: Rumor has it that during oral arguments for the case, Warren was sizing up Thurgood Marshall, pleading for the appellants and sent a page scurrying off to find out how tall he was.)

Griswold v. Connecticut (1964) (see fig. 2)

The case that made contraception safe for America was a nail-biter. Thirty-three years later, a man who watched the game while clerking for Hugo Black was still bitter as he recalled the improbable 30-foot shot William Douglas made at the buzzer: 'Two defenders hanging all over him, absolutely no arch, and it goes in – I mean, he should have apologized to everyone. But instead of acknowledging he was lucky, he goes and writes that crap about the "penumbra of privacy" to rub our noses in it. What a prick.'

FIG. 2. In the final frantic moments of *Griswold* v. *Connecticut*, with the game tied, William Douglas of the liberal bloc (ovals) had the ball at the top of the key being guarded by John Harlan of the conservative bloc (square).

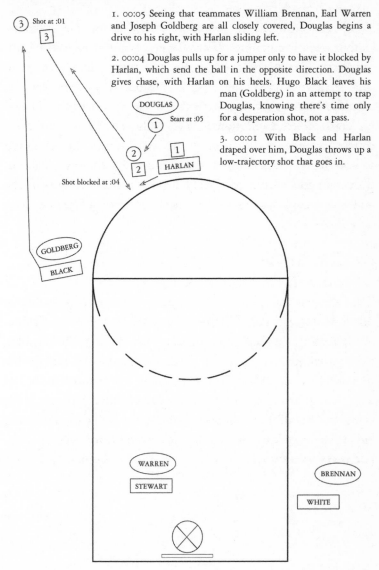

1. 00:05 Seeing that teammates William Brennan, Earl Warren and Joseph Goldberg are all closely covered, Douglas begins a drive to his right, with Harlan sliding left.

2. 00:04 Douglas pulls up for a jumper only to have it blocked by Harlan, which send the ball in the opposite direction. Douglas gives chase, with Harlan on his heels. Hugo Black leaves his man (Goldberg) in an attempt to trap Douglas, knowing there's time only for a desperation shot, not a pass.

3. 00:01 With Black and Harlan draped over him, Douglas throws up a low-trajectory shot that goes in.

Miranda v. Arizona (1966)

The case leading to the requirement that criminal suspects be informed of their rights. Warren again (14 points, 9 rebounds, 21 assists), making it seem like there were eight players on his team instead of four. He also blocked out Stewart and defended Byron White so effectively that White threw the ball at Warren's head and drew a costly technical. The Court's legal historian put it in perspective: 'Some justices – I'm thinking of Oliver Wendell Holmes here – had really high point totals, but their teammates suffered because of it. Earl made everyone else play better, and three men playing great is better than one any day.'

New York Times v. United States (1971)

The 'Pentagon Papers' game, in which Hugo Black and William O. Douglas, teammates for once, shared MVP honors. More than one clerk said that Black clearly was the game's outstanding player but that Douglas burned an indelible image into every brain with a monster dunk midway through the second half. 'It got completely quiet for a few seconds, and then everyone – justices, clerks, refs – started to applaud. Then we had to wait another 20 minutes while they fixed the rim.'

Furman v. Georgia (1972)

The death penalty game, when everything went to hell. Not only did several fistfights break out between sides, but justices were furious at their own teammates. After a while there was no passing; it got to be like a playground game where every person who grabbed a rebound turned and tried to take it himself to the other end. The result: a 16–16 final score, not even a pretense of choosing an MVP, and nine separate opinions. Bad law all around, which was overturned just a few years later. A disgusted clerk who witnessed the game summed it up: 'I don't care how many lives are at stake – you don't play like a bunch of municipal court thugs. A lot of my idealism died that day.'

Roe v. Wade (1973)

'I've never seen someone take control of a game the way [Harry] Blackmun did that day,' said one of his clerks. 'He was on a mission. You could tell he had stopped being intimidated and had come into his own. He ran up and down the court for 40 minutes, and after the first 15 the conservatives were just holding their sides and wheezing. Nobody there was thinking about abortion or right-to-privacy – it was just, "Look at Harry go!"'

Bakke v. California (1978)

Bakke wasn't the only one standing up to be heard; this was Lewis Powell's coming-out party as a player. He surprised everyone by his finesse, so fluid and graceful – almost courtly, in his Southern way, the way he ran the floor, dishing assists, getting everyone their points. But every time the defense collapsed on him and dared him to hit from outside, he arced shots that would melt in your mouth. Marshall was baiting him the entire game – understandable when you consider that the case threatened affirmative action – but Powell wouldn't bite, even after being elbowed again and again. Nobody remembers him hitting the rim the entire game.

Bowers v. Hardwick (1986)

Was a Georgia law against sodomy in violation of the Constitution? Perhaps more to the point, why couldn't Byron 'Whizzer' White realize he didn't have it anymore as an athlete? His teammates voted him MVP to keep him happy, even though he was cherry-picking the entire game. Brennan, whom White was supposed to be guarding, was scoring from all over, but all Whizzer cared about was his own total. His teammates were banking on his hints that he was about to retire, and thought giving him the honor would speed him out the door. It still took seven long years.

As you can see, the games have their own rich history, sometimes even overlapping with the Official Truth that made it into textbooks. Oliver Wendell Holmes actually did make the notorious statement, 'Three generations of imbeciles are enough' but he was not, as widely believed, referring to the state-sanctioned sterilization of a retarded woman. He directed it at a referee, the grandson of an official whose incorrect interpretation of the rulebook gave Justice Roger Taney an extra throw in the Dred Scott horseshoe match. (The ref was a bit touchy about the whole subject; nobody wants to hear that their granddad prolonged slavery, so Holmes got tossed.) And, yes, Potter Stewart did say 'I know it when I see it,' but he was not talking about pornography, he also was arguing with a ref about what constitutes traveling. The official did not accept his definition and responded, 'Why don't you try playing defense and see how you like it?'

But enough about justices running their mouths. Let's focus on overall athletic skills. Since this is the first written account to make it to the public, a lot of inside info on earlier justices has died with the men who knew it firsthand. But with most former clerks of the past few decades . . . still alive, it's possible to piece together fairly accurate descriptions of the recent ones. The general consensus is that, like in the outside world, the modern players have it all over their counterparts from 60 years ago. It's a markedly different game. Dunks are so common now that no one bats an eye. It's also impossible to ignore the influence that steroids have had on the players. (Needless to say, Supreme Court justices do not submit to drug tests.) Strength and conditioning regimens allow the players to bring off athletic displays that were unimaginable in the '30s and '40s.

Still, steroids and conditioning only gets you so far. As any sports fan knows, a lot depends on how well you play as a team and what you're willing to give after tip-off. After years of what they considered judicial overstepping by the Warren Court, conservative justices had high hopes for Warren Burger's boys. But when the games were on the line, the conservatives in the Burger Court just didn't want it as much.

Of course, they weren't helped by the fact that Burger was the worst player of all time. He was as bad as Ben Cardozo, although Cardozo could at least make free throws. Once, after Burger missed his 8th consecutive shot from the line, White gave him a withering look and said, 'Thank you, Nixon.'

Blackmun, though he had flashes of brilliance, was too often timid. White, of course, still was a formidable athlete when Kennedy appointed him, but he had lost a lot by the 1970s, even if he refused to admit it. (Marshall and Brennan constantly bickered over who got to guard him.)

The liberal holdovers from the Warren Court liked to torment the more conservative newcomers just to show who was boss. One example stands out in particular: It was said that Marshall, cantankerous in his final years, enjoyed taunting Scalia by mocking his fondness for hypothetical questions during oral argument. During one-on-one games that they played strictly for pride, every possession became an opportunity for Marshall to humiliate him: 'What if one justice were to back in slowly – like this, say – dribbling the ball methodically, while his fellow justice stood there powerless to stop him? And what if the first justice then dunked over him, like . . . this?'

As for scouting reports on the current nine:

CHIEF JUSTICE REHNQUIST: Bad back, hates to reach low for balls. Tends to turn it over if you force him to go to his left. Still no one is able to see the whole court better.

FIG. 3. The 'S-T Zone' (for 'Scalia-Thomas') has been used effectively by moderates to force turnovers. With Scalia and Thomas inseparable, moderates can use one man (usually Kennedy) to defend them both, leaving an extra moderate player for double-teams. In this example, Rehnquist has the ball on top, guarded by Ginsburg and Breyer. When he passes to a fellow conservative, one of the two slides over to double-team the recipient, with the other defender staying put. Lately, Rehnquist and O'Connor have been able to negate the defensive scheme with back-door cuts. (Stevens: abstaining.)

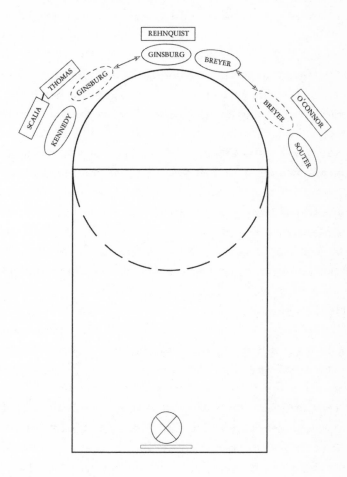

Opponents often think he's not even paying attention, and suddenly he's stolen the ball from them.

DAVID SOUTER: Finesse player; doesn't like to bang. Moves well without the ball; it's almost impossible to keep track of him. Drives defenders nuts and wears them out.

JOHN PAUL STEVENS: Often wants to switch teams halfway through the game; it's hard to count on him in the late minutes.

ANTHONY KENNEDY: Nondescript and workmanlike out there, but within the first week on the Court, he had memorized the dead spots on the floor and began forcing dribblers into them.

SANDRA DAY O'CONNOR: Got pushed around at first, but now uses her speed, and elbows. Runs the point well.

ANTONIN SCALIA: Real trash talker. Constantly comparing himself to Warren, Black, and the other 'maestros.' Even the refs hate him.

CLARENCE THOMAS: Was held in disdain by the other justices until his first game, when he let loose an eye-popping barrage of three-pointers. (The 'Natural Law Fury From Above,' as he called it.)

RUTH BADER GINSBURG: One of the best passers ever. Hooks up with Breyer in no-look alley-oops.

STEPHEN BREYER: Well-liked because he refuses to play dirty, even after taking cheap shots. Boxes out well.

Anyway, there you have the truth; it's up to you to handle it as best you can. And remember: I'll be judged by history. I don't know where the Court will go from here now that the secret's out. Will they continue issuing opinions with their *faux* precision in how the votes broke down? Will people be so outraged that political pressures will force – God forbid – an actual Supreme Court that tries to thrash out legal decisions based on logic?

The best we can hope is that everyone will submit to the higher power and let the shots fall where they may. Because at those critical moments when time stands still, as six of the justices clear out of the lane and one stands alone on top, dribbling the ball and eyeing the lone defender, this country reaches its full potential, a nation defined not by the past but by the moment. As the justice jukes and then brushes past his opponent and begins his rise to the goal, we all are lifted with him knowing one thing at heart: If he can finish, so can we.

Flush

JUDY BUDNITZ

I called my sister and said: What does a miscarriage look like?

What? she said. Oh. It looks like when you're having your period, I guess. You have cramps, and then there's blood.

What do people do with it? I asked.

With what?

The blood and stuff.

I don't know, she said impatiently. I don't know these things, I'm not a doctor. All I can tell you about anything is who you should sue.

Sorry, I said.

Why are you asking me this? she said.

I'm just having an argument with someone, that's all. Just thought you could help settle it.

Well, I hope you win, she said.

I went home because my sister told me to.

She called and said: It's your turn.

No, it can't be, I feel like I was just there, I said.

No, I went the last time. I've been keeping track, I have incontestable proof, she said. She was in law school.

But Mich, I said. Her name was Michelle but everyone called her Mich, as in Mitch, except our mother, who thought it sounded obscene.

Lisa, said Mich, don't whine.

I could hear her chewing on something, a ball-point pen probably. I pictured her with blue marks on her lips, another pen stuck in her hair.

It's close to Thanksgiving, I said, why don't we wait and both go home then?

You forget – they're going down to Florida to be with Nana.

I don't have time to go right now. I have a job, you know. I do have a life.

I don't have time to argue about it, I'm studying, Mich said. I knew she was sitting on the floor with her papers scattered around her, the stacks of casebooks sprouting yellow Post-its from all sides, like lichen, Mich in the middle with her legs spread, doing ballet stretches.

I heard a background cough.

You're not studying, I said. Neil's there.

Neil isn't doing anything, she said. He's sitting quietly in the corner waiting for me to finish. Aren't you, sweetheart?

Meek noises from Neil.

You call him sweetheart? I said.

Are you going home or not?

Do I have to?

I can't come over there and make you go, Mich said.

The thing was, we had both decided, some time ago, to take turns going home every now and then to check up on them. Our parents did not need checking up, but Mich thought we should get in the habit of doing it anyway. To get in practice for the future.

After a minute Mich said: They'll think we don't care.

Sometimes I think they'd rather we left them alone.

Fine. Fine. Do what you want.

Oh all right, I'll go.

I flew home on a Thursday night and though I'd told them not to meet me at the airport, there they were, both of them, when I stepped off the ramp. They were the only still figures in the terminal; around them people dashed with garment bags, stewardesses hustled in pairs wheeling tiny suitcases.

My mother wore a brown coat the color of her hair. She looked anxious. My father stood tall, swaying slightly. The lights bounced off the lenses of his glasses; he wore jeans that were probably twenty years old. I would have liked to be the one to see them first, to compose my face and walk up to them unsuspected like a stranger. But that never happened – they always spotted me before I saw them, and had their faces ready and their hands out.

Is that all you brought? Just the one bag?

Here, I'll take it.

Lisa honey, you don't look so good. How are you?

Yes, how are you? You look terrible.

Thanks, Dad.

How are you, they said over and over, as they wrestled the suitcase from my hand.

Back at the house, my mother stirred something on the stove and my father leaned in the doorway to the dining room and looked out the window at the backyard. He's always leaned in that door-frame to talk to my mother.

I made that soup for you, my mother said. The one where I have to peel the tomatoes and pick all the seeds out by hand.

Mother. I wish you wouldn't do that.

You mean you don't like it? I thought you liked it.

I like it, I like it. But I wish you wouldn't bother.

It's no bother. I wanted to.

She was up until two in the morning pulling skin off tomatoes, my father said, I could hear them screaming in agony.

How would you know? You were asleep, my mother said.

I get up at five thirty every morning to do work in the yard before I go in to the office, he said.

I looked out at the brown yard.

I've been pruning the rose bushes. They're going to be beautiful next summer.

Yes, they will.

Lisa, he said, I want you to do something for me tomorrow, since you're here.

Sure. Anything.

I want you to go with your mother to her doctor's appointment. Make sure she goes.

Okay.

She doesn't have to come, my mother said. That's silly, she'll just be bored.

She's supposed to get a mammogram every six months, my father said, but she's been putting it off and putting it off.

I've been busy, you know that's all it is.

She's afraid to go. She's been avoiding it for a year now.

Oh stop it, that's not it at all.

She always finds a way to get out of it. Your mother, the escape artist.

She crossed her arms over her chest. There was a history. Both her mother and an aunt had had to have things removed.

It's the same with all her doctors, my father said. Remember the contact lenses?

That was different. I didn't need new contacts.

She stopped going to her eye doctor for fifteen years. For fifteen years she was wearing the same contacts. When she finally went in, the doctor was amazed, he said he'd never seen anything like it, they don't even make contact lenses like that anymore. He thought she was wearing dessert dishes in her eyes.

You're exaggerating, my mother said.

Mich I mean Lise, my father said. He's always gotten our names confused; sometimes, to be safe, he just says all three.

She's afraid to go because of the last time, he said.

What happened last time? I said.

I had the mammogram pictures done, she said, and then a few days later they called and said the pictures were inconclusive and they needed to take a second set. So they did that and then they kept me waiting for the results, for weeks, without telling me anything, weeks where I couldn't sleep at night and I kept your father up too, trying to imagine what it looked like, the growth. Like the streaks in bleu cheese, I thought. I kept feeling these little pains, and kept checking my pulse all night. And then finally they called and said everything was fine after all, that there was just some kind of blur on the first pictures, like I must have moved right when they took it or something.

You were probably talking the whole time, my father said. Telling them how to do their job.

I was probably *shivering*. They keep that office at about forty degrees and leave you sitting around in the cold in a paper robe. The people there don't talk to you or smile; and when they do the pictures they mash your breast between these two cold glass plates like a pancake.

My father looked away. He had a kind of modesty about some things.

My mother said to me: All those nights I kept thinking about my mother having her surgery; I kept feeling for lumps, waking up your father and asking him to feel for lumps.

Leah, my father said.

He didn't mind that. I think he might have enjoyed it a little.

Please.

Didn't you?

Promise me you'll go, he said.

She's not coming, she said.

The next day we drove to the clinic an hour early. My mother had the seat drawn as close to the steering wheel as she could get it; she gripped the wheel with her hands close together at twelve o'clock. She looked over at me as often as she looked out at the road.

There were squirrels and possums sprawled in the road, their heads red smears.

It's something about the weather, my mother said, makes them come out at night.

Oh.

We're so early, my mother said, and we're right near Randy's salon. Why don't we stop in and see if he can give you a haircut and a blowout?

Not now.

He wouldn't mind, I don't think. I talk about you whenever I go see him to have my hair done. He'd like to meet you.

No.

If you just got it angled on the sides, here, and got a few bangs in the front –

Just like yours, you mean.

You know, I feel so bad for Randy, he looks terrible, circles under his eyes all the time, he says his boyfriend is back in the hospital. Now whenever I go to get my hair cut, I bake something to bring him, banana bread or something. But I think the shampoo girls usually eat it all before he can get it home.

That's nice of you.

I worry about him. He doesn't take care of himself.

Yes.

Why are you still getting pimples? You're twenty-seven years old, why are you still getting pimples like a teenager?

Not everyone has perfect skin like you, I said. Green light. Go.

I do not have perfect skin, she said, bringing her hands to her face.

Both hands on the wheel please. Do you want me to drive?

No, I don't. You must be tired.

I touched my forehead. Small hard bumps like Braille.

She drove. I looked at the side of her face, the smooth taut skin. I wondered when she would start to get wrinkles. I already had wrinkles. On my neck, I could see them.

So, how is it going with this Piotr?

He's all right.

Still playing the – what was it? Guitar?

Bass guitar.

She turned on the radio and started flipping through stations. Maybe we'll hear one of his songs, she said brightly.

I said: I told you he was in a band. I didn't say they were good enough to be on the radio.

Oh. I see. So the band's just for fun. What else does he do?

Nothing. Yet.

So. What kind of name is Piotr? Am I saying it right?

Polish, I said.

I did not feel like telling her that only his grandmother lived in Poland; his parents were both born in Milwaukee, and he had grown up in Chicago and had never been to Poland; Piotr was a name he had given himself; he was not really a Piotr at all, he was a Peter with pretensions and long hair. I did not tell her this.

A black car cut into the lane in front of us. My mother braked suddenly and flung her right arm out across my chest.

Mother! Keep your hands on the wheel!

I'm sorry, she said, it's automatic. Ever since you kids were little . . .

I'm wearing a seatbelt.

I know honey, I can't help it. Did I hurt you?

No, of course not, I said.

When we reached the parking garage my mother rolled down her window but couldn't reach; she had to unfasten her seatbelt and open the car door in order to punch the button and get her parking ticket. I looked at her narrow back as she leaned out of the car, its delicate curve, the shoulder blades like folded wings under her sweater, a strand of dark hair caught in the clasp of her gold necklace. I had the urge to slide across the seat and curl around her. It only lasted for a second.

She turned around and settled back into her seat and the yellow-and-black-striped mechanical bar swung up in front of the car, and I tapped my feet impatiently while she slammed the door shut and rolled up the window. Now she was fiddling with her rearview mirror and straightening her skirt.

Come on, I said, watching the bar, which was still raised but vibrating a little.

Relax honey, that thing isn't going to come crashing down on us the minute we're under it. I promise you.

I know that, I said, and then closed my eyes until we were through the gate and weaving around the dark oil-stained aisles of the parking lot. I would have liked to tell her about some of the legal cases Mich had described to me: freak accidents, threshing machines gone awry, people caught in giant gears or conveyor belts and torn limb from limb, hands in bread slicers, flimsy walkways over vats of acid. Elevator cases, diving board cases, subway train cases, drowning-in-the-bathtub cases, electrocution-by-blender cases. And then there were the ones that were just called Act of God.

I didn't tell her.

Remember where we parked, she said.

Okay.

But she did not get out of the car right away. She sat, gripping the wheel.

I don't see why we have to do this, she said. Your father worries . . .

He'll be more worried if you don't go, I said, and anyway there's nothing to worry about because everything's going to be fine. Right? Right.

If there's something wrong I'd just rather not know, she said to her hands.

We got out; the car shook as we slammed the doors.

She was right about the clinic. It was cold, and it was ugly.

She signed in with the receptionist and we sat in the waiting room. The room was gray and bare, the chairs were old vinyl that stuck to your thighs. The lights buzzed and seemed to flicker unless you were looking directly at them.

We sat side by side and stared straight ahead as if we were watching something, a movie.

There was one other woman waiting. She had enormous breasts. I could not help noticing.

I took my mother's hand. It was very cold, but then her hands were always cold, even in summer, cool and smooth with the blue veins arching elegantly over their backs. Her hand lay limply in mine. I had made the gesture thinking it was the right thing to do, but now that I had her hand I didn't know what to do with it. I patted it, turned it over.

My mother looked at me strangely. My hand began to sweat.

There was noise, activity, somewhere, we could hear voices and footsteps, the crash and skid of metal, the brisk tones of people telling each other what to do. But we could see nothing but the receptionist in her window and the one woman who looked asleep, sagging in her chair with her breasts cupped in her arms like babies.

I need to use the restroom, my mother said and pulled her hand away.

The receptionist directed us down the hall and around the corner. We went in, our footsteps echoing on the tiles. It was empty, and reeked of ammonia. The tiles glistened damply.

Here, do something with yourself, my mother said and handed me her comb. She walked down to the big handicapped stall on the end and latched the door.

I combed my hair and washed my hands and waited.

I looked at myself in the mirror. The lights were that harsh relentless kind that reveal every detail of your face, so that you can see all sorts of flaws and pores you didn't even know you had. They made you feel you could see your own thoughts floating darkly just under your skin, like bruises.

Mother, I said. I watched her feet tapping around.

Lisa, she said, there's a fish in the toilet.

Oh, please.

No, I mean it. It's swimming around.

You're making it up.

No I'm not. Come see for yourself.

Well, it's probably just some pet goldfish someone tried to flush.

It's too big to be a goldfish. More like a carp. It's bright orange. Almost red.

You're seeing things – maybe it's blood or something, I said; then I wished I hadn't. The clinic was attached to the county hospital; all sorts of things were liable to pop up in the toilets – hypodermic needles, appendixes, tonsils.

No, no, it's a fish, it's beautiful really. It's got these gauzy fins, like veils. I wonder how it got in here. It looks too large to have come through the pipes. It's swimming in circles. Poor thing.

Well then come out and use a different one, I said. I suddenly started to worry that she was going to miss her appointment. You're just stalling, I said.

Come in and see. We have to save it somehow.

I heard her pulling up her pantyhose, fixing her skirt. Then she unlatched the door to the stall and opened it. She was smiling. Look, she said.

I followed her into the stall.

Come see, she said. Together we leaned over the bowl.

I saw only the toilet's bland white hollow, and our two identical silhouettes reflected in the water.

Now where did he go? my mother said. Isn't that the strangest thing?

We looked at the empty water.

How do you think he got out? she said. Look, you can see, the water's still moving from where he was. Look, look – little fish droppings. I swear. Lisa honey, look.

My mother is going crazy, I thought. Let's go back to the waiting room, I said.

But I still have to use the bathroom, she said.

I stood by the sink and waited. You're going to miss your appointment, I said. I watched her feet. Silence.

I was making her nervous. I'll wait for you in the hall, I said.

So I left, leaned against the wall, and waited. And waited. She was taking a long time. I started to wonder if she had been hallucinating. I wondered if something really was wrong with her, if she was bleeding internally or having a weird allergic reaction. I didn't think she was making it all up; she couldn't lie, she was a terrible, obvious liar.

Mother, I called.

Mom, I said.

I went back into the bathroom.

She was gone.

The stall doors swung loose, creaking. I checked each cubicle, thinking she might be standing on the toilet seat, with her head ducked down the way we used to avoid detection in high school. In the handicapped stall the toilet water was quivering, as if it had just been flushed. I even checked in the cabinets under the sink and stuck my hand down in the garbage pail.

I stood there, thinking. She must have somehow left and darted past me without my noticing. Maybe I had closed my eyes for a minute. She could move fast when she wanted to.

Had she climbed out the window? It was a small one, closed, high up on the wall.

She had escaped.

I walked slowly down the halls, listening, scanning the floor tiles.

I thought of her narrow back, the gaping mouth of the toilet, pictured her slipping down, whirling around and vanishing in the pipes.

I tried to formulate a reasonable question: Have you seen my mother? A woman, about my height, brown hair, green eyes? Nervous-looking? Have you seen her?

Or were her eyes hazel?

I came back to the waiting room with the question on my lips, I was mouthing the words she's disappeared, but when I got there the receptionist was leaning through the window calling out in an irritated voice: Ms. Salant? Ms. Salant? They're ready for you, *Ms. Salant*.

The receptionist was opening the door to the examining rooms; the nurses and technicians were holding out paper gowns and paper forms and urine sample cups, Ms Salant, Ms Salant, we're waiting, they called; people were everywhere suddenly, gesturing impatiently and calling out my name.

So I went in.

Later I wandered up and down the rows of painted white lines in the lot. I had forgotten where she parked the car. When I finally came upon it I saw her there, leaning against the bumper. For a moment I thought she was smoking a cigarette. She didn't smoke.

When I drew closer I saw that she was nibbling on a pen.

We got in the car and drove home.

All of a sudden I thought of something I wanted to pick up for dinner, she said at one point.

Some fish? I said.

We drove the rest of the way without speaking.

So how did it go today, ladies? my father said that evening.

My mother didn't say anything.

Did you go with her? he asked me. Yeah, I said.

So, you'll hear results in a few days, right? he said with his hand on my mother's back.

She looked away.

Right, I said.

She looked at me strangely, but said nothing.

I told them not to but they both came to the airport Sunday night when I left.

Call me when you get the news, all right? I said.

All right, she said.

I wanted to ask her about the fish in the toilet, whether it had really been there. Whether she had followed the same route it had. But I couldn't work myself up to it. And the topic never came up by itself.

We said goodbye at the terminal. My hugs were awkward. I patted their backs as if I were burping babies.

I told them to go home but I knew they would wait in the airport until the plane took off safely. They always did. I think my mother liked to be there in case the plane crashed during take-off so she could dash onto the runway through the flames and explosions to drag her children from the rubble.

Or maybe they just liked airports. That airport smell.

I had a window seat; I pushed my suitcase under the seat in front of me. A man in a business suit with a fat red face sat down next to me.

I wondered if my mother even knew what I had done for her. I had helped her escape. Although at the time I hadn't thought of it that way; I hadn't really thought at all; I had gone in when I heard my name, automatic schoolgirl obedience, gone in to the bright lights and paper gowns and people who kneaded your breasts like clay. I began to feel beautiful and noble. I felt like I had gone to the guillotine in her place, like Sydney Carton in *A Tale of Two Cities*.

I called Piotr when I got home. I'm back, I said.

Let me come over, he said, I'll make you breakfast.

It's seven thirty at night.

I just got up, he said.

My apartment felt too small and smelled musty. I'd been gone three days but it seemed longer. Piotr came and brought eggs and milk and his own spatula – he knew my kitchen was ill-equipped for anything but sandwiches.

He seemed to have grown since I last saw him, and gotten more hairy; I looked at the hair on the backs of his hands, the chest hair tufting out of the collar of his T-shirt.

He took up too much space. As he talked his nose and hands popped out at me huge and distorted, as if I were seeing him through a fish-eye lens. He came close to kiss me and I watched his eyes loom larger and larger and blur out of focus and merge into one big eye over the bridge of his nose.

I was embarrassed. My mouth tasted terrible from the plane.

What kind of pancakes do you want? he asked.

The pancake kind, I said.

He broke two eggs with one hand and the yolks slid out between his fingers.

I can do them shaped like snowmen, he said, or rabbits or flowers.

He was mixing stuff up in a bowl; flour slopped over the edges and sprinkled on the counter and the floor. I'll have to clean that up, I thought.

Round ones please, I said.

There was butter bubbling and crackling in the frying pan. Was that pan mine? No, he must have brought it with him – it was a big heavy skillet, the kind you could kill someone with.

He poured in the batter, it was thick and pale yellow; and the hissing butter shut up for a while. I looked in the pan. There were two large lumpy mounds there, side by side, bubbling inside as if they were alive, turning brown on the edges.

He turned them over and I saw the crispy undersides with patterns on them like the moon; and then he pressed them down with the spatula, pressed them flat and the butter sputtered and hissed.

There was a burning smell.

I'm not feeling very hungry right now, I said.

But I brought maple syrup, he said. It's from Vermont, I think.

The pan was starting to smoke. Pushing him aside, I took it off the flame and put it in the sink. It was heavy; the two round shapes were now charred and crusted to the bottom.

Well, we don't have to eat them, he said. He held out the

bottle of syrup. Aunt Jemima smiled at me. She looked different, though. They must have updated her image; new hairstyle, outfit. But that same smile.

There's lots of stuff we can do with syrup, he said, it's a very romantic condiment.

He stepped closer and reached out and turned the knob on the halogen lamp. His face looked even more distorted in the dimness.

What? I said. Where did you get such a stupid idea?

Read it somewhere.

I'm sorry, I'm just not feeling very social tonight, I said. Peter, I said.

Oh come on.

I missed my parents very much suddenly. You're so insensitive, I said. Get out.

Hey, I *am* sensitive. I'm *Mr* Sensitive. I give change to bums. Pachelbel's Canon makes me cry like a baby.

Like a what? I said.

Why are you screaming at me? he said.

Don't let the door hit you in the ass on the way out, I said. I thought I was being smart and cutting. But he took it literally; he went out and closed the door behind him with great care.

My sister called later that night.

So how were they? she asked.

Fine, I said. Same as always.

Your voice sounds funny; what happened? she said.

Nothing.

Something's wrong. Why don't you ever tell me when something's wrong?

There's nothing, Mich.

You never tell me what's going on; when you think I'll worry about something you keep it to yourself.

I tell you everything.

Well then, tell me what was wrong with you earlier this fall.

Nothing . . . I don't know . . . there's nothing to tell.

That was the truth. All that happened was I got tired of people for a while. I didn't like to go out, didn't shower, and didn't pick up the phone except to call my office with elaborate excuses. The smell of my body became comforting, a ripe presence, nasty but familiar. I lay in bed telling myself that it was just a phase, it would pass. Eventually the bulb on my halogen lamp burned out and after two days of darkness I ventured out to buy a new one. The sunlight out on the street did something to my brain, or maybe it was the kind bald man who sold me the bulb. I went back to work.

So how are you? How's Neil?

Oh we broke up, she said. We had a big fight, and he couldn't see that I was right and he was wrong. It was high drama, in a restaurant with people watching, us screaming and stuff, and this fat waitress pushing between us using her tray as a shield and telling us to leave. So we finished it outside on the street, I made my points, one two three, and did my closing arguments. If we were in court I would have won.

I'm sorry, I said. Why didn't you tell me right away?

Oh, I didn't want you feeling bad for me. I'm glad, really. Small-minded jerk. Did I ever tell you he had all this hair on his back? Gray hair, like a silverback gorilla.

Yes, well. I don't know that I'll be seeing Piotr any more either.

That's too bad.

No, it's not.

That night as I lay in bed I thought of my mother and I felt my body for lumps the way she said she felt hers, and I put two fingers to the side of my throat. And I began to think of her and think of an undetected cancer, spreading through her body unnoticed. It began to dawn on me that I had done a very stupid thing.

I thought of her lying in bed beside my father at that moment, oblivious to the black thing that might be growing and thickening inside her, maybe in tough strands, maybe in little grainy bits, like oatmeal. She would avoid thinking about it for another six months or a year or two years; she'd deny it until her skin turned gray and she had tentacles growing out of her mouth and her breasts slid from her body and plopped on the floor like lumps of wet clay. Only when all that happened would she give in and say, Hmmm, maybe something is wrong, maybe I should see a doctor after all.

I lay awake for most of the night.

At one point I got up to use the bathroom, and as I sat on the toilet in the dark I suddenly became convinced that there was something horrible floating in the water below me. I was sure of it. A live rat. Or a length of my own intestines lying coiled bloody in the bowl. I sat there afraid to turn on the light and look, yet couldn't leave the bathroom without looking.

I sat there for half an hour, wracked with indecision. I think I fell asleep for a bit.

And when I finally forced myself to turn on the light, turn around and look – I was so convinced there would be something floating there that I was horribly shocked, my stomach lurched to see only the empty toilet.

I went back to work on Tuesday.

Did I miss anything? I asked one of the men.

You were gone? he said.

I didn't know his name; all the men who worked there looked alike. They were all too loud, and had too much spit in their mouths.

I had a cubicle all my own, but I dreamed of an office with a door I could close.

A few days later my father called. Your mother heard the results from the clinic, he said, the mammogram was fine.

That's great, I said.

She doesn't seem happy about it, he said, she's acting very strange.

Oh, I said.

What's going on, Lisa? he said. There's something fishy going on here.

Nothing, I said. Ask your wife, I said. Can I talk to her?

She just dashed out for an appointment, told me to call you. She said you'd be relieved.

Yes.

I'm going to call your sister now, she was waiting to hear. Or do you want to call her?

I'll do it, I said.

It seemed strange to me then that I would need to call Mich; a phone call implied distance, but our family seemed so close and entwined and entangled that we could hardly tell each other apart. Why should you need a phone to talk to someone who seems like she's living inside your skin?

*

We both went home for Christmas.

Later Mich visited them.

Then I visited.

Then it was Mich's turn again.

When I called home during Mich's visit my father said: Your mother was due for another mammogram, so I sent Lisa with her to make sure she goes.

You mean you sent Mich, I said. I'm Lisa.

Yes, right, you know who I mean.

A few days later my father called, his voice sounding strained. Your mother talked to the mammography clinic today, he said, but she won't tell me anything. She's been in her room, crying. She's been talking on the phone to your sister for an hour. I guess the doctors found something, but I'll let you know when we know for sure.

Okay.

I hung up and called Mich.

Hello, she said. She sounded like she was choking on one of her pens.

Mich, I said, it's yours, isn't it?

She sighed and said: It's ridiculous, but I thought I was doing her a favor, I thought I was sparing her some worry.

You went in for her, didn't you?

You know, Mich said, she's more worried about this than if she was the one with a lump in her breast. She feels like it's her lump, like it was meant for her, like she gave it to me somehow.

That's ridiculous, I said. I felt like I was talking to myself.

Although, you know, if it were possible, I would, Mich said. I mean, if there was somehow a way to magically take a lump out of her breast and put it in mine, I'd do it in a second.

I wish I could do that for you, I said.

Yeah, we could all share it.

One dessert and three forks, I said.

And later as I sat alone on the floor in the apartment I started to lose track of where I stopped and other people began, and I remembered standing in a white room with my breast clamped in the jaws of a humming machine, and I felt for the lump that I thought was mine, and sometimes I thought it was my mother's, and I imagined the mammogram pictures like lunar landscapes. Then I could not remember who had the lump anymore, it seemed we all did, it was my mother's my sister's and mine, and then the phone rang again and I picked it up and heard my father call out as he sometimes did: Leah–Lise–Mich.

Saint Chola

K. KVASHAY-BOYLE

Skater. Hesher. Tagger. Lesbo-Slut. Wanna-be. Dweeb. Fag. Prep. What-up. Bad-ass. Gangster. Dork. Nerd. Trendy. Freaky. In a few weeks it'll be solid like cement, but right now nobody knows yet. You might be anything. And here's an example: meet Mohammadee Sawy. Hypercolor T-shirt, over-sized overalls with just one hook fastened, the other tossed carefree over the shoulder like it's no big thing. In walks Mohammadee, short and plump and brown, done up for the first day with long fluffy hair and a new mood ring, but guess what, it's not *Mohammadee* anymore. Nope, because dad's not signing you up today, you're all by yourself and when you get the form where it says Name, Grade, Homeroom, you look around and take the pen Ms Yoshida hands you and you write it in big and permanent: Shala M. Sawy. And from now on that's who you are. Cool.

It's tough to do right but at least you learn what to want. You walk the halls and you see what's there. I want her jeans, I want her triple-pierce hoops, I want her strut, I want those boobs, I want that crowd, I want shoes like those, I want a wallet chain, I want a baby-doll dress, I want safety pins on my backpack, I want a necklace that says my name. Lipstick. I want lipstick. Jelly bracelets. Trainer bras from Target. It could be me. I could be anyone. Kiss FM, Power 106, Douche-bag,

Horn-ball. Fanny packs! Biker shorts! And suddenly, wow, Shala realizes that she has a surge of power inside that she never knew was there. Shala realizes that she's walking around and she's thinking, Yup, cool, or No way! Lame!

Shala? That sounds good. And that's just the way tiny Mrs Furukawa says it in homeroom when she calls roll. She says *Shala*. And Shala Mohammadee Sawy? She smiles. (But not so much as to be uncool because she's totally cool.) And she checks out the scene. There's a powerhouse pack of scary Cholas conspiring in the back row, there's aisle after aisle of knobby, scrawny white-boy knees sprouting like weeds from marsh-mallow sneakers, and there are clumps of unlikely allies hap-hazardly united for the first time by the pride of patriotism: Serrania Avenue, row three, Walnut Elementary, row five, or MUS, first row. Forty faces. Shala knows some of them. Ido, Farah, Laura Leaper, Eden, Mori Leshum, oh great, and him: Taylor Bryans. Barf. But the rest? They're all new.

In Our World, fourth period, Shala learns current events. It's social studies. The book's heavy. But then there's a war. And then Shala's embarrassed to say Niger River out loud, and she learns to recognize Kuwait and a kid named Josh gets a part in a movie with Tom Hanks, but that's nothing she tells Lucy because she used to roller-skate at Skateland with the kid from *Terminator II*. And he's cuter. Way cuter.

It's LA Unified where there's every different kind of thing, but it's just junior high so you're just barely starting to get an idea of what it means to be some different kind of thing. There are piercings. There are cigarettes. Even drug dealers. And with all that, there's the aura of danger all around, and you realize, for the first time, that you could get your ass kicked. You could get pounded after school, you could get jumped in the bathroom, you could get jacked-up, beat-up, messed-up, it's true, and the omnipresent possibility swells every exchange.

Mrs. Furukawa's new husband is in the Army. She says so. She wears the highest heels you've ever seen a person wear. Her class reads *The Diary of Anne Frank* but you know you're set, you already read it. Plus *A Wrinkle in Time*, and you read that one too. At home your mom says Get out the flag, we want them to know what side we're on.

On television every night Bush says Sad-dum instead of Suhdom and your dad says it's a slap in the face. Your dad, the Mohammad Sawy from which your Mohammadee came, says it's on purpose, just to drive that bastard nuts. You practice saying the name both ways, the real way and the slap-his-face way.

Gym class is the worst because you have to get naked and that is the worst. Gym is what your friends feared most in fifth grade when you thought about junior high and you tried so hard to imagine what it would be like to be with other people and take your clothes off (Take your clothes off? In front of people? Strangers-people? Oh yeah right. Get real. No way) and you started trying to think up the lie you'd have to tell your parents because they just wouldn't get it. A big important thing is Modesty. You know that. It's your cultural heritage, and naked is certainly not Modesty. On the first day, just to be sure, you raise your hand and ask, If you were a non-strip every day would you fail? And Ms. DeLuca says Yes.

Some kids ditch but it's been three months. It's too late now. You're stuck with who you are by now and even though you're finally Shala you're still a goody-good brainy dweeb.

And dweebs just don't ditch. Not like you want to anyway. Except in Gym. That's when you do want to. You sit on the black asphalt during roll call with your gym shirt stretched over your knees so that it's still all bagged out twenty minutes later when the volleyball crashes bang into your unprotected head for the fifteenth time like it's been launched from some mystery rocket launcher and it's got a homing device aimed straight for you.

At twelve, no one knows anything yet, so what kind of name is Shala? Who can tell? And, plus, who'd even consider the question if parents didn't ask it? Sometimes kids slip up to you in the crush of the lunch line and speak quick Spanish and expect you to answer. Sometimes kids crack jokes in Farsi and then shoot you a sly glance just before the punch line. Sometimes you laugh for them anyway. Sometimes you'll try and answer *Sí*, and disguise that Anglo accent the best you can. *Sí, claro*. But the best is when a sleep-over sucks and you want to go home and you call up your mom and mumble Urdu into the telephone and no one knows when you tell your mom I hate these girls and I want to leave.

On Tuesday a kid wears a T-shirt to school and it says 'NUKE EM' and when Mrs. Furukawa sees it she's pissed and she makes him go to the office and when he comes back he's wearing it inside out. If you already saw it you can still kind of tell though. ME EKUN.

After school that day your cousin asks if you want to try Girl Scouts with her. Then she gets sick and makes you go alone. When you get there it's totally weird for two reasons. First, your cousin's older by one year and she already wears a hijab and when you went over to get her she dressed you up.

So now you're wearing a hijab and lipstick and your cousin's shirt, which says 'Chill Out.' Uncool. But what could you say? She's all sick and she kept cracking up whenever you put something else of hers on and she's so bossy all the time and then before you knew it the carpool's honking outside and your aunt shouts that you have to go right now. So you do. Then, second of all, you don't know anybody here. They're all seventh graders. It sucks.

They're baking banana nut bread and the girl who gave you a ride says that you smell funny. What's worse than smelling funny? The first thing you do is you go to the bathroom and wash your hands. Then you rinse out your mouth. You try to keep the lipstick from smearing all over the place. You sniff your armpits. As far as you can tell, it seems normal. In the mirror you look so much older with Aslana's hijab pinned underneath your chin like that.

When you walk out of the bathroom you bump into the Girl Scout mom and almost immediately she starts to yell at you like you spilled something on the carpet.

Um, excuse me but this is a feminist household and hello? Honey, that's degrading, she says.

She must be confused. At first you wonder, is she really talking to me, and like in a television sitcom, you turn around to check if there's someone else standing behind you.

Don't you know this is America, sweetheart? I mean have you heard of this thing feminism?

Yeah I'm one too, you say, because you learned about it in school and it means equality between the sexes and that's a good idea.

That's sweet. She looks at you. But get that thing off your head first, she says. You know you don't have to wear it. Not here. No one's gonna arrest you. I didn't call the police or anything, honey – what's your name?

The Girl Scout mom shakes her Girl Scout head and she's wearing a giant Girl Scout outfit that fits her. She looks weird. Like an enormous kid, super-sized like French fries. You can just be yourself at our house, honey, she assures you. You can. What, your mom wears that? She's forced to? Right? Oh, Jesus Christ. Look at you. Well you don't have to, you hear me? Here, you want to take it off? Here, com'ere, honey.

And when you do she helps you and then after you're ashamed that you let her touch it. Then you mix the banana nut dough and you think it looks like throw-up and that same girl says that you still smell like a restaurant she doesn't like. You really, really want to leave. Maybe if you stand still, you think, no one will notice you. On the wall there's a picture of dogs playing cards. Your cousin's hijab is in your backpack and you hold your whole self still and imagine time flowing away like milk down your throat until it's gone and you can leave.

There are Scud missiles, yeah, but in sixth grade at LAUSD, there are more important things. Like French kisses. There's this girl who claims she did one. You just have to think What would that be? because no one would ever kiss you. At least until you're married. Lucy Chang says it's slutty anyway. Lucy Chang is your best friend. You tell her about Girl Scouts and she says Girl Scouts is lame.

On the way home from school you get knocked down by a car. With a group of kids. It's not that bad, kind of just a scary bump, from the guy doing a California-stop which means rolling through the stop sign. At first he says sorry and you say it's okay. But when you suck up all your might and ask to write down his license plate number he says no. Your dad must be a lawyer, he says, is that it? What, look, you're not even hurt, okay? Just go home.

You have some friends with you. You guys were talking about how you could totally be models for a United Benetton ad if someone just took a picture of you guys right now. You're on your way to Tommy's Snack Shack for curly fries and an Orange Julius. Uhh, I think we should probably just go, alright, Noel says, It's not that bad so we should just go.

Yeah, go, the man says. Don't be a brat, he says, Just go.

Okay fine, you say, fine I'll go, but FIRST I'm gonna write it down.

He's tall and he looks towards the ground to look at you. Just mind your own business, kid, she doesn't want you to. No one wants you to, he says.

Well I'm gonna, you say.

Look, you're not hurt, nobody's hurt, what do you need to for?

Just in case, you say. If it scares him you're happy. You're in junior high. You know what to do. Stand your ground. Make your face impassive. You are made of stone. You repeat it more slowly just to see if it freaks him out. *Just. In. Case*, you say and you're twelve and if you're a brat then wear it like a badge.

At mosque there's a broken window. It's a disgrace, your father says, Shala, I tell you it's a damn disgrace. The hole in the window looks jagged like a fragile star sprouting sharp new points. It lets all the outside noise in when everybody's trying to pray and cars rush past grinding their brakes.

There's a report in Language Skills, due Monday, and you have to have a thesis so on the way home from mosque your mom helps you think of one. Yours is that if you were living in Nazi times you would have saved Anne Frank. Your mom says that's not a thesis. Hers is that empathy and tolerance are essential teachings in every religion. You settle for a compromise: Because of Anne Frank's tolerance she should be a saint.

At home while your mom makes dinner she stands over the stove as you peel the mutant-looking ginger root and there are lots of phone calls from lots of relatives. What are we going to do, your mom keeps demanding each time she talks into the phone, What? Tell me. What are we going to do?

Saddam does something. You know it because there are television reports. Everyone's worried for your older brother. He's studying in Pakistan with some friends and if he leaves now then he'll be out one whole semester because his final tests aren't for two more months. He's big news at the mosque. Also people are talking about the price of gas and how much it costs just to drive downtown.

Then Bush does something back, and the phone cord stretches as your mom marches over and snaps the TV off like she's smashed a spider.

The ginger and the asafetida and the mustard seed sauté for a long time until they boil down and then it is the usual moment for adding in the spinach and the potato and the butter but instead the moment comes and goes and the saag aloo burns for the first time that you can remember and the delicate smell of scorched spice swirls up through the room as you watch your mom demand her quite angry Urdu into the receiver and you realize that she doesn't even notice.

You know why she's upset. It's because everyone can tell Ahmad's American and he can't disguise it. He smells American, he smiles American, and his T-shirts say 'Just Do It' like a dare. And lots of people hate America. Plus, in that country, in general in that country, it's much more dangerous. Even just every time you visit, you swallow giant pills and still your weak sterile body gets every cold and all the diarrhea and all the fevers that India has to offer. It's because of the antiseptic lifestyle, your mother insists. Too clean.

In Science, fifth period, you learn that everything is made out of stardust from billions of years ago. Instead of it being as romantic as Mr Kane seems to think it is, you think that pervasive dust feels sinister. You know what happened to Anne Frank, and you can't believe that when she died she turned back into people dust, all mixed up with every other kind of dust. Just piles and piles of dust. And all of it new.

There are plenty of other Muslim kids. Tons of them at school. Everyone's a little freaked out. In the hall, after Science, you see an eighth grader get tripped on purpose and the kid who did it shouts, Send Saddam after me, MoFo, I'll kick his ass too!

After school that day at Mori Leshum's house everyone plays a game called Girl Talk, which is like Risk, except it takes place at the mall. It gets old fast. Next: crank calls! 1–800-SURVIVAL is 1, 8, 0, 0, 7, 8, 7, 8, 4, 8, 2, 5. Uh hi, I just got in a car accident and YOU SUCK A DICK! You laugh and laugh but when it comes time for your turn to squeal breathy oinks into the phone the way you've heard in movies, you chicken out and everyone concludes that oh my God you're such a prude. Well at least I'm not a total perv, you say. Oi, oi, oh! Wooo! Ahh! moans Jackie and when Mori's shriveled grandma comes in the room to get you guys pizza, you all shut up fast for one quick second and then burst into hilarity. The grandma laughs right back at you and she has a dusty tattoo on her arm and it's not until years later that you realize what it is. Oh that, says Mori, It's just her boyfriend's phone number. She says she put it there so she won't get it lost.

Some things that you see you can't forget. On your dad's desk in his office where you're not supposed to touch anything, you see a book called *Vietnam*, and it's as thick as a dictionary and it has a glossy green cover. At random you open it up and flip. In the middle of a sentence is something about sex so you start to read quick. And then you wish you didn't. You slam it shut. You creep out of the office. You close your eyes and imagine anything else, and for a second the shattered starshape of your mosque window flashes to the rescue and you cling tight and you wish on it and you wish that you hadn't read anything at all. *Please*, you think, and you try to push the devastation shoved out through the sharp hole the same way you try to push out the sound of horns and shouts when you say prayer. *Please*, you think, but it doesn't work and nothing swoops in to rescue you.

Sex Ed is only one quarter so that for kids like you, whose parents won't sign the release form, you don't miss much. Instead of switching mid-semester, you take the biology unit twice and you become a bit of an expert on seed germination. Lucy tells you everything anyway. Boys get wet dreams and girls get cramps, what's that all about? she says. You look at her handouts of enormous outlined fallopian tubes and it just sort of looks like the snout of a cow's face and you don't see what the big deal is. You do ask, though, Is there a way to make your boobs grow? And Lucy says that Jackie already asked and No, there isn't. Too bad. Then Lucy says, I must, I must, I must increase my bust! And then you call her a Horndog and she calls you a Major Skank and then you both bust up laughing.

When it happens it happens in the stall at McDonald's. Paula Abdul is tinny on the loudspeaker. Lucy's mom asks what kind of hamburger you want and you say you don't eat meat, it has to be Fish Filet, please. With Sweet-and-Sour sauce, please. Then Lucy says Grody! and then you and Lucy go off to the bathroom together and while she's talking to you about the kinds of jeans that Bongo makes, and every different color that there is, and how if you got scrunchies to match, wouldn't that be cool? you're in the stall and you realize it like a loose tooth. Lucy, oh my god Lucy, check this out, wow! It happened!

Are you serious, she says, Are you serious? Oh my God, are you sure?

I'm sure, you say, and you breathe in big chalky breaths that stink of bathroom hand-soap, powdered pink. When you guys come back to the table and you eat your meal it seems like a whole different thing being in the world. And it is.

That night you ask your mom if you can stay home from school on account of the occasion. She doesn't let you. She does ask you if you want to try her hijab on, though, and you don't tell her about Aslana's. Shala, she says, Shala, I don't know about right now. This just may not be the time. But it has to be your choice. You don't have to if you don't want to, but you do have to ask yourself how do you represent yourself now as a Muslim woman in this country where they think that Muslims are not like you, Shala, and when you choose this, Shala, you are showing them that they know you and that you are nice and that you are no crazy, no religious nut. You are only you, and that is a very brave thing to show the world.

Now when you guys walk home, you're way more careful about not trusting any cars to do anything you expect them to. When you get to the 7–11, you try different ways of scamming a five-finger-discount on the Slurpees. The woman behind the counter hates kids. Timing is everything. Here's how it goes: one person buys and you mix every color all together and try to pass from mouth to mouth and suck it gone before it melts. It's hard because of brain freeze. You try to re-fill and pass off, which the woman says counts as stealing and is not allowed, but that's only when she catches you. Trick is, you have to look like you're alone when you buy the cup or she'll be on to you and then she'll turn around and watch the machine. So everyone else has to stand outside with the bum named Larry and then go in one by one and sit on the floor reading trashy magazines about eyeshadow while the buyer waits in line. Today that's you. You wait in line. You've got the collective seventy-nine cents in your hand. You freeze your face still into a mask of passivity and innocence.

As the trapped hotdogs roll over sweating on their metal coils, you hear the two men in front of you discussing politics and waiting with their own single flavor Slurpees already filled to the brim and ready to be paid for in full.

Same goddamn ground war we had in 'Nam, and hell knows

nobody wants to see their baby come home in a body bag. Hey.

The way I see it is, you got two choices, right? Nuke the towel-heads, use your small bombs, ask your questions later, or what you do is convert.

With you on the first one, buddy.

No, no listen: *convert*. Hell yeah, whole country. To Islam. To mighty Allah.

Shit, man, you and the rag-heads?

But I got a point, right? Right? 'Cause what'd you think these fuckers want? Right? Oh yeah, hey uh, pack of Lucky Strikes, huh? And how 'bout Superlotto? Yeah, one of those, thanks.

Next: you. You try to gauge how much this straggly woman sees. Can she tell? Muslim? Mexican? Does she know that your clothes are Trendy, that your grades are Dweeby, that your heart is Goody-goody? Your face: unreadable, innocent, frozen. One Slurpee. Please.

You walk around the counter and towards the magazines and when your friends see you, you try to look triumphant and cool and with it. But you feel like a cheat. Like maybe if it is stealing, you might not be such a good Muslim, you might be letting your kind of people look bad.

Not *stealing*, says Lucy. Sharing. It's just sharing.

So you share. You slurp cherry-cola-blueberry-cherry layers until your forehead aches. Then Jackie opens up her mouth and throws her head back and gets down on her knees and another girl pulls the knob and you all stop to watch the Slurpee slurped straight from the machine. Gross, someone says, but you're all impressed with the inventiveness and Jackie's daredevil status is elevated in everyone's eyes.

Oh, for Christssake! Give me a break! You goddamn good-for-nothing kids, get out of here! Get! Never again! You're banned, you hear me? Banned! Out! Get out!

Scatter giggling and shrieking across the parking lot, and the very next day dare each other to go back like nothing happened and you know you can because you know she can't tell the difference between any of you anyway. You could be anyone for all she knows.

The day you try it out as a test, someone yanks hard from behind and when it gets ripped off your head, a lot of hair does too. You think about how when hard-ass what-up girls fight they both stop first and take out all their earrings. It hurts enough to make you cry but you try hard not to. *Please don't let me cry, please, please don't let me cry.* First period, and Taylor Bryans sees your chubby lower lip tremble and he remembers the time you corrected his wrong answer in front of the whole class (Not pods! *Seeds*! Duh!) and he starts up a tough game of Shala-Snot-Germs and the cooties spread from hand to hand all around the room as your face gets hotter and hotter and your eyeballs sting and your nose drips in sorrow. Your dignity gathers and mounts as you readjust the scarf and re-pin the pin. You can't see anyone pass Germs, you can't hear anyone say your name. You are stone. You are cool. You will not cry. Those are not tears. The bell rings.

Then the bell rings six more times at the end of six periods and when you get home that day you have had the hijab yanked on seven occasions, four times in first period, and you've had your feet stomped twice by Taylor Bryans in the lunch line, and after school a group of eighth graders, all of them past puberty and huge with breasts in bras, surrounded you to gawk and tug in unison. And you've made up your mind about the hijab. It stays. No matter what. The fury coils in your veins like rattlesnake lava, the chin pushes out to be held high, the face is composed and impervious and a new dignity is born outraged where there used to be just Shala's self-doubt. It stays, you think, No matter what.

Still, at home you cry into your mom's sari and you shout at her like she's one of the merciless, I'm just regular, you wail. I'm the same as I ever was!

Oh baby, come on, shhh, it's going to be okay, she says. And then your mom suggests that maybe right now might not be the right time to start wearing this. She assures you that you are okay either way, that you can just take it off and forget about it. She says all this, sure, but she wears hers knotted firmly underneath her own chin as she strokes your back with reassurance.

That night, before you get into bed, you think about your brother and what it must be like for him. You look in the bathroom mirror and you slip the hijab on over your young hair and you watch like magic as you're transformed into a woman right before your very eyes. You watch like magic as all of the responsibilities and roles shift and focus.

You get it both ways. In your own country you have to worry, you have to get your hair pulled. And in India there you are: the open target, so obvious with your smooth American feet and your mini Nike backpack, the most hated. With anger and envy and danger all around you. The most hated. The most spoiled. An easy mark. A tiny girl. With every thing in the world, and all of it at your disposal.

You think about your brother and you wonder if he's scared.

As you get dressed for bed you check things out with a hand mirror. You poke at the new places you hadn't looked at before. You look at the shape in the hand mirror and you think, *Hello me*. It's embarrassing even though it's only you. You feel a whole new feeling. You think about how much you hate Taylor Bryans. Indignation rises up like steam. You stand there in the bathroom with blood on your hands and you know it. *I am Muslim*, you think, *I am Muslim, hear me roar.*

In third period PE the waves of hot Valley sun bake off the blacktop asphalt and from a distance you see squiggly lines of air bent into mirage and your head is cooking underneath the scarf and your ears feel like they're burning in the places where they touch the cloth and your hair is plastered to the back of your neck with sticky salty sweat and when you group up for teams, someone yanks hard. You topple right over. You scrape your knees and through the blood they're smudged sooty black. Everyone turns around to look, and a bunch of girls laugh quietly behind hands. The hijab is torn from where the pin broke loose and your dad is right, it's way better that it isn't a knot or you might choke. Your neck is wet with a hair-strand of blood from where the popped-open pin tip slipped along skin. And you figure, That's it. Forget it. I quit. I'm ditching. I hate you.

Someone says, Aw shit, girl, you okay?

You scramble up and walk tall and leave the girls in their bagged out PE uniforms and you go back into the cool dank locker room where you can get naked all by yourself for once. As you wash the gravel out of your hands you stare at yourself in the mirror. You think *Bloody Mary* and squeeze your eyes shut tight, but when you open them it's still just your face all alone with rows and rows of lockers. No demon to slice you down.

Now when you walk in late you're not Nobody anymore, you're not Anyone At All. Instead, now, when you walk in you have to brace yourself in advance, and you have to summon up a courage and a dignity that grows strong when your eyes go dull and you stare into unfocused space inches away while Taylor Bryans and Fernando Cruz snicker and snicker until no one's looking and then they run up and shout in your face: Arab! Lardass! Damn, you so ugly you ooogly!

Your inner reserves fill to full when Fernando stomps on your feet and your white Reeboks get all smeared up and your face doesn't even move no matter how much it hurts.

The bell rings. Lunch. You push and shove your way into the cluster of the girls' room, and there's no privacy and you try to peer into the tagged-up piece of dull-shine metal that's bolted to the wall where everyone wants a mirror, but there are girls applying mascara and girls with lip-liner and the only air is a fine wet mist of aerosol Aqua-net and it's too hard to breathe and you can't see if it's still pinned straight, because that last snatch was like an afterthought and it didn't even tug all the way off. But you can't make your way up to the reflection and you can't see for sure. So here it comes, and then you're standing there in the ebb and flow of shoulders and sneakers and all of a sudden here it comes and you're sobbing like you can't stop.

Hey girl, why you crying? You want me to kick some motherfucker's ass for you, girl? 'Cause I'll do it, bitch, I'm crazy like that. You just show me who, right, I'll do it, homegirl.

And through your tears you want to throw your arms around
the giant mountainous Chola and her big-hearted kindness
and you want to kiss her Adidas and you want to say Taylor
Bryans's name and you want to point him out and you want
his ass kicked hard, but you stop yourself. You picture the
outcome, you picture the humiliation he'd feel, a skinny sixth
grader, a scrub, the black eye, the devastation of public boy-
tears, the horror of having someone who means it hit you like
an avalanche. You look over your back and past all the girl-
heads, the stiff blondes and permed browns and braided
weaves, the dye jobs, the split ends, all of them elbowing
and pushing in to catch a dull distorted glimpse in graffitied
monochrome, and you smooth over the folds of your safe solid
black hijab and you snuffle up teary dripping snot and you
picture what it would be.

You picture her rush him: Hey BITCH, yeah I'm talking
to you, *pendejo*, that's right you better run outta my way
whiteboy, cuz I'm going to whup your ass, punkass motherfucker! You picture her and she's like a truck. Taylor Bryans
stops cold and then he startles and turns to flee but she's
already overcome him like a landslide, and she pounds him
like muddy debris crushing someone's million-dollar home.
You picture the defeat, the crowd of jeering kids, Fight! Fight!
Fight! The tight circle of locked arms, elbow in elbow so the
teachers can't break it up, the squawk of adult walkie-talkies
and then the security guards, the assistant principal, and all
the teachers on yard duty, all of them as one, all charging over
to haul kids out of the fray and into detention, and all the
while you can picture him like he's a photograph in your hand:
the tears, the scrapes, the bruises, the giant shame in his guilty
nasty eyes and you know that it wouldn't solve a thing and

you suspect that it probably wouldn't even stop him from pulling your hair out and stomping on your feet and you picture it and you open up your heart and you forgive him.

Then you gather up all that new dignity, and then you look up at her, stick your covered head out of the girls' bathroom, and point.

God Lives in St Petersburg

TOM BISSELL

God, in time, takes everything from everyone. Timothy Silverstone believed that those whose love for God was a vast, borderless frontier were expected to surrender everything to Him, gladly and without question, and that those who did so would live to see everything and more returned to them. After college he had shed America like a husk and journeyed to the far side of the planet, all to spread God's word. Now he was coming apart. Anyone with love for God knows that when you give up everything for Him, He has no choice but to destroy you. God destroyed Moses; destroyed the heart of Abraham by revealing the deep, lunatic fathom at which his faith ran; took everything from Job, saw it did not destroy him, then returned it, which did. Timothy reconciled God's need to destroy with God's opulent love by deciding that, when He destroyed you, it was done out of the truest love, the deepest, most divine respect. God could not allow perfection – it was simply too close to Him. His love for the sad, the fallen, and the sinful was an easy, uncomplicated love, but those who lived along the argent brink of perfection had to be watched and tested and tried.

Timothy Silverstone was a missionary, though on the orders of his organization, the Central Asian Relief Agency, he was not allowed to admit this. Instead, when asked (which he was, often and by everyone), he was to say he was an English teacher. This was to be the pry he would use to widen the sorrowful, light-starved breach that, according to CARA, lay flush across the heart of every last person in the world, especially those Central Asians who had been cocooned within the suffocating atheism of Soviet theology. 'The gears of history have turned,' the opening pages of Timothy's CARA handbook read, 'and the hearts of 120 million people have been pushed from night into day, and all of them are calling out for the love of Jesus Christ.'

As his students cheated on their exams Timothy drifted through the empty canals between their desks. His classroom was as plain as a monk's sleeping quarters; its wood floors groaned with each of his steps. Since he had begun to come apart, he stopped caring whether his students cheated. He had accepted that they did not understand what cheating was and never would, for just as there is no Russian word which connotes the full meaning of *privacy*, there is no unambiguously pejorative word for *cheat*. Timothy had also stopped trying to teach them about Jesus because, to his shock, they already knew of a thoroughly discredited man who in Russian was called *Hristos*.

Timothy's attempts to create in their minds the person he knew as Jesus did nothing but trigger nervous, uncomfortable laughter Timothy simply could not bear to hear. Timothy could teach them about Jesus and His works and His love, but *Hristos* grayed and tired his heart. He felt nothing for this impostor, not even outrage. Lately, in order to keep from coming apart, he had decided to try to teach his students English instead.

'Meester Timothy,' cried Rustam, an Uzbek boy with a long,

thin face. His trembling arm was held up, his mouth a lipless dash.

'Yes, Rustam, what is it?' he answered in Russian. Skull-clutching hours of memorizing rows of vocabulary words was another broadsword Timothy used to beat back coming apart. He was proud of his progress with the language because it was so difficult. This was counterbalanced by his Russian acquaintances, who asked him why his Russian was not better, seeing that it was so simple.

After Timothy spoke, Rustam went slack with disappointment. Nine months ago, moments after Timothy had first stepped into this classroom, Rustam had approached him and demanded (actually using the verb demand) that Timothy address him in nothing but English. Since then his memorized command of English had deepened, and he had become by spans and cubits Timothy's best student. Timothy complied, asking Rustam 'What is it?' again, in English.

'It is Susanna,' Rustam said, jerking his head toward the small blonde girl who shared his desk. Most of Timothy's students were black-haired, sloe-eyed Uzbeks like Rustam – the ethnic Russians able to do so had fled Central Asia as the first statues of Lenin toppled – and Susanna's blonde, round-eyed presence in the room was both a vague ethnic reassurance and, somehow, deeply startling. Rustam looked back at Timothy. 'She is looking at my test and bringing me distraction. Meester Timothy, this girl cheats on me.' Rustam, Timothy knew, had branded onto his brain this concept of cheating, and viewed his classmates with an ire typical of the freshly enlightened.

Susanna's glossy eyes were fixed upon the scarred wooden slab of her desktop. Timothy stared at this girl he did not know what to do with, who had become all the children he did not know what to do with. She was thirteen, fourteen, and sat there, pink and startled, while Rustam spoke his determined English. Susanna's hair held a buttery yellow glow in the long plinths of sunlight shining in through the windows; her small smooth hands grabbed at each other in her lap. All around her, little heads bowed above the clean white rectangles on their desks, the classroom filled with the soft scratching of pencils. Timothy took a breath, looking back to Rustam, unable to concentrate on what he was saying because Timothy could not keep from looking up at the row of pictures along the back wall of his classroom, where Ernest Hemingway, John Reed, Paul Robeson, and Jack London stared out at him from plain wooden frames. An identical suite of portraits – the Soviet ideal of good Americans – was found in every English classroom from here to Tbilisi. Timothy knew that none of these men had found peace with God. He had wanted to give that peace to these children. When he came to Central Asia he felt that peace as a great glowing cylinder inside of him, but the cylinder had grown dim. He could barely even feel God anymore, though he could still hear Him, floating and distant, broadcasting a surflike static. There was a message woven into this dense noise, Timothy was sure, but no matter how hard he tried he couldn't decipher it. He looked again at Rustam. He had stopped talking now and was waiting for Timothy's answer. Every student in the classroom had looked up from their tests, pinioning Timothy with their small impassive eyes.

'Susanna's fine, Rustam,' Timothy said finally, turning to erase the nothing on his blackboard. 'She's okay. It's okay.'

Rustam's forehead creased darkly but he nodded and returned to his test. Timothy knew that, to Rustam, the world and his place in it would not properly compute if Americans were not always right, always good, always funny and smart and rich and beautiful. Never mind that Timothy had the mashed nose of a Roman pugilist and a pimply face; never mind that Timothy's baggy, runneled clothing had not been washed for months; never mind that once, after Rustam had asked about the precise function of 'do' in the sentence 'I do not like to swim,' Timothy stood at the head of the class for close to two minutes and silently fingered his chalk. Meester Timothy was right, even when he was wrong, because he came from America. The other students went back to their exams. Timothy imagined he could hear the wet click of their eyes moving from test to test, neighbor to neighbor, soaking up one another's answers.

Susanna, though, did not stir. Timothy walked over to her and placed his hand on her back. She was as warm to his touch as a radiator through a blanket, and she looked up at him with starved and searching panic in her eyes. Timothy smiled at her, uselessly. She swallowed, picked up her pencil and, as if helpless not to, looked over at Rustam's test, a fierce indentation between her yellow eyebrows. Rustam sat there, writing, pushing out through his nose hot gusts of air, until finally he whirled around in his seat and hissed something at Susanna in his native language, which he knew she did not understand. Again, Susanna froze. Rustam pulled her pencil from her hands – she did not resist – snapped it in half, and threw the pieces in her face. From somewhere in Susanna's throat came a half-swallowed sound of grief, and she burst into tears.

Suddenly Timothy was standing there, dazed, rubbing his hand. He recalled something mentally blindsiding him, some sort of brainflash, and thus could not yet understand why his palm was buzzing. Nor did he understand why every student had heads bowed even lower to their tests, why the sound of scratching pencils seemed suddenly, horribly frenzied and loud. But when Rustam – who merely sat in his chair, looking up at Timothy, his long face devoid of expression – lifted his hand to his left cheek, Timothy noticed it reddening, tightening, his eye squashing shut, his skin lashing itself to his cheekbone. And Timothy Silverstone heard the sound of God recede even more, retreat back even farther, while Susanna, between sobs, gulped for breath.

Naturally, Sasha was waiting for Timothy in the doorway of the teahouse across the street from the Registan, a suite of three madrasas whose sparkling minarets rose up into a haze of metallic, blue-gray smog. Today was especially bad, a poison petroleum mist lurking along the streets and sidewalks and curbs. And then there was the heat – a belligerent heat; to move through it felt like breathing hot tea.

Timothy walked past the tall, bullet-shaped teahouse doorway, Sasha falling in alongside him. They did not talk – they rarely talked – even though the walk to Timothy's apartment in the Third Microregion took longer than twenty minutes. Sasha was Russian, tall and slender with hair the color of new mud. Each of Sasha's ears were as large and ornate as a tankard handle, and his eyes were as blue as the dark margin of atmosphere where the sky became outer space. He walked next to Timothy with a lanky, boneless grace, and wore blue jeans and imitation-leather cowboy boots that clomped emptily on the sidewalk. Sasha's mother was a history teacher from Timothy's school.

When his drab building came into sight Timothy felt the

headachy swell of God's static rushing into his head. It was pure sound, shapeless and impalpable, and as always he sensed some egg of sense or insight held deep within it. Then it was gone, silent, and in that moment Timothy could feel his spirit split from his flesh. *For I know*, Timothy thought, these words of Paul's to the Romans so bright in the glare of his memory they seemed almost indistinct from his own thoughts, *that nothing good dwells within me, that is, in my flesh. I can will what is right, but I cannot do it.*

As they climbed the stairs to Timothy's fifth-floor apartment, Sasha reached underneath Timothy's crotch and cupped him. He squeezed and laughed, and Timothy felt a wet heat spread through him, animate him, flow to the hard, stony lump growing in his pants. Sasha squeezed again, absurdly tender. As Timothy fished for the keys to his apartment door Sasha walked up close behind him, breathing on Timothy's neck, his clothes smelling – as everyone's clothes here did – as though they had been cured in sweat.

They stumbled inside. Sasha closed the door as Timothy's hands shot to his belt, which he tore off like a rip-cord. He'd lost so much weight his pants dropped with a sad puff around his feet. Sasha shook his head at this – he complained, sometimes, that Timothy was getting too skinny – and he stepped out of his own pants. Into his palm Sasha spit a foamy coin of drool, stepped toward Timothy and with the hand he spit into grabbed his penis. He pulled it toward him sexlessly, as if it were a grapple he was making sure was secure. Sasha laughed again and he threw himself over the arm of Timothy's plush red sofa. Sasha reached back and with medical indelicacy pulled himself apart. He looked over his shoulder at Timothy, waiting.

The actual penetration was always beyond the bend of

Timothy's recollection. As if some part of himself refused to acknowledge it. One moment Sasha was hurling himself over the couch's arm, the next Timothy was inside him. *I can will what is right, but I cannot do it.* It began slowly, Sasha breathing through his mouth, Timothy pushing further into him, eyes smashed shut. What he felt was not desire, not lust; it was worse than lust. It was worse than what drove a soulless animal. It was some hot tongue of fire inside Timothy that he could not douse – not by satisfying it, not by ignoring it. Sometimes it was barely more than a flicker, and then Timothy could live with it, nullify it as his weakness, as his flaw. But without warning, in whatever dark, smoldering interior shrine, the flame would grow and flash outward, melting whatever core of Timothy he believed good and steadfast into soft, pliable sin.

Timothy's body shook as if withstanding invisible blows, and Sasha began to moan with a carefree sinless joy Timothy could only despise, pity, and envy. It was always, oddly, this time, when perched on the edge of exploding into Sasha, that Timothy's mind turned, again, with noble and dislocated grace, to Paul. *Do not be deceived!* he wrote. *Fornicators, idolaters, adulterers, male prostitutes, sodomites – none of these will inherit the kingdom of God. And this is what some of you used to be. But you were washed, you were sanctified, you were justified in the name of Lord Jesus Christ and in the Spirit of our God.* It was a passage Timothy could only read and reflect upon and pray to give him the strength he knew he did not have. He prayed to be washed, to be sanctified in the name of Jesus, but now he had come apart and God was so far from him. His light had been eclipsed, and in the cold darkness that followed, he wondered if his greatest sin was not that he was pushing himself into non-vaginal warmth but that his worship was now for man and not man's maker. But such taxonomies were of little value. God's world was one of cruel mathematics, of right and wrong. It was a world that those who had let God fall from their hearts condemned as repressive and awash in dogma – an accurate but vacant condemnation, Timothy knew, since God did not anywhere claim that His world was otherwise.

A roiling spasm began in Timothy's groin and burst throughout the rest of his body, and in that ecstatic flooded moment nothing was wrong, nothing, with anyone, and he emptied himself into Sasha without guilt, only with appreciation and happiness and bliss. But then it was over, and he had to pull himself from the boy and wonder, once again, if what he had done had ruined him for ever, if he had driven himself so deeply into darkness that the darkness had become both affliction and reward. Quickly Timothy wiped himself with one of the throw pillows from his couch and sat on the floor, sick and dizzy with shame. Sasha, still bent over the couch, looked back at Timothy, smirking, a cloudy satiation frosting his eyes. '*Shto?*' he asked Timothy. *What?*

Timothy could not – could never – answer him.

The next morning Timothy entered his classroom to find Susanna seated at her desk. Class was not for another twenty minutes, and Susanna was a student whose arrival, on most days, could be counted on to explore the temporal condition between late and absent. Timothy was about to wish her a surprised 'Good morning' when he realized that she was not alone.

A woman sat perched on the edge of his chair, wagging her finger and admonishing Susanna in juicy, top-heavy Russian. Her accent was unknown to Timothy, filled with dropped

Gs and a strange, diphthongal imprecision. Whole sentence fragments arced past him like softballs. Susanna merely sat there, her hands on her desktop in a small bundle. Timothy turned to leave but the woman looked over to see him caught in mid-pirouette in the door-jamb. She leapt up from his chair, a startled gasp rushing out of her.

They looked at each other, the woman breathing, her meaty shoulders bobbing up and down, her mouth pulled into a rictal grin. '*Zdravstvuite,*' she said stiffly.

'*Zdravstvuite,*' Timothy said, stepping back into the room. He tried to smile and the woman returned the attempt with a melancholy but respectful nod. She was like a lot of women Timothy saw here – bull-necked, jowled, of indeterminate age, as sexless as an oval. Atop her head was a lumpen yellow-white mass of hairspray and bobby pins, and her lips looked as sticky and red as the picnic tables Timothy remembered painting, with his Christian youth group, in the parks of Green Bay, Wisconsin.

'Timothy Silverstone,' she said. *Teemosee Seelverstun.* Her hands met below her breasts and locked.

'Yes,' Timothy said, glancing at Susanna. She wore a bright, bubble-gum-colored dress he had not seen before, some frilly, ribboned thing. As if aware of Timothy's eyes on her, Susanna bowed over in her chair even more, a path of spinal knobs surfacing along her back.

'I am Irina Dupkova,' the woman said. 'Susanna told me what happened yesterday – how you reacted to her . . . problem.' Her joined hands lifted to her chin in gentle imploration. 'I have come to ask you, this is true, yes?'

Her accent delayed the words from falling into their proper translated slots. When they did, a mental deadbolt unlocked, opening a door somewhere inside Timothy and allowing the memory of Rustam's eye swelling shut to come tumbling out. A fist of guilt clenched in his belly. *He had struck a child.* He had hit a boy as hard as he could, and there was no place he could hide this from himself, as he hid what he did with Sasha. Timothy felt faint and humidified, his face pinkening. 'Yes, Irina Dupkova,' he said, 'it is. And I want to tell you I'm sorry. I, I—' He searched for words, some delicate, spiraled idiom to communicate his remorse. He could think of nothing, entire vocabularies lifting away from him like startled birds. 'I'm sorry. What happened made me . . . very unhappy.'

She shot Timothy a strange look, eyes squinched, her red lips kissed out in perplexion. 'You do not understand me,' she said. This was not a question. Timothy glanced over at Susanna, who had not moved, perhaps not even breathed. When he looked back to Irina Dupkova she was smiling at him, her mouthful of gold teeth holding no gleam, no sparkle, only the metallic dullness of a handful of old pennies. She shook her head, clapping once in delight. 'Oh, your Russian, Mister Timothy, I think it is not so good. You do not *vladeyete* Russian very well, yes?'

'*Vladeyete*,' Timothy said. It was a word he was sure he knew. '*Vladeyete*,' he said again, casting mental nets. The word lay beyond his reach somewhere, veiled.

Irina Dupkova exhaled in mystification, then looked around the room. 'You do not know this word,' she said in a hard tone, one that nudged the question mark off the end of the sentence.

'Possess,' Susanna said, before Timothy could lie. Both Timothy and Irina Dupkova looked over at her. Her back was still to them, but Timothy could see that she was consulting her CARA-supplied Russian–English dictionary. '*Vladeyete*,' she said again, her finger thrust onto the page. 'Possess.'

Timothy blinked. 'Da,' he said. '*Vladeyete*. Possess.' For the benefit of Irina Dupkova he smacked himself on the forehead with the butt of his palm.

'Possess,' Irina Dupkova said, as if it had been equally obvious to her. She paused, her face regaining its bluntness. 'Well, nevertheless, I have come here this morning to thank you.'

Timothy made a vague sound of dissent. 'There is no need to thank me, Irina Dupkova.'

'You have made my daughter feel very good, Timothy. Protected. Special. You understand, yes?'

'Your daughter is a fine girl,' Timothy said. 'A fine student.'

With that Irina Dupkova's face palled, and she stepped closer to him, putting her square back to the doorway. 'These filthy people think they can spit on Russians now, you know. They think independence has made them a nation. They are animals, barbarians.' Her eyes were small and bright with anger.

Timothy Silverstone looked at his scuffed classroom floor. There was activity in the hallway – shuffling feet, children's voices – and Timothy looked at his watch. His first class, Susanna's class, began in ten minutes. He moved to the door and closed it.

Irina Dupkova responded to this by intensifying her tone, her hands moving in little emphatic circles. 'You understand, Timothy, that Russians did not come here willingly, yes? I am here because my father was exiled after the Great Patriotic War Against Fascism. Like Solzhenitsyn, and his careless letters. A dark time, but this is where my family has made its home. You understand. We have no other place but this, but things are very bad for us now.' She flung her arm toward the windows, and looked outside, her jaw set. 'There is no future for Russians here, I think. No future. None.'

'I understand, Irina Dupkova,' Timothy said, 'and I am sorry, but you must excuse me, I have my morning lessons now and I—'

She seized Timothy's wrist, the ball of her thumb pressing harshly between his radius and ulna. 'And this little hooligan Uzbek thinks he can touch my Susanna. You understand that they are animals, Timothy, yes? *Animals*. Susanna,' Irina Dupkova said, her dark eyes not leaving Timothy's, 'come here now, please. Come let Mister Timothy see you.'

In one smooth movement Susanna rose from her desk and turned to them. Her hair was pulled back into a taut blonde ponytail and lay tightly against her skull, as fine and grained as sandalwood. She walked over to them in small, noiseless steps, and Timothy, because of his shame for striking Rustam before her eyes, could not bear to look at her face. Instead he studied her shoes – black and shiny, like little hoofs – and the thin legs that lay beneath the wonder of her white leggings. Irina Dupkova hooked Susanna close to her and kissed the top of her yellow head. Susanna looked up at Timothy, but he could not hold the girl's gaze. He went back to the huge face of her mother, a battlefield of a face, white as paraffin.

'My daughter,' Irina Dupkova said, nose tilting downward into the loose wires of Susanna's hair.

'Yes,' Timothy said.

Irina Dupkova looked over at him, smiling, eyebrows aloft. 'She is very beautiful, yes?'

'She is a very pretty girl,' Timothy agreed.

Irina Dupkova bowed in what Timothy took to be grateful

acknowledgment. 'My daughter likes you very much,' she said, looking down. 'You understand this. You are her favorite teacher. My daughter loves English.'

'Yes,' Timothy said. At some point Irina Dupkova had, unnervingly, begun to address him in the second-person familiar. Timothy flinched as a knock on the door sounded throughout the classroom, followed by a peal of girlish giggling.

'My daughter loves America,' Irina Dupkova said, ignoring the knock, her voice soft and insistent.

'Yes,' Timothy said, looking back at her.

'I have no husband.'

Timothy willed the response from his face. 'I'm very sorry to hear that.'

'He was killed in Afghanistan.'

'I'm very sorry to hear that.'

'I live alone with my daughter, Timothy, in this nation in which Russians have no future.'

Lord, please, Timothy thought, make her stop. 'Irina Dupkova,' Timothy said softly, 'there is nothing I can do about any of this. I am going home in three months. I cannot – I am not able to help you in that way.'

'I have not come here for that,' she said. 'Not for me. Again you do not understand me.' Irina Dupkova's eyes closed with the faint, amused resignation of one who had been failed her whole life. 'I have come here for Susanna. I want you to have her. I want you to take her back to America.'

Struck dumb had always been a homely, opaque expression to Timothy, but he understood, at that moment, the deepest implications of its meaning. He had nothing to say, *nothing*, and the silence seemed hysterical.

She stepped closer. 'I want you to take my daughter,

Timothy. To America. As your wife. I will give her to you.'

Timothy stared her in the face, still too surprised for emotion. 'Your daughter, Irina Dupkova,' he said, 'is too young for such a thing. *Much* too young.' He made the mistake of looking down at Susanna. There was something in the girl Timothy had always mistaken for a cowlike dullness, but he could see now, in her pale eyes, savage determination. The sudden understanding that Susanna's instigation lay behind Irina Dupkova's broke through Timothy's sternum.

'She is fourteen,' Irina Dupkova said, moving her hand, over and over again, along the polished sheen of Susanna's hair. 'She will be fifteen in four months. This is not so young, I think.'

'*She is too young*,' Timothy said with a fresh anger. Again he looked down at Susanna. She had not removed her eyes from his.

'She will do for you whatever you ask, Timothy,' Irina Dupkova was saying. 'Whatever you ask. You understand.'

Timothy nodded distantly, a nod that both understood but did not understand. In Susanna's expression of inert and perpetual unfeeling, he could see that what Irina Dupkova said was right – she would do whatever he asked of her. And Timothy Silverstone felt the glisten of desire at this thought, felt the bright glint of a lechery buried deep in the shale of his mind. *My God*, he thought. *I will not do this*. He was startled to realize he had no idea how old Sasha was. Could that be? He was tall, and his scrotum dangled between his legs with the heft of post-adolescence, but he was also lightly and delicately haired, and had never, as far as Timothy could tell, shaved or needed to shave. Sasha could have been twenty-two, two years younger than Timothy; he could have been sixteen. Timothy shook the idea from his head.

'I have a brother,' Irina Dupkova was saying, 'who can arrange for papers that will make Susanna older. Old enough for you, in your nation. It has already been discussed. Do you understand?'

'Irina Dupkova,' Timothy said, stepping backward, both hands thrust up, palms on display, 'I cannot marry your daughter.'

Irina Dupkova nearly smiled. 'You say you cannot. You do not say you do not want to.'

'Irina Dupkova, *I cannot do this for you.*'

Irina Dupkova sighed, chin lifting, head tilting backward. 'I know why you are here. You understand. I know why you have come. You have come to give us your Christ. But he is useless.' Something flexed behind her Slavic faceplate, her features suddenly sharpening. '*This* would help us. *This* would save.'

Timothy spun around, swung open his classroom door, poked his head into the hallway and scattered the knot of chattering children there with a hiss. He turned back toward Irina Dupkova, pulling the door shut behind him with a bang. They both stared at him, Irina Dupkova's arm holding Susanna close to her thick and formless body. 'You understand, Timothy,' she began, 'how difficult it is for us to leave this nation. They do not allow it. And so you can escape, or you can marry.' She looked down at herself. 'Look at me. This is what Susanna will become if she remains here. Old and ugly, a ruin.' In Irina Dupkova's face was a desperation so needy and exposed Timothy could find quick solace only in God, a mental oxbow that took him to imagining the soul within Susanna, the soul being held out for him to take away from here, to sanctify and to save. That was God's law, His imperative: *Go therefore and make disciples of all nations.* Then God's distant broadcast filled his mind, and with two fingers placed stethoscopically to his forehead Timothy turned away from Irina Dupkova and Susanna and listened so hard a dull red ache spread behind his eyes. The sound disappeared.

'Well,' Irina Dupkova said with a sigh, after it had become clear that Timothy was not going to speak, 'you must begin your lesson now.' Susanna stepped away from her mother and like a ghost drifted over to her desk. Irina Dupkova walked past Timothy and stopped at his classroom door. 'You will think about it,' she said, turning to him, her face in profile, her enormous back draped with a tattered white shawl, 'you will consider it.' Timothy said nothing and she nodded, turned back to the door, and opened it.

Students streamed into the room on both sides of Irina Dupkova like water coming to a delta. Their flow hemmed her in, and Irina Dupkova's angry hands fluttered and slapped at the black-haired heads rushing past her. Only Rustam stepped aside to let her out, which was why he was the last student into the room. As Rustam closed the door after Irina Dupkova, Timothy quickly spun to his blackboard and stared at the piece of chalk in his hand. He thought of what to write. He thought of writing something from Paul, something sagacious and unproblematic like *We who are strong ought to put up with the failings of the weak.* He felt Rustam standing behind him, but Timothy could not turn around. He wrote the date on the board, then watched chalkdust drift down into the long and sulcated tray at the board's base.

'Meester Timothy?' Rustam said finally, his artificial American accent tuned to a tone of high contrition.

Timothy turned. A bruise like a red-brown crescent lay

along the ridge of Rustam's cheekbone, the skin there taut and shiny. It was barely noticeable, really. It was nothing. It looked like the kind of thing any child was liable to get, anywhere, doing anything. Rustam was smiling at him, a bead of wet light fixed in each eye. 'Good morning, Rustam,' Timothy said.

Rustam reached into his book bag, then deposited into Timothy's hand something Timothy remembered telling his class about months and months ago, back before he had come apart; something that, in America, he had said, students brought their favorite teachers. It got quite a laugh from these students, who knew of a different standard of extravagance needed to sway one's teachers. Timothy stared at the object in his hand. An apple. Rustam had given him an apple. 'For you,' Rustam said softly, turned and sat down.

Timothy looked up at his classroom to see five rows of smiles. Meester Timothy will be wonderful and American again, these smiles said. Meester Timothy will not hit us, not like our teachers hit us. Meester Timothy will always be good.

Woolen gray clouds floated above the Registan's minarets, the backlight of a high, hidden sun outlining them gold. Some glow leaked through, filling the sky with hazy beams of diffracted light.

Timothy walked home, head down, into the small breeze coming out of the Himalayan foothills to the east. It was the first day in weeks that the temperature had dipped below 38°C, the first day in which walking two blocks did not soak his body in sweat.

Sasha stood in the tall doorway of the teahouse, holding a bottle of orange Fanta in one hand and a cigarette in the other.

Around his waist Sasha had knotted the arms of Timothy's gray-and-red St Thomas Seminary sweatshirt (Timothy didn't recall allowing Sasha to borrow it), the rest trailing down behind him in a square maroon cape. He slouched in the doorway, one shoulder up against the frame, his eyes filled with an alert, dancing slyness. Sasha let the half-smoked cigarette drop from his fingers and it hit the teahouse floor in a burst of sparks and gray ash. He was grinding it out with his cowboy-boot-tip when Timothy's eyes pounced upon his. '*Nyet*,' Timothy said, still walking, feeling on his face the light spume of rain. '*Ne sevodnya*, Sasha.' *Not today, Sasha.* Timothy eddied through the molded white plastic chairs and tables of an empty outdoor café, reached the end of the block and glanced behind him.

Sasha stood there, his arms laced tight across his chest, his face a twist of sour incomprehension. Behind him a herd of Pakistani tourists was rushing toward the Registan to snap pictures before the rain began.

Timothy turned at the block's corner even though he did not need to. In the sky a murmur of thunder heralded the arrival of a darker bank of clouds. Timothy looked up. A raindrop exploded on his eye.

Timothy sat behind his workdesk in his bedroom, a room so small and diorama-like it seemed frustrated with itself, before the single window that looked out on the over-planned Soviet chaos of the Third Microregion: flat roofs, gouged roads that wended industriously but went nowhere, the domino of faceless apartment buildings just like his own. The night was impenetrable with thick curtains of rain, and lightning split the sky with electrified blue fissures. It was the first time in months it had rained long enough to create the conditions Timothy associated with rain: puddles on the streets, overflowing gutters, mist-cooled air. The letter he had started had sputtered out halfway into its first sentence, though a wet de facto period had formed after the last word he had written ('here') from having left his felt-tip pen pressed against the paper too long. He had been trying to write about Susanna, about what had happened today. The letter was not intended for anyone in particular, and a broken chain of words lay scattered throughout his mind and Timothy knew that if only he could pick them up and put them in their proper order, God's message might at last become clear to him. Perhaps, he thought, his letter was to God.

Knuckles against his door. He turned away from his notebook and wrenched around in his chair, knowing it was Sasha from the lightness of his three knocks, illicit knocks that seemed composed equally of warning and temptation. Timothy snapped shut his notebook, pinning his letter between its flimsy boards, and winged it onto his bed. As he walked across his living room, desire came charging up in him like a stampede of fetlocked horses, and just before Timothy's hand gripped the doorknob he felt himself through his Green Bay Packers sweatpants. A sleepy, squishy hardness there. He opened the door. Standing in the mildewy darkness of his hallway was not Sasha but Susanna, her small nose wrinkled and her soaked hair a tangle of spirals molded to her head. 'I have come,' she said, 'to ask if you have had enough time to consider.'

Timothy could only stare down at her. It occurred to him that he had managed to let another day go by without eating. He closed his eyes. 'Susanna, you must go home. Right now.'

She nodded, then stepped past him into his open, empty living room. Surprise rooted Timothy to the floorboards. 'Susanna—' he said, half reaching for her.

After slipping by she twirled once in the room's center, her eyes hard and appraising. This was a living room that seemed to invite a museum's velvet rope and small engraved plaque: Soviet Life, circa 1955. There was nothing but the red sofa, a tall black lamp which stood beside nothing, and a worn red rug that did not occupy half the floor. Susanna seemed satisfied, though, and with both hands she grabbed a thick bundle of her hair and twisted it, water pattering onto the floor. 'We can fuck,' she said in English, not looking at him, still twisting the water from her hair. She pronounced it *Ve con foke*. She took off her jacket and draped it over the couch. It was a cheap white plastic jacket, something Timothy saw hanging in the bazaars by the thousand. Beneath it she was still wearing the bubble-gum dress, aflutter with useless ribbonry. Her face was wet and cold, her skin bloodless in the relentless wattage of the lightbulb glowing naked above her. She was shivering.

Timothy heard no divine static to assist him with Susanna's words, only the awful silent vacuum in which the laws of the world were cast and acted upon.

'We can fuck,' Susanna said again.

'Stop it,' Timothy said.

'We can,' she said in Russian. 'I will do this for you and we will go to America.'

'No,' Timothy said, closing his eyes.

She took a small step back and looked at the floor. 'You do not want to do this with me?'

Timothy opened his eyes and stared at the lamp that stood

next to nothing. He thought that, if he stared at it long enough, Susanna might disappear.

'I have done this before with men.'

'You have,' Timothy said – it was a statement – his throat feeling dry and paved.

She shrugged. 'Sometimes.' She looked away. 'I know what you think. You think I am bad.'

'I am very sad for you, Susanna, but I don't think that.'

'You will tell me this is wrong.'

Now both of Timothy's hands were on his face, and he pushed them against his cheeks and eyes as if he were applying a compress. 'All of us do wrong, Susanna. All of us are bad. In the eyes of God,' he said with listless conviction, 'we are all sinners.'

A knowing sound tumbled out of Susanna. 'My mother told me you would tell me these things, because you believe in *Hristos.*' She said nothing for a moment. 'Will you tell me about this man?'

Timothy split two of his fingers apart and peered at her. 'Would you like me to?' he asked.

She nodded, scratching at the back of her hand, her fingernails leaving a crosshatching of chalky white lines. 'It is very interesting to me,' Susanna said, 'this story. That one man can die and save the whole world. My mother told me not to believe it. She told me this was something only an American would believe.'

'That's not true, Susanna. Many Russians also believe.'

'God lives for Russians only in St Petersburg. God does not live here. He has abandoned us.'

'God lives everywhere. God never abandons you.'

'My mother told me you would say that, too.' From her

tone, he knew, she had no allegiance to her mother. She could leave this place so easily. If not with him, she would wait for someone else. She shook her head at him. 'You have not thought about marrying me at all.'

'Susanna, it would be impossible. I have a family in America, friends, my church . . . they would see you, and they would know. You are not old enough to trick anyone with papers.'

'Then we will live somewhere else until I do.' She looked around, her wet hair whipping back and forth. 'Where is your bed? We will fuck there.'

'Susanna—'

'Let me show you what a good wife I can be.' With a shoddy fabric hiss her dress lifted over her head and she was naked. For all her fearlessness, Susanna could not anymore meet Timothy's eye, her xylophonic ribcage heaving, the concave swoop of her stomach breathing in and out like that of a panicked, wounded animal. She hugged herself, each hand gripping an elbow. She was smooth and hairless but for the blond puff at the junction of her tiny legs. She was a thin, shivering fourteen-year-old girl standing naked in the middle of Timothy's living room. Lightning flashed outside – a stroboscope of white light – the room's single bright lightbulb buzzing briefly, going dark, and glowing back to strength.

His bedroom was not dark enough to keep him from seeing, with awful clarity, Susanna's face tighten with pain as he floated above her. Nothing could ease the mistaken feeling of the small tight shape of her body against his. After it was over, he knew the part of himself he had lost with Sasha was not salvaged, and never would be. *I can will what is right, but I cannot do it.* He was longing for God to return to him when His faraway stirrings opened Timothy's eyes. Susanna lay beside him, in fragile, uneasy sleep. He was drawn from bed, pulled toward the window. The beaded glass was cool against his palms. While Timothy waited – God felt very close now – he imagined himself with Susanna, freed from the world and the tragedy of its limitations, stepping with her soul into the house of the True and Everlasting God, a mansion filled with rooms and rooms of a great and motionless light. Even when Susanna began to cry, Timothy could not turn around, afraid of missing what God would unveil for him, while outside, beyond the window, it began to rain again.

The Woman Who Sold Communion

KATE BRAVERMAN

When Amy Cruz heard she had been denied tenure, she stumbled into her office and picked up her telephone directory. She leafed through the book, name by name, and the pages felt fragile between her fingers. They might be petals or antiquities. There were disasters between the lines. This was her private ritual of nostalgia and how she let herself know she was unhappy.

However, on this particular morning, she actually dialed her mother and waited for her to answer. Raven Cruz was an integral component in her arsenal of weapons of personal destruction. Raven was the core, the plutonium centerpiece. Amy needed an action to definitively express her rage and grief, something like a hand grenade or bullet. Raven could pull the trigger.

Cellular service, with static intermittent voids and uncertainties involving wind currents and angles, had finally come to Espanola. Theoretically, they could now communicate directly. But she couldn't actually talk to her mother. They spoke as if with flags the way people do at sea, where conditions are mutable, possibilities limited and primitive. She choreographed pieces of cloth. The air was so many fabrics. Raven removed language and logic. Her mother had a cell phone now, but Amy was still rendered childlike and vulnerable. She

215

pressed the phone hard against her ear and the metal hurt. This was foreshadowing. Amy counted the rings. Twenty-five.

'They didn't give me the job,' Amy began.

'You're surprised?' Raven said. 'You're not a team player. You've always wanted a rank and serial number. The right uniform. Play first string for the military industrial complex.'

Amy Cruz was in her office at the university where she staggered after Alfred Baxter Coleman, the ABC of the History Department, stage-whispered the terminal news to her in the corridor. What he actually said was, 'No way, sweetie. Told you.' This was true. He had been intimating this to her all year. She had ignored him.

'Do you know how long it's been?' Raven asked. 'Since you called?'

'To the hour,' Amy answered. Then she told her mother precisely how many years, months, and days had passed since their last conversation.

'I'm impressed,' Raven admitted.

'You're always impressed by the wrong things,' Amy said. She glanced out the window, palm trees stunted by sun, air oily and smeared. 'Men who added fast and didn't need scratch paper. Chess players and piano players, no matter how bad. Women with trust funds who sew their own clothes and bake breads from scratch. Christ.'

'I'm a simple country girl. You were always too smart for me,' Raven said. 'I'm just an old hippie. We sit around listening to Bob Dylan and monitoring our hep C. I'm hoping to live long enough to get Medicare.'

'You have hepatitis C?' Amy asked, startled.

'We all do,' Raven said.

Outside was a slice of Los Angeles in early summer. The

hills were a brutal stale green with brittle shrubs like dry stubble. The air seemed to be leaking away.

'You still doing that AA nonsense?' Raven asked.

'I've got it under control,' Amy replied, much too quickly. 'I want to see you now.' Her words tumbled into the hot-stripped morning like dice hitting a wall and she wondered if she meant them. Amy thought of water in a creek, how it accommodated rocks. She considered the fluid spill.

'Get in your car now. You'll be here tomorrow,' Raven said with surprising urgency. 'Just check that AA crap at the border.'

'I'll leave half my IQ, too,' Amy offered. 'As a sign of good will.' After a pause in which Raven failed to construct a reply, Amy asked, 'How will I find you?'

'Ask in the plaza. Anyone can tell you where.'

Her mother hung up. No more details. Just anyone. In the plaza. It was like a treasure hunt. It was like dropping acid or eating peyote and letting it happen.

That's what they did for years. Let it happen. They camped in the mesas and canyons. Raven had a boyfriend with a Jeep and a sawed-off 12-gauge under the seat, a 9-millimeter in his suitcase or backpack, and a .32 semi-automatic in his pocket. A man, one man or another, who played drums or guitar in a band that had just come back from Australia or Japan. They stayed out for weeks. Finally, insect bites, sunburn and infected cuts made them return. Sometimes Raven just wanted a hot bath.

'I want perfume,' Raven would laugh, standing half-dressed on a plateau, her bare shoulders sculpted as if by centuries of wind and a gifted potter's hands. 'I want musk and a new hat with a feather.'

They would find a town with a hotel sporting an Old West motif in Durango or Aspen or Santa Fe. Her childhood is a sequence of lead glass windows and red floral carpets, mahogany paneling and saloon doors. The air is cool and the amber of honey and whiskey. It is the color of an afternoon shoot-out.

This was the era of the commune and before boarding-school. Raven's boyfriends had what they called business in town. They took sudden flights to Los Angeles and Miami. Raven drove them to and from airports. Small planes landed in the desert and Raven had flares, flashlights, and a Jeep. Amy was in the backseat wrapped in a down blanket. She was certain they were dealing drugs.

But she didn't confront her mother. They already spoke in code, in a network of implications and arrested partial sounds like passwords. Between them were flannel and denim and gingham scraps in a basket waiting to become a quilt that was never stitched. Plans for a house built of adobe on the mesa above Espanola her mother somehow owned remained a rolled-up document, a parchment hollow inside a rubber band. It was a navigational chart for a sea they would never sail. Their ideas drifted off. Soon their bodies would follow.

Amy was already leaving. She had been accepted to a boarding-school in San Diego. The director pronounced her test scores impressive. He seemed convinced a university scholarship would be eventually granted. She was already studying brochures for colleges in New York and Massachusetts.

In between, during summers and holidays, she was just letting it happen. Amy remembers returning from a camping trip, a vision quest Raven called it, their clothing filthy and stuffed randomly into plastic trash bags. It was the best hotel in town and the bellman carried their trash bags to their room with the gravity afforded real luggage. It was always a suite. Her mother's boyfriend of the moment entered cautiously, his hand touching the gun in his pocket. He eased into rooms, opening closet doors and shower curtains. He glanced at the street from behind the window shades as if scanning for gunmen below.

After weeks in canyons of juniper, sage, pinion, and rock, coffeeshops and boutiques were a fascination. Amy understood this was another form of foraging. She spent afternoons in tourist gift stores. She had lost so much weight on their vision quests on the plateaus, eating only dried fruit and crackers, she could wear size twos on the sale racks in Pocatello, Alamosa, and Winslow where the women had either run away or gone to fat the way domesticated animals do.

Once she bought a hot-pink miniskirt in what felt like Teflon. Eventually Raven had to cut it off her with scissors. Amy wore the skirt with a silver blouse that had the texture of steel wool. She bought pink spike heels. She imagined she was Brazilian. She rode a dawn bus to work from the projects. She was a clerk with ambitions. Her boss was married and took her to hotels on Sundays after mass. Through the slatted terrace windows were the sounds of birds and cathedral bells in cobblestone plazas, old trolley cars with electric spokes that sizzled, and something insistent that might have been an ocean.

We are all clerks with ambitions, Amy thought then, lounging on a brocade bedspread in a restored hotel suite in Colorado or New Mexico. She was fourteen years or fifteen years old. Raven and her current boyfriend were out doing business. They left her three hundred-dollar bills and instructed her to get an ice-cream soda and go shopping. Somewhere beyond town was thunder and the San Diego Pacific Academy. Boarding-school was similar to the commune. But the sleeping and eating arrangements were superior. There were desks and electricity and a library. Bells rang and they had a specific and reliable meaning.

Now it's noon in Los Angeles. It's time to pack her office. It's the end of the semester and she won't be back in the fall. Alfred Baxter Coleman, chair of the promotion and tenure committee, has successfully convinced his colleagues they don't need her. Amy wraps a pottery vase in the school newspaper. Ink smudges her fingers and she feels soiled to the bone. She doesn't want to put her books in cardboard boxes again. It's an obsolete rite of empty repetition. The square book caskets, carrying the dead texts from state to state, up and down flights of apartment steps with views of alleys and parking lots, bougainvillea and oleander strangling on wire fences. In truth, Amy realizes she doesn't want the books anymore, period.

What she wants is a wound that will bleed and require sutures and anesthesia. What she wants is a cigarette. Amy gathers her cosmetics and tape cassettes from her desk drawer. She takes her gym bag containing her tennis racket, bathing suit, blue jeans, diamondback rattlesnake boots, flashlight, and mace. She wraps her raincoat across her shoulders and thinks, I'm down the road. I'm out of here.

She hopes someone will say, 'Professor Cruz?' Then she could reply, 'Not anymore.' Her response would be fierce and laconic. It would deconstruct itself as you watched. It would explode in your face. She walks to the lobby alone and begins driving.

She shoves U2's *Joshua Tree* into the cassette player. She replaces it with a ZZ Top cassette. Yes, it's time for the original nasty boys from Texas. It's time to consider an entire further dimension of the concept of garage band. After all, you don't have to just rehearse there. You could throw a mattress on the floor, invite your friends, drink a case of bourbon, shoot coke, and stage a gang rape. Maybe she should consider getting down even further. Maybe it's a moment for chainsaws and a massacre.

As she turned onto the freeway, Amy considered her final encounter with Professor Alfred Baxter Coleman. In instant replay, Amy noticed her knees wobbled and she almost went down. But she didn't. She had the presence of mind to stay on her feet and give Alfred the finger. If she had really been on top of it, she would have maced him. Los Angeles is at her back. It feels like a solid sheet of grease and it's not entirely unpleasant. That's why she's been able to inhabit this city. The ugliness is a kind of balm. Beauty makes her uncomfortable. She instinctively averts her eyes from a flawless face the way others recoil from the sight of a car crash.

Amy Cruz has relentlessly attempted to annihilate all certified versions of perfection, she recognizes that now. The conventionally sanctioned snow-dusted peaks above wildflowers in alpine meadows that look like they should be photographed and sold as posters fill her with disgust. She is repelled by images that resemble the covers of calendars. And towns with contrived lyrical names that could be in the titles of country-and-western songs.

That's why she left Raven the southwest interior of the country. She took the coasts and gave her mother everything else. That was the real division of assets. She took abstraction and hierarchy, she took systematic knowledge and left Raven the inexpressible, the preliterate, the region of magic and herbs. It was a sort of divorce. Her mother could have Colorado, Arizona, and New Mexico and she would get her doctorate.

Raven accepted landscape as her due. She collected it. In her memories, Raven is perpetually staring at a sun setting in a contagion of magenta and purple. The sky seems like it's begging to be absolved. Raven nods at it, in acknowledgment, shaking her waist-length black hair at clouds passing like a flotilla above her face, and pauses, as if expecting the skies to actually part.

Raven, windblown and prepared for clouds to form a tender lavender mouth and confess everything. Raven, on the third or fourth day of a peyote fast, is a pueblo priestess, accustomed to tales of routine felonies and necessary lies. Amy watches Raven taking her form of communion beneath an aggressively streaked sunset the texture of metal. Amy already knows the sky is a deceit, a subterfuge of malice.

Her childhood seems incoherent, the images stalled and stylized, somehow suspect. They might be postcards. That's curious, she thinks, they never took pictures. Even when her mother married the magazine photographer, there were no cameras, no artifacts.

'You can't paste this between album pages,' Raven was saying, standing in a meadow, her bare arms stretched out like twin milk snakes, her paisley skirt wind-swirled. This what, precisely, Amy wanted to know.

Raven is topless on a mesa festooned by pinion and juniper, tilting her face to the sky, memorizing the spectrum of purple. It's an alphabet bordered by blue and a magenta that has gone a step too far, left the fold and committed itself to red. Amy wondered what could be discerned from such a sequence. You couldn't arrange it like paint on a palette, or orchestrate it to sound like flutes or bells. You couldn't put it into stanzas or paragraphs. It was entirely useless.

Her mother exists in a series of indiscriminate moments, each already framed and merely waiting for lighting cues. Raven is posed with a lagoon or a canyon as a backdrop. Amy half-expects the afternoon to dissolve into a car commercial. This is what she resists. No to the plateaus of northern New Mexico in wind. No to the vivid orange intrigues of sunsets that look designed to be stenciled on T-shirts. No to men who spend summers in sleeping bags, backpacks filled with Wild Turkey and kilos of marijuana and cocaine. No to Raven in August, scented with dope and pinion, sleeping oblivious under lightning and an outrage of stars.

'I've been tattooed,' Raven laughed in the morning, making coffee over a fire of purple sage. 'Look,' she angled her face toward the new boyfriend, her face that was tanned peach, without a single line or freckle. Amy had a secret accumulation of invisible scratches. Those were the most exquisite. If there was an entity Raven called the Buddha, it was by these internal lacerations that you could know he was watching.

'You can live myth or be buried by it. You have a choice,' Raven said. It was her cocaine voice, vague and distant and leaking light. Her mother was taking sunset like a sacrament. 'I've been more intimate with this canyon than all my husbands combined,' she confided. 'It's had more to reveal and more to give.'

Amy is on the periphery, simultaneously chilled and parched. She is not a team player. The sky is relentlessly alien. The plateaus are layered like a chorus of red mouths that have nothing to say to her.

Before nightfall and the desert, Amy Cruz stops for gas. She stands in a convenience store, fixed in the glare of anonymous waxy light, and decides, on inexplicable impulse, to change her life. She deliberately buys a pack of cigarettes, even though she hasn't smoked in eight years.

'Vodka,' she says, pointing to a fifth. The word sounds inordinately white and mysterious, like something you cannot procure on this planet. It takes her breath away. I've been too long without the traditions, she thinks. Eight years. I've become estranged from my true self. I'm broken off at the root, amputated. I must graft myself back. Now she knows why she must go home.

Amy wonders if she could buy amphetamines in a truck stop. It would probably be just kitchen bennies. White crosses, manufactured in basement labs, and sold as the trucker's other fuel. Last time she copped roadside speed, she took a handful, and got a two-day stomach ache accompanied by the sensation that a 747 was landing in her head. Still, the scenarios of possible dangers excite her. Once she glided between trucks somewhere near Albuquerque, walked beside the enormous cabs oily with streaks of red and yellow like war paint on their faces. She considered the vastness of their wheels and how it felt to say, 'Got any whites?' in her fake Southern accent.

Amy smoked a cigarette, drank vodka and smiled. There is no other way to cross the Mojave, she assured herself. At 3 a.m. she turned off the highway, placed her gym bag under her head as a pillow, and fell asleep, holding the mace in her right hand.

She woke stiff and feverish and drove to Santa Fe, singing with ZZ Top and drinking vodka and orange juice. She poured the vodka into the juice bottle. One of Raven's husbands had taught her how to do that. He had coached her on the

Southern accent and how to carry, conceal, and shoot a weapon.

'I did all I could,' he said to Raven when she left for the San Diego Pacific Academy. He sounded disappointed.

He was serious, Amy is startled to realize. He had positioned beer bottles on sand banks and taught her how to put bullets in them. He found her snakes to shoot, demonstrated how to remove the rattles and make them into earrings. He explained spoor on trails and how to determine what coyotes, raccoons, and rabbits had been eating. She remembers her mother nodding sympathetically at the man who was named Big Red or Big Sam, Jeb or Hawk or Wade.

Amy didn't encounter men with multisyllabic names until boarding-school. She was stunned when strangers offered their last names. It had never occurred to her that people voluntarily revealed this information. The first time she was asked her name, she automatically gave an alias.

Amy Cruz checks into a new hotel near the plaza in Santa Fe. Everything is some manifestation of adobe, a tainted orange and pink. She has erased clay in all its permutations from her memories. That had been simple. Now she walks to the swimming-pool.

The water reminds her of Hawaii. The blues are so vivid and unadulterated, the elements so participant, that landscape becomes paramount. As a child, they had lived in Maui for three years. Her mother was married to a drummer named Ed. Big Ed. The ocean beyond their lanai possessed a clarity only certain sunlight, purified currents, and cloud configurations can impart.

The swimming-pool is the turquoise of Indian jewelry. There is an enticement to this blue, with its suggestion of revelation and sacrament, of opening an enormous chamber into the world as it once was, into thunder and stone and the sacrificial beating heart just as it is yanked out. Such a blue is baptismal. It announces the rising of an incandescent intelligence. It is the turquoise of time travel, camouflaged bridges at dusk, and smuggled contraband.

Yes, this terrain renders ideas and its artifacts inconsequential. That's why everyone was moving to Santa Fe and Taos, the ones who hadn't already migrated to Hawaii or Mexico. But she has no interest in being stripped by so obvious and generic a surrender. That would admit the squalor of her ambitions and what they implied about the incontrovertible value of the acquisition of systemic knowledge. Then she swims three hundred laps. It does not clear her head.

Amy puts on jeans and the red silk blouse she had worn to work two days ago and walks to the plaza. The late afternoon air is the adobe of dust and apricots. The sky is a swarm of storm clouds. Earlier, rainbows appeared in two perfect arches. It occurred to her, as the rainbows broke into fragments, that this was a DNA of the sky. Then Amy looks across the plaza straight at her mother.

'Amethyst,' her mother cries, already moving towards her, awkward and determined. They embrace and Raven smells unexpectedly sweet, like vanilla ice-cream and rain. Raven's hair is entirely white and tied into a ponytail with a piece of rawhide. Raven in dusty black jeans. Her Saturday-night end-of-the-trail look. She is profoundly tanned. It is not a skin coloration one can receive through ordinary daily living. It is clearly a statement, no doubt the result of pronouncing the diminishing ozone layer an establishment rumor that has nothing to do with her.

'Too many tourists,' Raven said. She seemed to be talking out the side of her mouth. 'Let's go.'

Amy checks out of her hotel and follows her mother's Jeep along the highway toward Taos, then off, up a winding dirt road. She parks alongside a small yellow trailer.

'It's temporary,' Raven said, indicating the structure with a dismissive flutter of her left hand. 'Like life.'

'Right,' Amy answered. They are protohumans, banging on stones. Language has barely been invented. She climbs three stairs to the trailer, and pauses, suddenly listless and disoriented.

'Old hippies don't die. They just quit drinking, take their milk thistle and liver-enzyme counts.' Raven laughs.

Raven sits at a miniature formica table and rolls a joint. When her mother offers it to her Amy takes it. She left AA at the border. And half of her IQ. Hadn't that been the deal?

And what had become of the Navajo rugs, the carved-oak furniture, the Mescalero Apache tribal wall hangings, Hopi baskets and masks? And where was the Santa Clara pottery?

Amy is remembering. It was the era of the Harmonic Divergence. The commune they called a tribe dwindled. First AIDS. Then the alteration no one had anticipated. Their foundation was the exploration of human consciousness. Insidiously and inexorably, their beliefs had been culturally degraded, marginalized, and then outlawed.

They were conceptual renegades, biochemical pioneers in an aesthetic frontier that was abruptly fenced. Suddenly, satellites provided surveillance. There was no glamour in being a designated leper. There were treatments for the disease. Antidepressants. Rehab. AA. Everyone took the cure.

'I'm too old for this,' one of the Big Eds or Jebs said. 'I'm not squatting in the mud in winter at forty-five.'

Yes, there had been attrition. Drugs were now controlled by men with computers in Nassau and Seattle. Big Wade and Big Jake had arthritis and the wrong skills for the new global marketplace. The survivors dispersed, took Prozac, called themselves Zen masters and meditated in shacks with canyon views and battery-powered tape decks. There were plans for houses that didn't get built. Some found apartments in town with electricity and watched CNN on sixteen-inch black-and-white televisions.

That's how the Espanola property had accrued to Raven. She was the last woman keeping the faith in derelict rooms of kerosene lamps, incense, and candles. The buildings collapsed around her. That's why she had gotten the trailer. And what was that green square outside? Was her mother growing marijuana? Was she taking the risk alone?

'Corn,' Raven seemed amused. 'Subsistence economy. Tomatoes. Squash. I put seeds in the ground. I eat the plants. A simple life. Much too boring for a professor like you. But you always thought me dull.'

Not dull, Amy wants to correct, just affected, predictable, and formulaic. The trailer reminds her of a boat, ingenuously compact, deceptively pulling in or out of the miniature closets and drawers. They had a boat in Maui, she remembers later, when winds rise and batter the metal sides, when there is a sudden squall with thunder and lightning. They are laying side-by-side in twin cots the size of berths, rocking. The trailer is swaying and Amy thinks, we are moving through metaphors, symbolic oceans. We make a telephone call, stand in the glaring light of a liquor store, and the course of our life is changed.

Once during the night storm, she sat bolt upright for one inconclusive moment, and thought she saw her mother standing barefoot at the tiny window, weeping. Her mother by moonlight, whitened, whittled. 'I'm a moon crone,' she thought Raven said, directly to the night.

Her mother sensed her movement, her intake of breath. 'I'm fifty-two and haven't had a period in years. I take hormones and I'm still burning up,' Raven was speaking into the darkness. 'You don't have to be afraid anymore. I'm not a competitor. You've removed my nine heads. Hydra is gone. See me as I am.'

'Are you lonely?' Amy may have asked, uncertain if she was awake.

'Lonely?' Raven repeated. 'I have two friends. New Mexico and Bob Dylan. They say he wrote the soundtrack for the sixties. Well, he wrote the soundtrack for my life. When he dies, I'll be a widow.'

Amy woke at noon. Raven had assembled sleeping bags, a tent, and stacks of camping equipment on the ground near the canopy in front of the trailer.

'Let's rock and roll,' Raven said. 'Mesa Verde. I feel a spiritual experience coming.'

This woman has absolutely no sense of irony, Amy thought. She inhabits an era of oral tradition and intuition. Science has not yet been codified. One worships flint and thunder. They drove north, Raven taking the curves too fast. Amy composed a random list of what she hated about the southwest. How everyone was making jewelry and searching for shrines. Santa Fe had become an outdoor theme mall. The silver was a wound that gleamed. It was a cancer. It laid itself out in strands of necklaces and belts, a glare of dead worms, obscene. The entire

Navajo nation was home in some stupor, watching TV while pounding out silver conches and squash blossoms. It was sickening.

Amy suddenly remembers a town on the way to Las Cruces. Shacks where she could see lava mountains out a broken window. Her real father was coming down from the reservation to see her. He was out of prison. Amy had never met him. Big Ed or Big Jeb was buying pot. Or perhaps he was selling it. The adults were eating peyote. Her mother and a woman she had never seen before were sitting on the floor stringing necklaces and laughing. The TV was on maximum volume, picture and sound wavering and distorted. She had become dizzy, perhaps fainted. She had been carried to a car. It was a special day. She is certain. Yes, it was her fourteenth birthday and her father didn't come down from the reservation to see her after all. Later, when the woman offered her beads, silver and turquoise, Amy refused.

'Mesa Verde is a revelation,' Raven said. 'The Buddha must have built it.'

'I thought extraterrestrials did the construction,' Amy said. 'Aliens from Roswell with green blood and implants in their necks.'

Raven was smoking a joint. Amy Cruz turned away. She despised the concept that enlightenment could be geographically pinpointed, that one could map a route, drive there, and purchase a ticket. Spirituality had become another commodity. Couldn't Raven comprehend that? Amy experienced a disappointment so overwhelming it erased the possibility of speech. She drank from her vodka bottle surreptitiously, leaned against the car window and let the afternoon fall in green and blue fragments around her face, as if the time–space continuum was fluid and it was flowing across her skin. Or breaking across her flesh in a series of glass splinters.

They spent the afternoon in Indian ruins, peering through holes and the implications of windows, climbing reconstructed stairs and wood ladders into the cliff dwellings. The constant repetition of identical ceremonial rooms. She imagined they smoked pot there, made jewelry, got drunk and engaged in acts of domestic and child abuse. Amy crawled through a tunnel, dust settling across her forehead like another coating of adobe filigree. They stood on the edge of the rim of the canyon, their shoulders brushing. It began to rain, thunder echoed off rock.

'It's the ancient ones talking,' Raven was out of breath. She was winded.

'Christ,' Amy said. 'You're going to end up as a tour guide.'

Amy felt for the emergency pint of vodka in her raincoat pocket. When Raven wasn't watching, she finished the bottle.

'You don't have to drink like that,' Raven said later. 'Pot is easier on the liver. And it's more enlightening.'

They stood in mud in the deserted campground. Raven was wearing a denim jacket. It had simply materialized. It was always like that with her mother, the costume changes, the inexplicable appearance of accessories, the sudden silver belt, the mantilla that was both a veil or shawl. Amy was shivering.

'West and south,' Raven decided. 'The first decent hotel where it's hot.'

Gallup was a few blocks of pawnshops and liquor stores, a community center with windows broken, the tennis-court pavement was ripped. The net had been hacked up with knives. She imagined playing on the court, bits of glass making her footing slippery. She could fall, sprain an ankle, get cut. Amy realized that was too simple. The wound she is searching for is more profound and permanent.

'The whole infrastructure is going,' Amy realizes, staring at the gutted swimming-pool, the brown lawn laced with glass. 'It's not just the cities.'

'My infrastructure is going. But Prozac and AA won't be my answer.' Raven stared at her. There was a long pause. 'Listen, I had boyfriends,' her mother began, voice almost a whisper. 'When you were ten, I was the same age you are now. But nobody ever laid a finger on you, Amethyst. You were my jewel. Everybody treated you right. I made sure.' Late afternoon was a chasm of red that looked vaguely Egyptian. Raven sat in the passenger seat. 'Your turn,' she said. 'Surprise me.'

Amy drove west across desert. She stopped in a liquor store and bought four pints of vodka and hid them. She drank and drove until her mother woke up. They were almost across Arizona.

'What's this?' Raven asked, mildly interested. She rubbed her eyes, couldn't find her eyeglasses and opened her map. She examined it. The map was upside-down.

'It's a *déclassé* Vegas on the Arizona–California–Nevada border. Feeds off the retirement dollar. It's nickel and dime all the way. They let them park their trailers free. Hope they'll toss a quarter in a slot machine on the way to the john. It's the fall of the Western world. It's the final capitalist terminal. Come on. We'll love it.' Amy felt incredibly festive.

She paused in the lobby. Here were men who had won a minor event at second-tier rodeo. Here were men who had just buried their wives and inherited ten thousand in insurance. That's what they got for their thirty years, five of it spent going to and from chemo. Here were women who had sold their mothers' wedding rings for four hundred dollars, their divorced husbands' bass boats and tool sets. This was the new American score. It wasn't a house and forty acres with a pond and waterfall anymore. It was the world of the shrinking dollar and the failure of words. It was about having one good weekend. On the seventeenth floor they had a view of the Dead Mountains, a swath of the Mojave and the Colorado River. Amy wondered how many people were standing at their windows, at this precise moment, drawing the curtains apart, realizing their lives were nothing they had thought they would be and feeling the sun like a slap across their mouths.

Amy Cruz feels a rising excitement as they ride the elevator back to the lobby. She listens to the bells from slot machines and the cascades of nickels falling into steel shells. Of course, this was what you heard at the end of the world. It wasn't a whimper at all. It had nothing to do with anything human, not with the mouth or the ear. It was the sound of symbol and motion. It was the sound of tin.

Raven is changing a ten-dollar bill for rolls of quarters. Raven, in a purple kaftan with gold sandals and a canary-yellow sash around her waist. She is wearing oversized sunglasses and two old men are staring at her.

Amy realizes she has never had the right accessories for any of the towns or situations of her life. Standing in the lobby of the Flamingo in Laughlin, Amy wishes she had bought silver in Aspen or a squash blossom in Taos. She should have taken the birthday beads she was offered. Or even a turquoise bracelet from a pawnshop in Flagstaff where she had seen thousands in display cases. The Navajo nation was divesting itself of its semiprecious stones for gin and crack and it was horrifying. She didn't want any of it, not even for free.

Now Amy thinks she missed something vital. She should have picked up a gold lamé shawl somewhere, big brass hoop earrings, a skirt in a floral print or anything in chiffon, fall-leaf colored, a light rust, perhaps. Or maybe a straw hat with a flagrant yellow silk flower.

There is something wrong with her body. Listening to the tinny chime of bells, which are not from cathedrals or ships but from the machine proclamations of impending cash falling out, it occurs to her that no accessories could possibly be right for this occasion.

'Let's check out the river,' Raven suggests. She is wearing mauve lipstick and a citrus perfume.

Outside the casino, air cracks against her face. It must be 108, Amy thinks. 110. It's a heat that rolls across the flesh, laminating it. This is how time takes photographs of you. This is how you got into the eternal lineup. It has nothing to do with Interpol.

Then they are walking into liquid heat. Huge insects sit on the ground. Clusters of scorpions.

'Crickets and grasshoppers,' Raven explains. Her skirt is a compendium of all possible shades of purple. Her skirt is wind across dusk mesas. Her mother wears sunset around her hips. 'Are you okay?'

Okay? Is that a state with borders or an emotional concept? Can you drive there, get a suite? Should she try to answer with a flag or a drum? And what is in the arc of light on the side of the parking lot? It's a confederation of hallucinatory swooping forms, too thin to be birds. They are creatures from myth. They have broken through the fabric. They have torn through time with their teeth.

'Bats,' Raven says. 'Can't you hear them?'

Everything is humming. It's some corrupted partial darkness, too overheated and streaked with red neon to be real night. It's grazing above the river that is surprisingly cold. Amy touches it with her hand. They are standing on a sort of loading dock. The terrain is increasingly difficult to decode. What is that coming toward them? A sea vessel? Yes, a mock riverboat calling itself a water taxi.

Raven reaches out her tanned arms, helps her climb down the stairs. 'You look like you're going to vomit,' her mother whispers. 'You're drinking too much. You could never maintain.'

The boat motion is nauseating. It simply crosses one strand of river, disgorges silent passengers, takes new ones on and crosses back again. They ride back and forth, back and forth, ferrying gamblers from Arizona across the river to Nevada where it is legal. Everyone is somber.

She closes her eyes and counts the rivers she has been on or in with her mother. The Snake, the Arkansas, Rio Grande, Mississippi, Columbia, Missouri, and Wailua, and now this ghastly Colorado in July where she doesn't have the right accessories, not a scarf or bracelet or shawl. Do they call this the Styx?

'You're not smoking,' Amy realizes, looking at her mother.

'Even the bank robbers quit,' Raven replies. 'Even guys in the can have quit.'

It's the last ride of the night. The driver tells them this twice. They've been in the boat for hours, Amy with her head in her mother's lap. Amy has finished her last emergency pint of vodka. She stands, and then pauses on the dock. There is anomalous movement in the river. Two young boys are doing something with white flowers. They are tossing bouquets into

235

the muddy cold water and the flowers are being savagely ripped apart. Amy bends down, startled by an agitation beneath the surface. Enormous fish circle in the shallows around the wood planks. They must be three feet long. There are severed palms in the water. People have removed their hands and these grotesque fish are eating them. The hideous dark gray fish. It's a ritual. They must supplicate themselves.

'My God,' Amy says, wondering if she should jump in. This is the moment. She understands that. She's an excellent swimmer. She knows CPR. She takes a breath.

'Just carp,' Raven seems tired. 'Hundreds of carp.'

'But what are they eating?' Amy feels an ache that begins in her jaw and runs through the individual nerves of her face. Fine wires are being pulled through her eyes. Perhaps they are going to use her skin for bait.

'Bread,' her mother says. 'Look. Pieces of bread.'

Yes, of course. Slices of white bread. It is not the torn-off hands of virgins. It's not the orchids the Buddha promised. It's bread from plastic bags. And we are released. We are reprieved. Enlightenment does not announce itself on the map. It is random, always.

'Where are you going?' Raven demands. 'You're sick. Let me help you.' She sounds frightened.

'I'll come back,' Amy says.

'You haven't been back in ten years,' Raven says. 'You left too soon, Amethyst. Fifteen was too early, baby. And you're not going anywhere now.'

She is moving through the lobby and she is way ahead of her mother. She's been way ahead of her since the beginning. That's why her attention wanders. It's always been too easy. Amy passes machines with glittering gutted heads. She possesses the secret of this age. It's about the geometry of cheap metal. And she knows where the parking lot is and she has the only set of keys.

Amy Cruz stops, paralyzed. She understands this moment with astounding clarity. No. She is not going to pack her office at the university. She is not going to carry books through corridors, one cardboard box, one square casket at a time, across any more parking lots. We decide the components of our necessities. We design our ceremonies of loyalty and propitiation. History does not explain the necessity of accessories.

Raven is reaching through the garish neon, her palms open, waiting to receive something. The original pages from the *Bhagavadgita*? The UFO invasion plan? An Anasazi document inscribed in glyphs on bark in a lime ink thought centuries extinct?

'Give me the keys. Give me the booze and cigarettes,' Raven commands. 'I'm taking you home.'

Her mother is a predator bird who was never captured. She's an albino, infertile, arthritic. She has no claws and osteoporosis. She has liver disease and refuses antidepressants. Her nest is lit by kerosene and candles. Amy will be safe there. She will receive the correct instructions and this time she will listen. When they drive through the Four Corners, through the region of the Harmonic Convergence, this time she will hear.

Her mother is driving, wearing eyeglasses, white and stiff in the darkness, a woman with lines like dried tributaries in her face. She gave birth to a daughter named for the distillation of all known purple. Raven has wrapped a shawl gold as a concubine's solstice-festival vestment around her shoulders. This woman loves her. Raven will give her tenure. Amy leans against her mother, her eyes close and she is completely certain.

The architectural drawings can be revised. They can build with hay bales now, it's cheaper. They could do it themselves. Some vestigial survivors would help with the foundation and carpentry. After the adobe walls and kiva-style beams, they'll tile the floors. Later they'll plant chilies. Then half an acre of lilies, calla lilies. They will have a roadside stand in April at Easter. They will be known throughout the northern plateaus as the women of the lilies. They would become famous for this the way some women are for their turquoise bracelets and hand-painted gourds. They will be called the women who sold communion. They will be known by rumor. It will be said that the solitary raven of the mesa received a miracle. There was a brutal severing and a long season of mourning. Then, inexplicably, since this is the nature of all things, the unexpected occurred. Hierarchies are irrelevant because they do not examine central and recurring events. As there is lightning and cataclysm, so too exists the inspired accident. Are we not reconfigured as we cross rooms, strike matches, catch moonlight on our skin? On the mesa above Espanola, where the Rio Grande is a muddy creek you can't even see from the highway, it is said that one day a lost daughter with the name of a sacred stone was somehow returned.

Red Ant House

ANN CUMMINS

The first time I saw this girl she was standing at the bottom of the coal pile. I thought she was a little wrinkled dwarf woman with her cheeks sucked in and pointed chin. She had narrow legs and yellow eyes. They had just moved into the old Perino house on West 2nd. This was the red ant house.

'I'm having a birthday,' the girl said. She was going around the neighborhood gathering up children she didn't know for her birthday party. She told us they had a donkey on the wall and beans in a jar.

'What kind of beans?' I asked her.

She shrugged.

'Hey you guys,' I said to my brothers, 'this bean wants us to go to her birthday party.'

'My name's not Bean.'

'What is it then?'

'Theresa Mooney.'

'You don't look like a Theresa Mooney.'

She shrugged.

'Hey you guys. This girl named Bean wants us to go to her birthday party.'

She didn't say anything then. She turned around and started down the street toward her house. We followed her.

In her yard was a grease monkey. Her yard was a junker

239

yard with car parts and cars all over the place, and a grease monkey was standing up against one car, smoking a cigarette.

'Joe,' the little dwarf girl says, 'what do you think of a name like Bean?'

He considered it. The man was a handsome man with slick black hair and blue eyes, and he gave the dwarf a sweet look. I couldn't think of how such a funny-looking child belonged to such a handsome man. 'It's an odd one,' he said. The girl looks at me, her eyes slant. 'One thing about a name like that,' he said, 'it's unusual. Everybody would remember it.'

That idea she liked. She looks at me with a little grin. She says, 'My name is Bean.'

Just as if the whole thing was her idea.

Rosie Mooney was this Theresa's mother. When she moved in she had not known there would be ants in the house. These were the ants that had invaded the Perinos' chickens two summers before. Nobody wanted to eat chicken after that.

The ants came through the cracks in the walls. Rosie Mooney had papered those walls with velveteen flower wallpaper. She had a red room and a gold room. She had wicked eyes to her, Rosie Mooney, could look you through and through.

These were trashy people, I knew. They had Christmas lights over the sink. They had hodge-podge dishes, and garlic on a string, and a book of matches under one table leg to make it sit straight. When the grease monkey came in, he kissed Rosie Mooney on the lips, a long wormy kiss, and then he picked the birthday girl up, swung her in a circle.

For us, he took off his thumbs.

'It is an optical illusion,' the girl told us.

He could also bend his thumbs all the way back, could tie

his legs in a knot, and could roll his eyes back and look at his brain.

'Your dad should be in the circus,' I told the girl.

'He's not my dad.'

'What is he?'

She shrugged.

The grease monkey laughed. It was the sort of shame-faced laugh where you put two and two together you come up with sin.

There were two prizes for the bean jar event, one for a boy, one for a girl. The boy's prize was a gumball bank. Put a penny in, get a ball of gum. When the gum was gone you'd have a bank full of pennies. Either way, you'd have something.

The girl's prize was a music box. I had never seen such a music box. It was black with a white ivory top made to look like a frozen pond, and when you wound it up, a white ivory girl skated over the top. It was a nice box.

We were all over that jar, counting the beans. It was me, my brothers, the Stillwell boys, the Murpheys, and the Frietags. As I was counting, I thought of something. I thought, this jar is an optical illusion. That was because there would be beans behind the beans. It occurred to me that there would be more beans than could be seen, thousands more.

The grease monkey was the official counter. He had written the exact number on a piece of tape and stuck it to the bottom of the jar. We all had to write our numbers down, and sign our names. I wrote 5,000. When Joe read that everybody laughed.

'There are beans behind the beans,' I informed them.

'This one's a shrewd one,' the grease monkey said. 'She's thinking.' But when he turned the jar over, the number on the tape said 730. This Joe winked at me. 'Don't want to be thinking too hard, though.'

I just eyeballed him.

'You want to count them? You can count them if you want,' he said.

'I don't care to.'

He grinned. 'Suit yourself.'

And he awarded the music box to the birthday girl who had written 600. Then I knew the whole thing had been rigged.

The birthday girl's mother said, 'Theresa, I bet you'd like some other little girl to have the music box since you have birthday presents. Wouldn't you?'

She didn't want to.

'That would be the polite thing,' she said. 'Maybe you'd like to give it to Leigh.'

'I don't want it,' I said.

This Theresa looked at me. She looked at the grease monkey. He nodded, then she held the box out to me.

But I didn't want it.

My mother was down sick all that summer. The doctor prescribed complete bed rest so the baby would stay in. For the last three years, she had gone to bed again and again with babies that didn't take.

Up until that point, there were six of us children.

There was Zip, named for my grandmother, Ziphorah. Zippy loved me until I could talk. 'You used to be such a sweet child,' she would say. 'We used to dress you up and take you on buggy rides and everybody said what a sweet child you were. Whatever happened to the sweet child?'

There was Wanda, named for my other grandmother. Wanda was bald until she was five, and my father used to take every opportunity to bounce a ball on her head.

There was me, Leigh Rachel, named by the doctor because my parents drew a blank. I'm the lucky one. Once when I was a baby I jumped out a window – this was the second-story window over the rock cliff. My mother, who was down sick at the time, had a vision about it. I was already gone. By the time she got herself out of her bed and up the stairs, I was in flight, but she leaped across the room, stuck her arm out, caught me by the diapers, just as she'd seen it in the vision.

Another time, I survived a tumble down Bondad Hill in my grandpa's Pontiac. We both rolled like the drunk he was. Drunks I know about. My dad's dad was one, and my mom's dad was another. I never knew my dad's mom. She weighed three hundred pounds and died of toxic goiter. My mom's mom weighed seventy-five at the time of her death. Turned her face to the sky and said, 'I despise you all.' Irish like the rest of us.

There were the boys, Thomas Patrick, Raymond Patrick, Carl Patrick.

Then there were the ones who didn't take. One of these I saw, a little blue baby on a bloody sheet. My mother said, 'Help me with these sheets,' to Wanda, but Wanda couldn't stop crying, so I helped pull the sheet away from the mattress, and my mother wadded the sheet up.

I said, 'We should bury that sheet.'

She said, 'It's a perfectly good sheet. We'll wash it.'

Then she took a blanket and went into the living room and wrapped herself up in it. When my father came home he found her half bled to death.

My mother has Jewish blood in her. When they took her to

the hospital, a Jewish man, Mr Goldman, gave blood. He was the only Jew in town.

That summer my mother had cat visions. She would begin yelling in the middle of the night. She would come into our dreams: 'The cats have chewed their paws off. They are under the bed.'

'Mother, there are no cats.'

'Look under the bed. See for yourself.'

But we didn't want to.

Each day that summer I had to rub my mother's ankles and legs before I could go out to see the shadow, Theresa Mooney, who had started living in my backyard. I woke up in the morning, there she was on the swing or digging in the ground with a spoon.

Once out of the house, I didn't like to go back. If I snuck back in for any little thing, I had to rub the legs again. This was my job. Zip's job was to clean the house.

Wanda cooked. Grilled cheese on Mondays, frozen pot pie on Tuesdays, Chef Boy R D ravioli on Wednesdays, frozen pot pie on Thursdays, and fish sticks on Fish Fridays. Saturdays were hamburger and pork and bean days, and Sundays, Sick Slim brought trout that he caught in the river. Sick Slim had a movable Adam's apple, and finicky ways. He used to exchange the fish for loaves of my mom's homemade bread until he found out that she put her hands in the dough. After that, he didn't care for bread, though he still brought the fish. 'I never thought she would have put her hands in it,' I heard him tell my father.

Slim was my dad's army buddy. He built his house on

West 1st, way back from the street, right up against Smelter Mountain. Slim didn't want anybody at his back, that's what my dad said.

We knew a secret on him. My brother, Tom, saw this with his own eyes. A woman drove to West 1st where Sick Slim lived. She had a little blonde girl with her, and when the girl got out of the car, Tom saw that she was naked. The mother didn't get out of the car. The little girl walked up that long sidewalk to the porch and up the steps to Slim's house and knocked on the door, and Slim opened the door, and he gave the girl money.

Slim was a bachelor and didn't have anything to spend his money on except naked children and worms for fish.

We all thought it would be a good idea to try and get some of Slim's money. My brothers thought I should take my clothes off and go up to his door, though I didn't care to. But, I thought Theresa might like to make a little money, so I told her that there was a rich man on West 1st who would give us twenty dollars if she took her clothes off and walked up the sidewalk and knocked on his door. She didn't know about that. She was not accustomed to taking off her clothes outside.

I said, 'Do you know how much twenty dollars is?'

She didn't know. She was poor as a rat.

'You go first, then I'll go,' she said.

'It's my idea.' I figured if it was her idea – which, she didn't have any – then she could say who went first.

'Mama says not to get chilled,' she said. She was prone to sore throats and earaches and whispering bones. Without notice, she would go glassy-eyed and stiff, and would lose her breath. When she caught it again, she'd say, 'My bones are whispering.'

'What are they saying?' I'd ask.

'They don't talk,' she said. 'They don't have words. Just wind.'

'You are a delicate flower,' I said to butter her up.

She liked that.

'I bet we could get thirty dollars for you. You're better looking than me.'

She looked at me slant.

'It's easy,' I said. 'Don't think about it. You just think, *I am running through the sprinklers*. You don't think, *I am naked*. If you don't think about it, it's easy.'

She told me she'd get beat if she took her clothes off outside.

'Maybe even forty dollars,' I said, 'because this particular gentleman likes itty-bitty things. Twenty for you, twenty for me. That's a lot of money. We could go places on that much money.'

She thought about that. 'I don't think we could go far on forty dollars.'

'You got to look on the bright side. You're always looking on the dark side.'

'No I'm not.'

'You are doom and gloom and whispering bones. Just ask your whispering bones. They'll say you're doom and gloom.'

'You go first,' she said. 'Then I'll go.'

'Maybe I will.'

'Okay,' she said.

'Okay then.'

My mother was curious about Theresa and her mother. 'Where does little Terry go when her mama's working?' my mother asked me. 'If we had any room at all, I'd have that child here. If we weren't doubled up already.'

'Hang her on a hook,' I said.

'Don't smart mouth. Do you think she would like to come here?'

Mother thought all children should like to come to our house because it was so pleasant to have a big family. To have children to do the cooking, and cleaning, and leg rubbing. Her legs were yellow logs. I didn't like to touch them, and so I would think of them as yellow logs at Cherry Creek – the dried logs split by lightening with worm silk inside. I would close my eyes and rub the cold legs. Sometimes, if my mother didn't talk to me, if she only closed her eyes and breathed, I would forget I was in her room. I would put myself someplace else, Cherry Creek or Jesus Rock, and I would think of running my hands through soft things, the sand below Jesus Rock, or worm silk.

But, mostly, she talked. She wanted to know about Mooney and Joe. She wanted to know about Theresa.

When she talked she would sit, propped up on pillows, her belly, a world under the sheet. Her eyes were all glitter.

'She doesn't stay with that man, does she?'

'Joe Martin is his name.'

'I don't care to know his name.'

'I don't know where she stays.'

My mother sighed. Except for the belly, she couldn't put weight on. She had trouble keeping food down, and she didn't have the strength to wash her hair so she kept it in a bandanna, one that bore the grease of her head.

'He has a wife and children, you know. Over in Dolores. I understand he has two little children. You mustn't say anything to the little girl, though. I'm sure she doesn't know. I understand,' my mother said, 'that he abandoned his family. I don't know how they make do.

'Now just look.' She laughed and held her hands out to me. Her fingers were thick. The one ring finger was especially plumped out and her wedding ring had sunk to the bone. 'I have no circulation,' she said, and she laughed again. They were cold, the fingers. 'I'll be glad when this is over, Leigh. I guess we'll all be glad, won't we? Let's get some soap and get this ring off,' she said.

I went for the soap and water. We soaped her hands good, and I started working the ring. She leaned back and closed her eyes. 'Don't you love the sound?' she said.

'What sound?'

'Of the children playing. Listen to them.' My brothers were kicking the can in the street. 'You should be out, Leigh. Your poor old mom is all laid up, but you should be out. Why don't you go on out, now?'

'Shall I tell Mr Richter he has to come and cut this ring off your finger?'

'Go on out,' she said, 'and tell little Terry what I told you.' She opened her eyes and smiled. 'I know you want to.' An ugly smile.

'I'm not going to say anything.'

She shook her head. 'I was wrong to tell you. I don't know why I told you. It was very, very wrong of me. I would not have told you if I were myself. You understand that?'

'Yes.'

She frowned and shook her head. 'It's only natural that you should go tell her now. A child cannot keep such a secret.'

'You want me to tell her?'

'Of course I don't want you to tell her. But you will.'

'No I won't.'

'Yes you will. You cannot keep a secret.'

I didn't say anything. Just soaped the fingers.

'Leigh?'

'What?'

'Can you keep it a secret?'

'Yes.'

'Look at me.'

I looked at her.

We looked at each other for a long time. She took my chin. She pinched it. She was pinching it. 'You are the one,' she said, 'who cannot keep a secret. Am I right?'

'I can,' I said, but she was pinching it. She shook my head back and forth.

'Here,' she said. She pulled the sheet back. She put my face against her belly. The baby was kicking. 'Feel that?' she said. 'That's your blood, too.' She put her hand on my cheek and held my face there. The baby stopped kicking, and my mother laughed. 'Well,' she said, 'it probably doesn't matter.' She let me go. 'It's just as well that little girl knows what kind of man is living under her roof.'

'I can keep a secret.'

She closed her eyes again, and leaned her head against the wall behind her.

She tried to twist the ring on her finger, but it wouldn't move. 'I believe,' she said, 'we're going to have to cut this ring off. I cannot feel this finger any more.'

This was the summer they announced they were closing the mill. They were opening a new mill in New Mexico on an

Indian reservation. Some workers got their walking papers. Some got transfers.

'What shall I do?' my father asked Wanda and me one night when we were walking down to the train depot. 'Shall I take the transfer? Tell me what to do, and I'll do it.'

We had to keep it secret because it was just the sort of news that would send my mother into a tizzy.

'It would mean a smaller house. You girls would all have to share one room, and the boys would have to share the other. But we'd eat good.'

'What else could you do?' Wanda wanted to know.

He shrugged. 'Collect the garbage?'

'You could do a lot of things,' she said. She was against moving. Wanda was fourteen. She and Zippy had limbo parties for their friends in our living room. My brother Tom and I could out-limbo everybody because we were bendable beyond belief.

'You could work for the post office,' Wanda said.

'I guess I could.'

'Or the lumber mill.'

'Mm hm. Hate to let old Mike Reed down, though.' Mike Reed was my father's boss. 'That gentleman's done a lot for me. But I want to be fair to you kids, too. What do you think, Leigh?'

'Let's go.'

'You'd have to leave all of your friends.'

'That's okay.'

'She doesn't have any friends,' Wanda said.

'I do, too.'

'It's different if you're a little kid,' she told my father.

'I think somebody's only thinking of herself,' I said. He winked and took my hand. Wanda gave me a look.

'Good jobs are not that easy to come by,' I said. My father squeezed my hand.

'We should put our fate in the hands of the Lord,' I said.

He laughed. 'Not bad advice,' he said.

Wanda crossed her arms and just stared at the sidewalk in front of her.

On our way home we saw Joe at Lucky's grill. We always stopped at Lucky's for ice-cream on our way home. Joe was in a booth with a blonde woman and two little boys. When he saw me a queer look came over him.

'That's the man who sniffs around Rosie Mooney,' I said, 'and I bet that's his wife and kids.'

My father looked at Joe. 'Wouldn't be the first time for old Joe Martin,' he said quietly. He nodded and Joe nodded back.

'Mr Martin, how you doing?' I called.

'I'm okay, Leigh. You?' The blonde woman smiles. She's wearing red lipstick that makes her look like she's all lips. That's how blond this woman is.

'Can't complain,' I said. 'I haven't seen Rosie and Theresa Mooney in a while, though.' The blonde woman keeps smiling. She's smiling at her french fries.

'That old boy,' I tell my father when we get outside, 'probably has a wife in every state. Don't you think?'

My father put his hands in his pockets. 'You shamed him, Leigh.'

'Joe?' I hooted.

He looked at me. 'You shamed me,' he said.

Wanda dug her elbow into me. 'You shamed that man's wife,' she said.

I dug her back.

'She shamed them, didn't she, Dad?'

My father didn't say anything. He watched the air in front of him.

'God wouldn't spit you from his mouth,' Wanda hissed.

Wanda's no saint. She'll knuckleball you in the back, and who are you going to scream to? The cats under the bed? The bloody cats?

Wanda's no saint, and Zip is no saint – *You used to be such a sweet child, we used to dress you up and take you in the buggy and everybody said what a sweet child you were, whatever happened to the sweet child?*

I'll tell you who's the saint. My father is the bloody saint. He'll say, 'When I was over there in Guam? When I was fighting the Japansies? I walked to holy mass every day. I'd walk five miles if I had to. If it kilt me, I was going to holy mass.'

So give the saint a hand.

The Bean was lying on our lawn, winding the music box. The skater skated. The Bean was keeping her finger on the skater head, and the music was chugalugging because she was pressing the head too hard.

'My dad'd never leave my mom,' I was telling her. 'He's a good Catholic.'

The Bean sucked her cheeks.

'This is why you want the holy sacrament of matrimony in the house. To keep 'em from leaving.'

She winds up that music box. Everywhere she goes, the music box goes. Terry was addicted to the skater on the pond.

'Joe'll be back, though,' I told her to give her comfort. That morning, we sat in the peach tree and watched Joe throw his clothes in the back of his truck while Rosie sat on the front porch and just smoked. 'Don't you think?'

The Bean lay on her back and let the skater skate on her stomach. She closed her eyes.

'I mean, what'd he say? Did he say, "I'm leaving you for ever", or did he say, "I need time to think", or did he say . . .'

She was holding the skater, letting her go, holding her, letting her go, and the music was revving up just to stop, and I said, 'Am I invisible?' Because she hadn't said a word all morning. 'Are you a mute?' I said.

She looked at me for a minute, then she screamed and laughed and the music box tumbled to the grass. 'We're invisible!' she shouted. She flung her arms and legs out like an angel. 'I'm a mute!' she yelled.

Then she started bawling. She says, 'Don't look at me.' She's put her hands over her face and she's bawling, a pitiful thing.

Me, I laid down next to her, and I didn't look at her, just lay there. The sky was blue-white. After a while she stopped bawling and started hiccuping. I said, 'Got the chuck-a-lucks?' She sort of laughs and hiccups. 'You know the difference between chuck-a-lucks and hiccups?'

I felt something scratchy on my hand, and it was her withered little paw. She whispered, 'Leigh, you are my best friend.'

I thought of how skinny she was, and how she'd probably never find anybody to marry her. I held her dry hand and we started to sweat.

I said, 'I know what'll cheer us up.'

She said, 'What?'

I let go her hand, rolled over on my side, propped my head on my hand. I said, 'That rich gentleman's money.'

*

We both peed ourselves. I tried to hold it in but the Bean's hotfooting down the sidewalk, doing a little sidewinder dance, trying to keep her knees together, her pointy bottom shining, and the pee's running down, and I don't know if she's laughing or crying, but I'm laughing so hard my stomach hurts. I peed his porch. Cars were honking. The Bean turned around and did a little dance for them, then scatted off around the house before we got the money. I pounded that door, and rang the bell. He was in there. The shades were open and then they closed. He was in there shaking in his boots.

After a while we went for our clothes, but then this car stops at the curb, and this lady gets out, yells, 'Hey!' We started running. I looked back, and the lady's my mom's friend, Mrs Malburg, who makes oily donuts and eats them, fat Mrs Malburg: 'Hey, Leigh!' She is standing on the curb looking at the bush where our clothes are. She shades her eyes. She looks straight at us.

We hid in the little cave under Jesus Rock up there on Smelter Mountain. Theresa Mooney's moaning, 'I'm dead.' She's scrunched in the dirt, shivering up against the rock, and I don't tell her there are ants there in the shadows. Last year I buried a box of crackerjacks there for a rainy day, but when the rainy day came, I dug them out and they were crawling with ants. I can't see Theresa Mooney's dirty feet where she's dug in. I don't know if the ants are awake.

The Bean moans, 'I am dead, I'm dead, I'm dead.' She says, 'Will she tell?'

I start digging in the dirt with a stick. 'Once,' I told her, 'there was an Indian maiden who got stole by the Calvary, and when she ran away back to her tribe, they buried her naked in an ant pile and the ants ate her. Her own people did that.'

'That's not true,' Theresa Mooney said.

I shrugged.

'First of all,' she said, 'ants can't eat people.'

'You don't know about all the species,' I told her. 'Sugar ants, no. But these were not sugar ants.'

She didn't say anything to that.

A train whistle was blowing – the Leadville train coming in. It was five o'clock. By now, my dad would be home. He'd be sitting at the kitchen table with his boots unlaced, stirring his coffee. Wanda'd be taking the pot pies out of their boxes.

'Will she tell?' the Bean whispered.

Mrs Malburg, muddy-eyed Mrs Malburg, would be sitting across the table from my dad, giving him trouble. They would be talking in whispers so my mother wouldn't hear. 'It is,' I said, 'against human nature to keep a secret.'

The Leadville train whistled again. It was probably pulling into the depot.

I closed my eyes and listened hard.

'I'm cold,' the Bean whispered.

'You can wrap yourself around me like a spider monkey,' I told her. 'I don't mind.'

She crawled from the back of the cave and wrapped her ice-cube self around me. She said, 'You smell like yellow urine.'

'So lick me,' I said, and the Bean laughed.

I was listening for my brothers who would be coming after us. Wanda would send them. She would say, *Jesus wouldn't spit you from his mouth*. They would all say it. 'The Calvary is coming,' I told the Bean. 'Mark my word.'

'We're dead,' the Bean said.

'We are dead under Jesus Rock,' I yelled so they'd know where to look.

'Shh!' the Bean hissed.

'This is Lazarus's cave!'

She unwrapped herself and scowled at me. She crawled to the edge of the hole, knelt there looking out, her little bottom tucked under her filthy heels. She stood up and stepped out in the sun. She stretched on her tiptoes and looked down the mountain. She turned around, her face twitching to go.

I crawled out, too. The evening breeze had a sting, and the sun was sitting on the mountain. Scrub oak leaves were crackling all around.

'Nobody's coming,' she whispered. She squinted down the path.

'That,' I said, 'is an optical illusion.'

At the bottom of the hill in the back of Sick Slim's house, a light went on, and then Sick Slim was standing at the window, looking up Smelter Mountain. We scatted back into the hole. Terry starts giggling and whimpering. 'He saw us,' she said. 'We're trapped.'

'Him?' I hooted. 'He's blind.' Then I remembered what my dad had said, how ever since he got back from playing soldier, Sick Slim didn't like anybody at his back. But we *were* at his back. Two naked children. I laughed.

'What?' the Bean said.

I crawled back out into the sun. I stood up and walked to the edge where he could see me good. I put my hands on my hips like King of the Mountain. I couldn't see his face, couldn't see him looking, but I knew he was.

I said, 'Next time, we'll *make* him give us money.'

'How?' the Bean said.

I didn't know exactly how. It was coming to me. It was a dream in the distance.

The Nista Affair

JONATHAN AMES

In June of 1987, I graduated from college. A week after commencement, I sold my senior thesis, a novella, to a New York publishing house. But there were two conditions: I had to expand the book into a full-length novel, and it was due in six months.

In July, a few weeks after selling my book, I found out that I had a fifteen-month-old son. His mother sent a letter with a photograph of him, a baby boy with red hair and blue eyes. I have red hair and blue eyes.

In late October, two chapters of my novel were stolen by a stranger who lured me into something of a trap. The theft occurred on the Upper West Side of Manhattan. I reported the crime to the 24th Precinct.

In November, after not drinking for twelve months and one week, I went on an alcoholic binge and ended up in a psychiatric hospital.

In November, while in the hospital, I discovered who stole my writing.

This story is about how those two chapters were taken from me. I'll start from the beginning.

The novella was twenty thousand words; I had to get it up to fifty thousand. I was given some money, not a lot, by the publishing house, but I was on top of the world. From New

Jersey, I moved to New York City. I sublet my cousin's rent-control apartment on the Upper East Side. I set up a writing desk – yellow pads and a typewriter. I had thirty thousand words to go.

That very first week I became scared: I couldn't write.

By the second week, I thought maybe it was the apartment. I learned about a special study room in the public library on Forty-second Street. It was for writers and was in the back of the long reading room. You had to have a key. It was a privilege. I applied and was allowed to use the room. I started going there like going to a job, but the writing didn't improve. The trip to the library would tire me out, and I'd use my privilege only to take naps, my head on the table.

In July I received the letter about my son. His mother was an older woman, a good woman, whom I had slept with once. She and my son lived down south. My plan was to go see her and the baby as soon as I finished the book. I couldn't handle my dream of being a writer and my unexpected fatherhood at the same time. So I was going to tackle the situations as they had arisen, first the book and then my son. I was only twenty-three; it was the best plan I could come up with.

One night in July – though I was half-crazy with fears and anxiety about everything – I went to a party. I was invited by a friend of mine who didn't show up. I didn't know anyone at the party and was going to leave, but the hostess, a woman named Marie, was very nice to me and insisted that I stay. She knew from my absentee friend that I was working on a book. She asked me how it was going, and I told her about the study room at the public library. I lied and said the library was a good place to work. I didn't want to tell her that I was crumbling under the pressure of a professional contract and couldn't write a word. I stayed at the party for two hours. Marie asked me for my number so that she could invite me to her next party.

The following day a woman called me and introduced herself as a friend of Marie's. Her name was Julia, and she apologized for bothering me, but explained that she was a writer and that Marie had told her about the study room in the library. She wanted to know how one could get a key to the room. I told her. She was very grateful. She called me two days later and said she had a key. She said we should meet some time at the library and go for coffee. She was very funny and flirtatious on the phone. At some point in the conversation, she said, 'You know who my father is, right?'

I didn't know who her father was. I hadn't made the connection with her last name. It turned out she was the daughter of an extremely famous writer. I did feel my heart leap a little at my closeness to celebrity, but not too much. I knew his fame, but hadn't read his books. I agreed to meet with her for coffee.

A few days later, I met Julia in front of the library, and the first thing she said to me was, 'You look like a Swedish sailor.' It was summer, and my hair was very light, almost blond. She meant the Swedish line as a compliment and I took it as one. She was in her late thirties and she wore a loose-fitting dress – she was heavy. Her face was long and pale. Her dark hair was curly from a permanent. Beneath her large brown eyes were deep purple rings of exhaustion.

We went to a coffee shop and we got along fine. I liked her. She was funny, and it was good to talk to her. We were both nervous about our writing: I was scared that I wouldn't be able to finish my novel, and she was scared that she would never be able to write hers and escape her father's shadow.

After our coffee together, Julia started calling me frequently, and we developed a phone friendship. We didn't see each other at the library, as she went in the evenings after work.

In August, I began to receive prank phone calls. Someone was calling my answering machine ten to fifteen times a day and hanging up. When I was home the same thing happened. Dialing star-69 didn't exist at that time, and I called the phone company only to learn that tracing calls was tedious and expensive. I hoped the calls would just stop. Julia told me that the same thing had happened to her a few months before, and she had tried to do the tracing but it didn't work, because the person was calling from payphones. I endured the constant ringing.

I wasn't sleeping well during this time and often had nightmares. I dreamt one night that the soles of my feet had slit open up like envelopes. When I looked inside my feet, I saw that they were hollow and rimmed with blood. The whole next day, remembering my dream, I could hardly walk. I thought I might be cracking up, but I kept going to the study room, so I could take naps.

One evening in August I became sick. I had food poisoning, some kind of stomach disturbance. Julia wanted to come over and take care of me. I told her that I would be all right, but she begged me to let her nurse me. I assented and she arrived with teas and a giant bottle of Pepto-Bismol and several boxes of antacid tablets. She had stocked up at a pharmacy.

She visited with me for at least two hours. She saw some of my novel on my desk and asked if she could read it. I told her no. I was feeling terrible about my work. She insisted that I let her read something. I kept saying no. She seemed hurt and offended by my refusal.

A few nights later, my stomach problem had cleared up,

and she invited me to her place for dinner. She had a nice apartment on the Upper East Side, and she made a good meal. After dinner, we drank coffee. We started talking about our childhoods and she told me a strange story from her high-school years. She went to an exclusive all-girls school on Fifth Avenue and, during her freshman year, fell in love – from a schoolgirl distance – with her music teacher, a handsome Swedish man in his thirties. She found out where he lived and spent her weekends spying on him. With a Super-8 camera, she filmed him leaving his building and followed him, or she wouldn't follow him and instead snuck into his building and stole some of his mail. If he did laundry and left the laundro-mat, she stole an item of his clothing. She did this for all four years of high school, taking his class every semester and never letting the music teacher know she loved him.

Her father eventually found out what was going on and sent her to a psychiatrist. But she didn't stop doing what she wanted. 'My father was the one who needed a shrink,' she said. At the end of her senior year, she gathered together her movies of the music teacher, the poems and stories and plays she had written about him, the photographs he had inspired, and his mail and clothing she had taken, and she put all of this material in eighteen shopping bags, which was symbolic to her because she was now eighteen.

Julia arranged to meet with the music teacher. She brought the bags to school and lined them up in the gym. She showed him all the bags. 'What's this?' he asked. She told him to look in the bags, and he did. She was very excited for him to see all she had done for him, the depth of her adoration and her love. After poking around in a few bags, he said to her, 'If you wanted to get laid, why didn't you just ask?'

Julia then stopped telling her story and just looked at me. I pictured very clearly the music teacher standing over eighteen shopping bags. I admired his calm reaction.

'Can you believe he said that to me?' Julia asked, still indignant twenty years later. 'I was just a girl. I was in love with him, and he couldn't see that.'

I knew she wanted me to take her side, but it was such a strange story. 'What did you do?' I asked.

'I just turned around and left him with the bags, and my crush was completely over. It hadn't been about sex. I was so disappointed in him. But what he said was the best thing for me. Worked a lot better than all the therapy. I felt nothing for him instantly.'

'Do you think he was angry about the mail?' It was a dumb question, but I loved to get mail and would have been very upset if mine was ever stolen.

'I never heard from him if he was,' she said, and she smiled. 'I hope he was angry.'

'That's some story,' I said.

'You can't ever write about it,' she said.

'I won't,' I said.

The conversation took on a lighter tone and I thought, Well, she was crazy twenty years ago, but now she's normal. We drank more coffee, and she told me she was invited every fall to a party that Woody Allen threw – she had met him through her father, but now was friends with him in her own right – and she suggested I should come with her to the party.

As I was leaving, she asked me at the door if she could kiss me. I wasn't attracted to her. I said, trying to be kind, 'I think I'd rather be friends.' But then, so as not to reject her completely, I said, foolishly, 'We could have a hug good-bye.'

So we hugged, and she held me tight. Her breasts were against my chest. I didn't mean to, but I became aroused.

'I thought you just wanted to be friends,' she said and went to kiss my mouth. I tried to kiss her on the cheek. Her lips brushed the corner of my mouth. I got out of her arms. I thanked her for dinner and left. It was an uncomfortable moment, but she didn't seem angry.

By the end of August, I was getting nowhere with my novel and thought that it must be New York. I gave up my rent-controlled apartment and moved back to Princeton. My hope was that I could write there, in the quiet. The book was due in three months, but even more importantly, I wanted to finish it so I could go see my son.

In Princeton, I rented a room in a house with two graduate students. I set up a phone line with one of them, listing my name in information. By the second day of phone service the hang-ups started again, five to ten times a day. I felt as if a sick taint had followed me from New York. My housemate kept picking up the phone. I didn't tell her I was the cause of it. I was frightened by the calls and was going to set up the trace this time, but I procrastinated, and then, after a few days, the calls stopped.

In mid-September I received a phone call from Marie, the woman whose party I had gone to in July. She was calling to ask me a favor on behalf of Julia. Marie told me that Julia had a bad relationship with her father and only visited him once a year, usually in September. Marie always went with Julia for these visits to provide support, but this year she couldn't make it, and Julia wanted me to go. For some reason Julia felt too embarrassed to ask me herself and so she had enlisted Marie to make the call. I told Marie that I could do it, and she said Julia would be very happy. I didn't feel good about my motivation, though. I wanted to meet the famous writer.

I hadn't seen Julia since the night she had tried to kiss me, but we had continued our friendship over the phone as if nothing had happened. After speaking to Marie, Julia called a little while later and thanked me for wanting to go with her. 'Every year,' she said, 'it was a difficult trip.'

'I'm happy to go with you,' I said, 'but don't you think you should take a friend you've known longer?'

'I want you to come,' she said. 'I've known you long enough to feel that you're a friend.'

The following weekend, I met Julia in New York, and we took the train out to the country. Her father had a beautiful home, and I was put up in a large guest cottage. Next to my bed was an enormous bookshelf with all the foreign translations of his books.

Over the course of the weekend Julia's father treated me like a lost son. On Saturday and Sunday mornings, he made oatmeal for me, a ritual with him. Supposedly he had never made a bowl of oatmeal for anyone else. Julia and her father's young girlfriend, who was Julia's age, made a big deal about this oatmeal.

He and I went for a bike ride on a path through the woods next to his house, and then we sat in his den and watched a baseball game. We talked about my writing and he said, 'Sounds very difficult to turn a novella into a novel. I've never tried to do it. Maybe it isn't supposed to become a larger story.'

This frightened me, because I suspected it was true. Then he said, 'But you can do it and you have to do it. Don't worry about plot. Just get your character into trouble.'

The two nights I was there he had dinner parties with

interesting and talented guests. One night there was a famous screenwriter and I regaled the table with the story of a fight I got into in Paris and how my nose was broken. The screen-writer said to the writer, 'Where did you get this kid? He has too many stories.'

Julia's father beamed, and then he joked, 'They're all lies,' and he smiled at me. Julia was very quiet.

The day we left, Julia's father gave me several first-edition hardbacks of his novels. He gave me all the books he had written in the first person since I was writing my novel in the first person. 'These should help you,' he said.

I left him feeling quite good about myself. A famous writer had liked me very much, and I liked him.

On the train back to the city, Julia said to me, 'My father had a talk with me this morning. Do you know what he told me?'

'I have no idea,' I said. My vanity had me hoping that I would hear some compliment about myself.

'He said to me, "Why don't you marry someone like Jonathan? He's substantial. You never bring men like him around. That last boyfriend of yours was anorexic."'

'What did you say?'

'Nothing. He's a horrible and rude man. It's none of his business. And then before we left, he said it again, "Marry him."'

'You could have explained to him that we're just friends.'

'Why would I tell him that?'

'So that he wouldn't bother you.'

'You don't understand my father,' she said, and she turned to look out the window, and I let the conversation drop.

It was a long train ride, and I started writing in my journal,

265

and for some reason, I wrote, 'I'm crazy. Julia's crazy. All my friends are crazy.'

I hadn't realized it, but she was watching me write and she said, 'You think I'm crazy?'

'I think you're crazy in a good way. See, I wrote that I'm crazy, that all my friends are crazy.'

She was silent and then she said, 'You know I brought you up there to spend time with me, not my father.'

'I'm sorry,' I said. 'He kept asking me to do things.'

'You could have said no.'

'I'm sorry . . . I didn't want to be rude.'

'So you were rude to me. You were *my* guest.'

I didn't say anything. I was in over my head. I regretted having gone with her. We were both silent. Then she said, 'I'm not angry at you, I'm angry at him. I can't stand the man, but I visit him once a year because he's my father.'

I left her at the station in New York, and vowed that I wouldn't have anything more to do with her. I had enough problems. Alone on the train to New Jersey, I wrote in my journal, 'Julia would kill me if she knew this, but I like her father more than her. She gives me the creeps. Scary to write this, but she reminds me of a brooding spider.'

In October, Julia left for California for eight days and sent me a package with eight presents. I was to open one present each day she was gone. I opened them all at once. They were strange presents: a Jackie Mason tape, fancy pencils, expensive fudge, potpourri, a little travel alarm clock, beautiful rubber erasers to go with the pencils, a thermometer to put out my window, and a small desk ornament – a tiny globe. The letter with the presents thanked me for going with her to her father, but then ended angrily: 'You didn't have to be so cold on the

train. You didn't have to tell me that we were only friends.
Don't be so pompous. Who do you think you are?'

I considered throwing the gifts away, but I thought this
would bring me bad luck. So I stored her presents in my closet
and pressed on with trying to write my book.

My son's mother sent me more photos to look at – we had
talked on the phone a few times – and I wrote back telling
her that I would come see them both very soon. I kept hoping
to go on some Kerouac-like writing jag and finish the book,
but no such jag occurred.

At the end of October, I received a phone call from a woman
who said that she was helping to organize a literary symposium
of young American writers to be held in Sweden, at Gothenburg University. The symposium was jointly sponsored by the
university and by a Swedish literary magazine called *Nista*.
The woman had a slight accent. Her name was Sara Sundstrom.

She told me that I was one of twelve candidates whom they
were considering. She was calling from New York and wanted
to interview me. Selection for the symposium was based on
this interview and a sample of my work. If chosen I would
receive an all-expenses-paid trip to Sweden in March. I readily
agreed to be interviewed and we made an appointment to meet
in New York in two days.

That night Julia called. She was just back from California,
and her voice was ebullient. She said, 'Did you receive my
package?'

'Yes,' I said and thought of mentioning the angry tone at
the end of her letter, but decided not to – she was sounding
friendly, and I didn't want any conflict.

'Did you only open one present each day? I wanted you to
think of me each day that I was gone,' she said.

'I opened one each day. The Jackie Mason tape was the first,' I said. I didn't like to lie, but it was a sort of half-truth. The Jackie Mason *had* been the first thing I unwrapped. 'It was an interesting assortment, thank you . . . How was your trip?'

'Terrible. I was practically blind the whole time. I had a problem with my contact lenses, they were scratching my eyes – I had to go to an eye doctor. I don't like to go to doctors I don't know.'

We talked for a little while longer. I told her about the symposium in Sweden, and then we rang off. I thought to myself that my friendship worked fine with her over the phone, but that in person it was a disaster.

Sara Sundstrom called back the next day, but I wasn't in, and she left a message on my machine asking me to bring a photograph of myself to our meeting. She didn't leave a number where I could reach her.

The following night, around nine o'clock, I met with her at Birdland on Broadway, up near Columbia, as we had planned. She was sitting at a table next to the large window that looked onto the street. She was a blonde woman in her mid-thirties. She was small and had handsome features. Her skin was a little worn from the sun. She seemed very European: mature and cool. She stood up to shake my hand and then we both sat down. She said, 'I don't have much time, so we have to do this quickly.'

'All right,' I said. Her attitude was as if I had requested the interview. She already had a drink, and I didn't bother to order one.

'Do you have your writing sample and the photograph?'

'Yes,' I said, and smiled, drawing them out of my backpack. I wanted to appear friendly and outgoing so I could get a free trip to Sweden. I handed her two chapters of my novel and the photograph. She put them in her bag, and then she put on the table a small tape recorder. She pressed 'record' and began to ask me questions: What would you offer to the symposium? What new things could you say about writing and literature in America today? Who are your influences? Are you calm in front of a large audience asking you questions?

She was stern and almost mean. I tried to give concise and intelligent answers, but I struggled. I said things like, 'I'd love to come and talk about American literature. There are so many American writers I've loved, I can hardly name them.'

Then the phone at the bar rang. The bartender answered and said to us, 'Is one of you a Dr Sundstrom?'

'That's me,' she said. She went up to the bar and took the phone for just a minute.

When she came back to the table, I said, 'You're a doctor?'

'I have a Ph.D.,' she said.

'In what?' I asked.

'The Russian language,' she said. It was the very end of the Cold War, and there was something spooky about her being a doctor of Russian. I was about to ask her who had called, but she said, 'So you'd like to come to Sweden?' It was the first time she smiled at me, and she seemed to soften.

'Yes, very much,' I said.

Then she told me that she needed cigarettes. She glanced out the window and said she was going to run across the street and get a pack. I looked out the window. Across Broadway there was a little tobacco and newspaper shop.

She picked up the tape recorder and her bag and said, 'I'll be right back.' She smiled at me. I sat at the window in Birdland and watched her cross the street. It was night, but

Broadway was well lit by the streetlights and the headlights of the cars.

Something was wrong. She had told me we didn't have much time, but suddenly she's going across the street for cigarettes. I wanted to follow her, but I wondered if I was just being paranoid. If I joined her across the street and she was simply getting a pack of cigarettes, then I would blow my chance at a free trip to Sweden by acting as if I didn't trust her.

She went into the store. The lights on Broadway changed, and the road filled with traffic. I tried to watch for her through the cars and buses, but it was difficult to see the other side of the street.

When the lights turned red again there was a clear view, but I didn't see her coming out of the store. I was getting anxious. The light changed once more, and I couldn't see across the street, and she didn't return to the bar. I asked the bartender if she had paid for her drink, and he said she had.

I ran across Broadway to the newspaper store, but she wasn't there. I asked the proprietor if a blonde woman had come into the store, and he said yes, but that she had left several minutes ago.

'She's not in the bathroom? Do you have a bathroom?'

He looked at me like I was crazy. I ran back across Broadway to Birdland.

'The woman I was with, has she come back?' I asked the bartender.

She hadn't. She had taken off with my photograph and my two chapters. I had other copies, but the idea that she had walked off with them sickened me. Something grotesque was happening. I had no way to find her. She had never given me a phone number or an address where I could reach her.

I called my agent – I didn't know who else to call – from a payphone on Broadway. I said to her, 'That person who was interviewing me for that symposium in Sweden . . . I know this sounds crazy, but she just stole two chapters of my novel.'

'Are you sure?' my agent asked. She probably thought I was drunk. I told her what happened, and she said, 'Go to the police. This way we'll have a record in case those pages get published somewhere.'

I went back to Birdland and asked the bartender where the closest precinct was. It was over on Amsterdam, the 24th. The station was in the middle of some tough-looking projects.

Except for a sergeant at the front desk, the station seemed deserted. The sergeant was a portly, soft-looking man with glasses and a bald head. His desk was elevated. I looked up at him and said, 'Excuse me, officer . . . This is very odd, but I'd like to report something stolen.'

'What?'

'I'm a writer . . . and somebody just took off with two chapters of my manuscript.'

'Fiction?'

'Yes,' I said.

'Really?'

'Yes.'

'This is right up my alley, then – I'm a fiction buff!' He smiled happily at me. 'I love to read. I'd like to write a book someday. As a cop you hear a lot of stories . . . But I have to say you're the first writer to come in because somebody stole his writing.'

He made a phone call, and another officer came into the room, a heavy-set woman. She led me to a desk and typed up my report and gave me a receipt. I took the train back to New Jersey.

The next day, first thing in the morning, I went to Firestone Library on the Princeton campus and did some research. There was no magazine called *Nista* in any listings. I did, however, find the phone number of Gothenburg University.

I rushed home, made the international call, and was connected to the English department. It was late in the afternoon in Sweden, and a secretary put me through to the head of the department, a man who spoke perfect British-accented English. I said I was an American novelist connected with Princeton University and asked if his department was having a symposium in March of young American writers.

'No, no such symposium.'

'I heard that there was going to be some kind of panel . . . Might it be held by another department?'

'No other department except this one would be interested in American writers.'

'Have you heard of a literary magazine called *Nista*?'

'No.'

'Is there such a word as "nista" in Swedish?'

'No.'

'Thank you for your help,' I said. 'There's been a misunderstanding.'

'Perfectly all right,' he said, and he laughed and we hung up.

I don't know what the professor made of such a strange overseas call, but my mind was reeling. The whole thing was a mad hoax. I felt sick. Who would hate me enough to arrange such an elaborate trick?

The following day, a message was left on my machine by a man with a phony-sounding foreign accent. He spoke with great urgency: 'This is Dr Bohanson. I am the editor of *Nista* magazine. I received your writing! It is very important that I speak to you! I am in Boston airport. Call me!'

That was all he said. He didn't leave a number. Boston airport. Not even Logan airport. Who was doing this to me?

The next morning I stepped out to get the paper and, when I came back, there was a message from Sara Sundstrom: 'Dr Bohanson wants to speak to you about your writing. Why don't you call?' She didn't leave a number. She had never given me a number.

Their torture of me was strange and absurd. The woman's voice was hateful. There was no way I could get any writing done. I was no closer to finishing my novel and seeing my son. I needed to clear my mind, so that afternoon I drove to the ocean.

I went to Asbury Park, a place I had often gone to for its downtrodden beauty: the rusted Ferris wheel with each car bearing the name of a Jersey town; the deserted boardwalk; the closed fudge and taffy shops; the warped and gigantic wooden casino, which looks as if it's going to topple into the ocean; and, of course, the Atlantic, gray and enormous and indifferent.

It took me an hour to drive from Princeton. When I got there, I sat on the beach. It was a cool November day, but the sun was bright. I was all alone except for a few stragglers on the boardwalk, and I stared at the ocean. Then I got on my knees, bent my head to the ground, resting it on my hands, and started praying. I was agnostic, but I prayed to God to help me. I was overwhelmed by everything. I needed help. I dug my hands into the sand. They got entangled in something wet and I lifted them up. Attached to my fingers were damp strips of disintegrating toilet paper, and on the paper were little black bugs. I screamed and thrashed my hands in the sand to get the bugs and paper off me.

I went running off the beach and into the bar of the Empress Hotel, across the street from the boardwalk. This wasn't a good thing for me to do. I was young, but I had quit drinking the year before and knew being sober had enabled me to write my novella and graduate. But I didn't care. I ordered a beer and a shot of whiskey.

The Empress was a transient hotel. Like the rest of Asbury Park, the Empress had probably been glorious in the fifties – it looked like something from Miami. The bar still operated, and the drinks were cheap. It was afternoon when I got in there, and I drank for hours. At some point I sat at a table with a borrowed pen and a piece of paper and wrote a long drunken letter to my son. I gave him lots of advice and apologized that I hadn't been able to come see him yet.

I remember looking up from the letter to see that I had been joined at the table by an old woman. She must have been seventy, her hair was gray and her eyes were crazy.

She told me that Abraham Lincoln was Jewish – you could tell because of his name, and that she had taken an accounting course with Frank Sinatra in Jersey City in the 1930s. At some point, she said she wanted to have sex with me if I wore a condom. She said she hadn't had sex in years.

I was crazy drunk and agreed to have sex with her. When we stood up from the table, I saw that she was incredibly tiny. She was about four-foot eight and used an old broomstick for a cane. She was wearing a housedress. I realized then that I was completely mad, and there was no way I could sleep with this woman. I told her that I was starving, that I had been drinking for hours. I suggested we go to a restaurant and have dinner rather than go to her room. She said, 'They won't let me in any restaurant the way I look. You go and come back. I'll be waiting.'

I went to another bar, spent the rest of my money, and then got into my car and blacked out.

I came to on some restricted roads of the Fort Dix military base. I have no idea how I got in there. I found my way out and, half-conscious, half-drunk, drove back to Princeton. I am beyond fortunate that I did not kill anyone. Somewhere I lost the letter I wrote to my son.

I drank for a week. I went to a psychologist and told him about getting a letter with a picture of my son, *Nista*, the miniature old woman I had almost slept with, and everything else. I asked him to put me somewhere to sober up. He said he wasn't sure if I had a drinking problem or if I was chemically imbalanced.

He put me in a psychiatric hospital that had an alcohol unit, covering all my potential problems. After a humiliating week on the locked-up psychiatric ward, I was transferred to the alcoholic wing.

I told my life story to the group and afterwards the head doctor said to me, 'You're an alcoholic and a maniac. Some day you're going to have a florid psychotic moment and end up in Bellevue. But because you're smart, when you come out of it you'll be able to talk your way out. But then it will happen again. If you don't go on lithium you'll lose your mind and never write that book.'

The doctor was chewing Nicaret gum while he gave me my life sentence. I refused to go on the lithium.

The doctor came by my room the next day and gave me

articles about manic-depressive alcoholic artists who commit suicide without lithium. He tried to convince me by saying, 'I want to help you be a writer who can write.'

But I kept refusing the drugs. He performed numerous tests on my blood, nervous system, and brain. He did this to a number of patients, milking their insurance companies for all he could get.

It was the closest I've come to jail: I couldn't leave the place against doctor's orders unless I wanted to absorb the expense of my hospitalization, which was something like a thousand dollars a day. I was stuck there until my insurance ran out.

The day after Thanksgiving, my father, whom I told all about Sara Sundstrom and *Nista*, called me at the hospital. He said, 'I know who was involved with stealing your writing.'

'Who?'

'Julia.'

'How do you know?'

'A woman called here yesterday looking for you. She said she was with *Nista* magazine. And I asked her for a number where you could reach her. I didn't let on that I suspected anything, and I heard her whisper, "Julia, the father wants a number." She gave me a California number. I had a feeling it was phony, and I called it for you. It was an optometrist's office. I asked where they were located – Berkeley. Why would she give an eye doctor's number? Then a few hours later Julia called to wish you a late, happy Thanksgiving. I didn't let on anything.'

I felt incredibly grateful to my father. 'Thank you for solving this,' I said. 'Julia went to an eye doctor in Berkeley.'

'Don't do anything about it, especially from there. You don't want to provoke her. She's crazy.'

'I won't do anything.'

'How was the Thanksgiving meal they gave you?' he asked.

'Horrible,' I said.

'You'll be out soon,' he said.

'I hope so,' I said.

I hung up with my father. The payphone was in the lounge. It was the rest hour before dinner, which was the only time we were allowed to receive and make phone calls. I went to my room and lay on my bed. My roommate, a toll clerk on the Garden State Parkway, was snoring loudly. His septum was badly damaged from cocaine abuse.

I went over in my mind all that had transpired between me and Julia. When something like this happens to you, you don't see the odd trail of evidence accumulating, but now, like a constellation, it was all laid out for me. The Swedish sailor remark when we first met. The music teacher story. The kiss at her door. The prank phone calls. The botched weekend at her father's. But who was Sara Sundstrom? What kind of friends did Julia have that would go along with her? Who was the man who had called me, claiming to be Dr Bohanson?

I felt a weak, impotent rage. What could I do to Julia? I got off my bed and went back to the phone and dialed her number. She answered, and we exchanged the usual greetings. I wanted to act as if nothing had happened to me, to show her that she hadn't affected me in the least.

'I'm just returning your call,' I said. 'How was your Thanksgiving?'

'Uneventful. And yours?' she asked.

'Very nice,' I said. They had served us artificially flavored pumpkin pie. 'Whatever happened to the party with Woody Allen?' I asked.

'He cancelled this year,' she said. 'How's your book coming?'

'Great,' I said. 'Almost finished. How's your writing?'

She talked about her book for a while, and then, as if it just occurred to her, she asked, 'What ever happened to your trip to Norway?'

'Oh, you mean Sweden,' I said. *Norway.* She was purposely feigning ignorance. She had masterminded the whole thing. Here was my small chance at revenge, to act as if it had meant nothing to me. She was probably dying to hear me describe my confusion and bewilderment and fear. 'Well, the trip didn't happen,' I said, laughing. 'It was just some silly hoax.'

Silly. I intended that word to be a dagger into her heart. But then I realized she had probably watched me run frantically out of Birdland to that news store. Most likely she had been right on Broadway, and from a payphone had called the bar to ask for Dr Sundstrom. And she had chosen Birdland for its big windows, so that she could see me sitting there, answering questions like a fool. I imagined she had listened to the tape recording.

'Oh, that's a shame,' she said. 'You deserved a trip like that.'

'Well, it was just a stupid hoax,' I said, and despite all my acting, it was terribly scary to speak to her. I was locked up, but she was the insane one. My dad was right. I didn't want to provoke her. I was afraid it would make her do something more drastic, and she had already proved very capable of hurting me. I then said, 'I better get going, my mom is calling me to dinner.' A few patients, men and women, all clothed in sweatpants, were starting to gather by the ward's locked door. In ten minutes we would be lead down the hall to the cafeteria.

'All right, Jonathan,' she said. 'Call me. Come into the city so we can get together.'

'Okay,' I said, and we rang off. I placed the phone on the cradle and wanted to strangle Julia. I saw my hands around her neck. Her eyes would have to meet mine, acknowledging her punishment and acknowledging that she hadn't gotten away with anything. But it didn't feel good to think about hurting her. I wasn't used to feeling violent, to wanting to really hurt someone.

After forty days, I was let out of the hospital. I didn't hear from Julia and didn't call her. I was told that the best way to deal with obsessed people was not to initiate any contact, to starve them of yourself until they became obsessed with someone else.

I started trying to write again, but still couldn't get anywhere. I kept thinking of the famous writer's words: 'Maybe it isn't supposed to become a larger story.' The fact that he was Julia's father made his off-hand remark even more ominous. The deadline for handing in the book passed. I was still 30,000 words short.

The new year came. On January 23, I wrote a desperate letter to Joyce Carol Oates, my teacher. Essentially, I was asking her to help me write my book – a ridiculous request. I didn't know how I could possibly mail the letter, but didn't know what else to do. I needed help. I had to finish the book so that I could go see my son.

Then before sending the letter, I opened a Hazelden book of daily meditations, which a friend had given me in the hospital. At the top of each day's meditation was a quote from a famous person. For January 23 it read, 'No person can save another.'

The author of those words was Joyce Carol Oates.

I didn't have to mail my letter. She had answered me.

From that point forward, I started to write and didn't stop until it was finished. Julia took one more shot at me though. A letter arrived on February 22, posted from Berkeley.

> *Nista*
> *Nonnensgatan 32*
> *Stockholm, Sweden*
>
> > *Berkeley*
> > *15 January*

Dear Mr. Ames,

Dr. Bohanson has asked me to write you to inform you that we have made our choices for the panel for our symposium in March.

I am afraid your qualifications for our agenda are sadly lacking. While we both agree that your writing contains a certain juvenile charm, our responsibility is to deliver something a bit more substantial.

Off the record, may I also offer a bit of personal advice for future interviews? When someone asks you what, if anything, you can contribute to a serious literary symposium, you might think of something other than that you would 'love to go'. I am afraid I was not impressed by your enthusiasm for a free trip to Europe, when you could hold the promise of so little in return.

Still, thank you for your interest in Nista, and as we say in Gothenburg, 'Många Hälsninger'!

Regards,
Sara Sundstrom

The signature, while nearly unintelligible, looks like 'Sara Sundstrom.' It was a letter from a fictional literary magazine, signed by someone with an assumed name, written or dictated by a madwoman, and yet I was hurt by the criticism of my writing.

I had thought the whole problem with Julia had come to an end, but holding that letter in my hands, I was devastated.

I had to end this somehow. I wanted revenge, but thought it best to forgive. My plan was to forgive and ask for forgiveness.

The side of me that wanted revenge imagined that by being morally superior I would come out ahead. But I tried to repress that thought. I wanted to act purely so as to stop her strange attacks against me.

I phoned Julia at her work number. After our initial greetings, I said, 'I know this comes out of the blue, but I just wanted to call and tell you I'm sorry if I hurt you or led you on in any way.'

Her voice took on a low, hushed, deeply appreciative tone, she said, 'Thank you . . . This means a great deal to me . . . I want to talk to you more, but things here are busy right now. Can I call you back in half an hour?'

'I just really wanted to say that I was sorry—'

'Are you telling me that you don't want anything to do with me?' Her voice was now harsh, angry. The change in tone was rapid.

'I just want to say I'm sorry—'

'I want to speak to you in half an hour,' she demanded.

'All right,' I said, weakly, and we hung up. Half an hour later she called me. She asked me how my work was coming; she said she was nearly done with her book. I was sick of this banter, of being afraid of her, and I finally said, 'What's been going on with you?'

'What do you mean?' she asked. Her voice was immediately odd and defensive.

'I know that you are involved with *Nista* magazine,' I said. It was exhilarating to finally get it out. To show her that I knew the truth.

'What are you talking about? You're very strange.' She was shouting.

'I know that you're involved,' I said.

'You're sick . . . I don't know what you're talking about . . . What are you accusing me of?'

'I know that you're involved with *Nista* magazine.' My voice was calm. She was hanging herself.

'You're sick . . . I don't like this . . . I don't like you . . . Why are you saying these things—'

She hung up the phone.

I was wiped out, destroyed. I lay on my bed. Five minutes later, the phone rang. I didn't pick it up. It was Julia. I listened to her leave a message on the machine, her voice was contrite, practically a whisper: 'Jonathan, I understand if you don't want to be my friend, but I'd like us to be friends. I want to talk to you. Please call me . . . I think you're a really good writer . . . If you don't call, I understand. But please call me.'

I have never spoken to or seen Julia again.

Epilogue

I finished my novel and met my son. I became very involved in his life. I became his dad. He's now fifteen years old. He has my last name. He's a wonderful boy.

For several years I waited for my florid psychotic moment. In my mind I called it the FPM. One night, I was alone in a diner in New Jersey, and a very overweight man approached my table. He said, 'I read your book.' I looked at him. 'I liked it,' he said.

I knew him from somewhere. Then I placed him – the head doctor from the psychiatric hospital. He was still talking down to me like I was his patient. But there was something wrong with him. He was heavy when I knew him, but now he was obese.

'Thank you for reading it,' I said. 'Are you still at the hospital?'

'I don't practice any more,' he said, and gave me a strange smile. I sensed that he had lost his license. That's when I stopped waiting for the FPM.

In 1989, a few months before my book came out, Julia sold her novel to the same publisher. This was incredible to me, but fitting. I had told my editor this whole story and one time, when I went to see him, he informed me that Julia was visiting her editor – there were troubles with her manuscript. My editor showed me the office where Julia was meeting with her editor. The door was slightly ajar. I walked past to try and catch a peek of her, but wasn't able to. My editor didn't want me to make trouble, so I left the building before her meeting was over.

Her book came out a year after mine. The reviews all mentioned that she was the daughter of the famous writer. She hadn't escaped his shadow. In a bookstore, I looked at her novel. The epigram was from Balzac: 'How fondly swindlers coddle their dupes.' I glanced through the book. I didn't expect to find my two chapters. Who knows what she did with my photograph. Drew a moustache on it? Horns? Cut it up?

Her book ends with a man, a famous writer, sitting by himself on a plane to Stockholm. He is going there to collect the Nobel Prize. The empty seat next to him is supposed to be for his ex-wife, but she didn't show up at the airport. He isn't terribly upset because they fight a great deal, and he's actually relieved to go to Stockholm without her. Under the seat in front of him is his briefcase, and he believes that his acceptance speech, which he has slaved over, is inside. But it isn't. The speech has been stolen by his ex-wife. She has stolen his writing.

And the last word of the last line is: Sweden.

NOTES

1. Regarding the letter sent to me by *Nista*: there is no street called Nonnensgatan in Stockholm. I think the hidden meaning could almost be: Nonsense Street. Många Hälsningar, directly translated, means 'many salutations', but is not a phrase used in Swedish letter-writing. Furthermore, Gothenburg is misspelled.
2. The names in this essay have been changed, unless they were false to begin with.

K is for Fake

JONATHAN LETHEM

'The birth of the sad-eyed waifs was in Berlin in 1947 when I met these kids,' Mister Keane said. 'Margaret asked for my help to learn to paint, and I suggested that she project a picture she liked on a canvas and fill it in like children do a numbered painting. Then the woman started copying my paintings.'

While he has sought redress in the courts twice, Margaret Keane has thus far emerged the winner. A lawsuit against her for copyright infringement was dismissed; she then sued Mister Keane for libel for statements he made in an interview with *USA Today*, and to back her suit, she executed a waif painting in front of the jury in less than one hour. She won a $4 million judgment. Walter Keane declined to participate in the paint-off, citing a sore shoulder.

The New York Times, February 26, 1995

K.'s phone rang while he was watching cable television, an old movie starring the Famous Clown. In the movie the Famous Clown lived in a war-torn European city. The Famous Clown walked down a dirt road trailed, like the Pied Piper, by a line of ragged children. The Famous Clown juggled three lumps of bread, the hardened heels of French loaves. K.'s phone rang twice and then he lifted the receiver. It was after eleven. He wasn't expecting a call. 'Yes?' he said. 'Is this painter called

K.?' 'Yes, but I'm not interested in changing my long distance –' The voice interrupted him: 'The charges against you have at last been prepared.' The voice was ponderous with authority. K. waited, but the voice was silent. K. heard breath resound in some vast cavity. 'Charges?' said K., taken aback. K. paid the minimums on his credit cards promptly each month. 'You'll wish to answer them,' intoned the voice. 'We've prepared a preliminary hearing. Meanwhile a jury is being assembled. But you'll undoubtedly wish to familiarize yourself with the charges.'

On the screen the Famous Clown was being clapped in irons by a pair of jackbooted soldiers. The ragamuffin children scattered, weeping, as the Famous Clown was dragged away. Through the window beyond K.'s television the cityscape was visible, the distant offices, lights now mostly extinguished, and the nearby apartments, from whose open windows gently arguing voices drifted like mist through the summer air. On the phone the sonorous breathing continued. 'Is it possible to send me a printed statement?' said K. He wondered if he should have spoken, whether he had in fact now admitted to the possibility of charges. 'No,' sighed the voice on the phone. 'No, the accused must appear in person; hearing first, then trial. All in due course. In the meantime a defense should be readied.' 'A defense?' K. said. He had hoped that whatever charges he faced could be cleared by rote and at a remove, by checking a box or signing a check. K. had once pleaded no contest to a vehicular infraction by voicemail. 'Press One for No Contest,' the recorded voice had instructed him. 'Press Two for Not Guilty. Press Three for Guilty With An Explanation.' 'A defense, most certainly,' said the voice on K.'s telephone now. 'Be assured, you are not without recourse to a defense.'

The voice grew suddenly familiar, avuncular, conspiratory. 'Don't lose heart, K. That is always your weakness. I'll be in touch.' With that K.'s caller broke the connection. More in curiosity than fear K. dialed *69, but his caller's number had a private listing. K. replaced the receiver. On his television the Famous Clown was in shackles in a slant-roofed barracks, his head being shaved by a sadistic commandant. Wide-eyed children with muddy cheeks and ragged hair peered in through a window. In the distance past them a sprawling barbed wire fence was visible, and at the corner of the fence a high wooden tower topped with a gunnery. K. thumbed the remote. The Sci-Fi channel was in the course of a *Twilight Zone* marathon. A man awoke alone in terror, in sweats, in a shabby black-and-white room. The camera boxed at him, the score pulsed ominously. K. fell asleep, comforted.

'The central European Jewish world which Kafka celebrated and ironized went to hideous extinction. The spiritual possibility exists that Franz Kafka experienced his prophetic powers as some visitation of guilt . . .'

George Steiner

'I consider him guilty . . . he is not guilty of what he's accused of, but he's guilty all the same.'

Orson Welles, on *The Trial*

K. was on his way to visit his art dealer, Titorelli, when the Waif appeared in the street before him. It was a cold day, and heaps of blackened snow lay everywhere in the street. The Waif wasn't dressed for the cold. The Waif stood shivering, huddled.

Titorelli's gallery was in Dumbo (Down Under the Manhattan Bridge Overpass) and though it was midday the cobblestone streets were empty of passers-by. Above them loomed the corroded pre-war warehouses, once Mafia-owned, now filled with artists' studios and desirable loft apartments. The sky was chalky and gray, the chill wind off the East River faintly rank. The Waif's huge eyes beckoned to K. They gleamed with tears, but no tears fell. The Waif took K.'s hand. The Waif's grip was cool, fingers squirming in K.'s palm. Together they walked under the shadow of the vast iron bridge, to Titorelli's building. K. wanted to lead the Waif to shelter, to warmth. Through the plate-glass window on which was etched Titorelli's name and the gallery's hours K. saw Titorelli and his art handler, Lilia, animatedly discussing a painting which sat on the floor behind the front desk. K. glanced at the Waif, and the Waif nodded at K. K. wondered how the Waif would be received by Titorelli and Lilia. Perhaps in the refrigerator in the back of the gallery a bit of cheese and cracker remained from the gallery's most recent opening reception, a small snack which could be offered to the Waif. K. pictured the Waif eating from a saucer on the floor, like a pet. In his imaginings the Waif would always be with him now, would follow him home and take up residence there. Now K. pushed the glass door and they stepped inside. Immediately the Waif pulled away from K. and ran silently along the gallery wall, moving like a cat in a cathedral, avoiding the open space at the center of the room. The Waif vanished through the door into the back offices of the gallery without being noticed, and K. found himself alone as he approached Titorelli and Lilia. The art dealer and his assistant contemplated a canvas on which two trees stood on a desolate grassy heath, framing a drab portion of gray sky.

As K. moved closer he saw that the floor behind the desk was lined with a series of similar paintings. In fact they were each identical to the first: trees, grass, sky. 'The subject is too somber,' said Titorelli, waving his hand, dismissing the canvas. Lilia only nodded, then moved another of the paintings into the place of the first. 'Too somber,' said Titorelli again, and again, 'Too somber,' as Lilia presented a third example of the indifferently depicted heathscape. Lilia removed it and reached for another. 'Why don't you hang them upside down?' remarked K., unable to bear the thought of hearing Titorelli render his verdict again, wishing to spare Lilia as well. 'Upside down?' repeated Titorelli, his gaze still keenly focused on the painting as though he hadn't yet reached a complete judgment. 'That may be brilliant. Let's have a look.' Then, looking up: 'Oh, hello, K.' K. greeted Titorelli, and Lilia as well. The assistant lowered her gaze shyly. She had always been daunted and silent in K.'s presence. 'Quickly, girl, upside down!' commanded Titorelli. K. craned his neck, trying to see into the back office, to learn what had become of the Waif. 'Have you got anything to drink, Titorelli?' K. asked. 'There might be a Coke in the fridge,' said Titorelli, waving distractedly. K. slipped through the doorway into the back room, where a cluttered tumult of canvases and shipping crates nearly concealed the small refrigerator. K. didn't see the Waif. He went to the refrigerator and opened the door. The Waif was inside the refrigerator. The Waif was huddled, arms wrapped around its shoulders, trembling with cold, its eyes wide and near to spilling with tears. The Waif reached out and took K.'s hand again. The Waif stepped out of the refrigerator and, tugging persistently at K.'s hand, led him to the vertical racks of large canvases which lined the rear wall of the office. Moving aside a large shipping tube which blocked its entrance the Waif stepped into the last of the vertical racks, which was otherwise empty. K. followed. Unexpectedly, the rack extended beyond the limit of the rear wall, into darkness, alleviated only by glints of light which penetrated the slats on either side. The Waif led K. around a bend in this narrow corridor to where the space opened again into a tall foyer, its walls made of the same rough lath which lined the racks, with stripes of light leaking through faintly. In this dark room K. discerned a large shape, a huge lumpen figure in the center of the floor. The glowing end-tip of a cigar flared, and dry paper crackled. As the crackle faded K. could hear the sigh of a long inhalation. The Waif again released K.'s hand and slipped away into the shadows. K.'s eyes began to adjust to the gloom. He was able to make out the figure before him. Seated in a chair was a tremendously fat man with a large, stern forehead and a shock of white eyebrows and beard. He was dressed in layers of overlapping coats and vests and scarves and smoked a tremendous cigar. K. recognized the man from television. He was the Advertising Pitchman.

The Advertising Pitchman was advocate for certain commercial products: wine, canned peas and pears, a certain make of automobile, et cetera. He loaned to the cause of their endorsement his immense gravity and bulk, his overstuffed authority. 'It is good you've come, K.,' said the Advertising Pitchman. K. recognized the Advertising Pitchman's voice now as well. It was the sonorous voice on the phone, the voice which had warned him of the accusation against him. K. 'We're overdue to begin preparations for your defense,' continued the Pitchman. 'The preliminary hearing has been called.' The Advertising Pitchman sucked again on his cigar; the tip flared; the

Pitchman made a contented sound. The cigar smelled stale. 'By any chance did you see a small child – a Waif?' asked K. 'Yes, but never mind that now. It is too late to help the child,' said the Pitchman. 'We must concern ourselves with answering the charges.' The Pitchman rustled in his vest and produced a sheaf of documents. He placed his cigar in his lips to free both hands, and thumbed through the papers. 'Not now,' said K., feeling a terrible urgency, a sudden force of guilt regarding the Waif. He wondered if he could trouble the Pitchman for a loan of one of his voluminous scarves; one would surely be enough to cloak the Waif, shelter it from the cold. 'I want to help—' K. began, but the Pitchman interrupted. 'If you'd thought of that sooner you wouldn't be in this predicament.' The Pitchman consulted the papers in his lap. 'Self-absorption is among the charges.' K. circled the Pitchman, feeling his way through the room by clinging to the wall, as though he were a small bearing circling a wheel, the Pitchman the hub. 'Self-absorption, Self-amusement, Self-satisfaction,' continued the Pitchman. K. found himself unable to bear the sound of the Pitchman's voice, precisely for its quality of self-satisfaction; he said nothing, instead continued his groping search, moving slowly enough that he wouldn't injure the Waif should he stumble across it. 'Ah, here's another indictment – Impersonation.' 'Shouldn't that be Self-impersonation?' replied K. quickly. He believed his reply quite witty, but the Pitchman seemed not to notice, instead went on shuffling papers and calling out charges. 'Insolence, Infertility, Incompleteness—' By now K. had determined that the Waif had fled the cul-de-sac he and the Pitchman currently inhabited, had vanished back through the corridor behind them, through the gallery racks, perhaps even slipping silently between K.'s legs to accomplish this feat. 'See under Incompleteness: Failure, Reticence, Inability to Achieve Consummation or Closure; for reference see also Great Chinese Wall, Tower of Babel, *Magnificent Ambersons*, et cetera,' continued the Pitchman. K. ignored him, stepped back into the narrow corridor. 'See under Impersonation: Forgery, Fakery, Ventriloquism, Impersonation of the Father, Impersonation of the Gentile, Impersonation of the Genius, Usurpation of the Screenwriter—' K. moved through the corridor back towards the gallery office and the Pitchman's voice soon faded. K. made his way through the glinted darkness of the gallery racks to Titorelli's office. The Waif was nowhere to be seen, but Lilia waited there, and when K. emerged she came near to him and whispered close to his ear. 'I told Titorelli I had to go to the bathroom in order to come find you,' she said teasingly. 'I didn't really have to go.' The shyness Lilia exhibited in front of Titorelli was gone now. Her sleek black hair had fallen from the place where it had been pinned behind her ears, and her glasses were folded into her blouse pocket. 'Perhaps you've seen a child,' said K. 'A little – Waif. In tatters. With big eyes. And silent, like a mouse. It would have just run through here a moment ago.' Lilia shook her head. K. felt that there only must be some confusion of terms, for Lilia had been standing at the entrance to the racks, apparently waiting for K. 'A small thing—' K. lowered his hand to indicate the dwarfish proportions. 'No,' said Lilia. 'We're alone here.' 'The Waif has been with me in the gallery all this time,' said K. 'We entered together. You and Titorelli were distracted and didn't notice.' Lilia shook her head helplessly. 'The Waif is like a ghost,' said K. 'Only I can see it, it follows me. It must have some meaning.' Lilia stroked K.'s hand and said, 'What a strange experience. It's practically Serlingesque.'

'Serlingesque?' asked K., unfamiliar with the term. 'Yes,' said Lilia. 'You know, like something out of *The Twilight Zone.*' 'Oh,' said K., surprised and pleased by the reference. But it wasn't exact, wasn't quite right. 'No, I think it's more—' K. couldn't recall the adjective he was seeking. 'Titorelli was very happy with your suggestion,' whispered Lilia. She put her lips even closer to his ear, and he felt the warmth of her body transmitted along his arm. 'He's hung them all upside down – you'll see when you go back into the gallery. But don't go outside yet.' K. was faintly disturbed; he'd intended the remark to Titorelli as a joke. 'What about the artist's intentions?' he asked Lilia. 'The artist's intentions don't matter,' said Lilia. 'Anyway, the artist is dead, and his intentions are unknown. He left instructions to destroy these canvases. You've saved them; the credit belongs to you.' 'There's little credit to be gained turning a thing upside down,' said K., but Lilia seemed oblivious to his reflections. She pulled at his collar, then traced a line under his jaw with her finger, closing her eyes and smiling dreamily while she did it. 'Do you have any tattoos?' she whispered. 'What?' said K. 'Tattoos, on your body,' said Lilia, tugging his collar further from his collarbone, and peering into his shirt. 'No,' said K. 'Do you?' 'Yes,' said Lilia, smiling shyly. 'Just one. Do you want to see it?' K. nodded. 'Turn around,' commanded Lilia. K. turned to face the rear wall of the gallery office. He wondered if Titorelli was occupied, or if the gallery owner had noticed K.'s and Lilia's absence. 'Now, look,' said Lilia. K. turned. Lilia had unbuttoned her shirt and spread it open. Her brassiere was made of black lace. K. was nearly moved to fall upon Lilia and rain her throat with kisses, but hesitated: something was evident in the crease between her breasts, a mark or sign. Lilia undid the clasp at the center of the brassiere and parted her hands, so that she concealed and also gently parted her breasts. The tattoo in her cleavage was revealed. It was an image of the Waif, or a child very much like the Waif, with large, shimmering eyes, a tiny, downturned mouth, and strawlike hair. Looking more closely, K. saw that the Waif in the tattoo on Lilia's chest also bore a tattoo: a line of tiny numerals on the interior of the forearm. 'I should go,' said K. 'Titorelli must be wondering about us.' 'You can visit me here anytime,' whispered Lilia, quickly buttoning her shirt. 'Titorelli doesn't care.' 'I'll call,' said K., 'or e-mail – do you e-mail?' K. felt in a mild panic to return to the front of the gallery, and to pursue the Waif. 'Just e-mail me here at the gallery,' said Lilia. 'I answer all the e-mails you send, anyway. Titorelli never reads them.' 'But you answer them in Titorelli's voice!' said K. He was distracted from his urgency by this surprise. 'Yes,' said Lilia, suddenly dropping her voice in impersonation to a false basso, considerably deeper than Titorelli's in fact, but making the point none the less. 'I pretend to be a man on the internet,' she said in the deep voice, dropping her chin to her neck and narrowing her nostrils as well, to convey a ludicrous satire of masculinity. 'Don't tell anyone.' K. kissed her cheek quickly and rushed out to the front of the gallery, where he found Titorelli adjusting the last of the small landscapes in its place on the wall. The paintings were hung upside down, and they lined the gallery now. 'There you are,' said Titorelli. He thrust a permanent marker into K.'s hand. 'I need your signature.' 'Did you see a – a child, a Waif?' said K., moving to Titorelli's desk, wanting to sign any papers quickly and be done with it. 'A wraith?' said Titorelli. 'No, a Waif, a child with large, sad eyes,' said K. 'Where are the papers?' K. looked through the front window of the gallery and thought he saw the Waif standing some distance away, down the snowy cobblestone street, huddled again in its own bare arms and staring in his direction. 'Not papers,' said Titorelli. 'Sign the paintings.' Titorelli indicated the nearest of the upside down oils. He tapped his finger at the lower right-hand corner. 'Just your initial.' In irritation K. scrawled his mark on the painting. 'I have to go—' he said. The Waif waited out in the banks of snow, beckoning to him with its sorrowful, opalescent eyes. 'Here,' said Titorelli, guiding K. by the arm to a place beside the next of the inverted heath-scapes. K. signed. Outside, the Waif had turned away. 'And the next,' said Titorelli. 'All of them?' asked K. in annoyance. Outside, the Waif had begun to wander off, was now only a speck barely visible in the snowy street. 'Please,' said Titorelli. K. autographed the remaining canvases, then headed for the door. 'Perhaps now we can market these atrocities,' said Titorelli. 'If they move I'll have her paint a few more; she can do them in her sleep.' 'I'm sorry,' said K., doubly confused. Market atrocities? Paint in her sleep? Outside, the Waif had vanished. 'Isn't the painter of these canvases dead?' K. asked. 'Not dead,' said Titorelli. 'If you really think she can be called an artist. Lilia is responsible for these paintings.' Outside, the Waif had vanished.

CITIZEN KAFKA
Name of punk band on flyer, San Francisco, circa 1990

As the babyfaced wunderkind awoke one morning from uneasy dreams he found himself transformed in his bed into a three-hundred pound advertising pitchman.

As Superman awoke one morning from a Red K Dream he found himself transformed in his bed into two Jewish cartoonists.

As the laughing-on-the-outside clown awoke one morning from uneasy dreams he found himself transformed in his bed into a gigantic crying-on-the-inside clown.

As the painter of weeping children awoke one morning from uneasy dreams he found himself transformed in his bed into his own defense attorney, a man who in his previous career in Hollywood had himself been accused of charlatanism, plagiarism, and dyeing Rita Hayworth's hair black. Great, he thought, this is just what I need. He found that he was so heavy he had to roll himself out of bed.

As Modernism awoke one morning from uneasy dreams it found itself transformed in its bed into a gigantic Postmodernism.

The Waif didn't have a bed.

Gregor Samsa ducked into a nearby phone booth. 'This looks', he said, 'like a job for a gigantic insect.'

In my masterwork I wanted to portray the unsolved problems of mankind; all rooted in war, as that vividly remembered sight of the human rats amid the rubble of Berlin so poignantly signified ... endless drawings, the charcoal sketches lay scattered along the years. Each in its groping way had helped lead me to this moment ...'

Walter Keane, in Walter Keane,
Tomorrow's Master Series

I've come up against the last boundary, before which I shall in all likelihood again sit down for years, and then in all likelihood begin another story all over again that will again remain unfinished. This fate pursues me.

Kafka, Diaries

On a gray spring morning before K.'s thirty-first birthday K. was summoned to court for his trial. He hadn't thought a trial so long delayed would ever actually begin, but it had. Go figure. K. was escorted from his apartment to the court by a couple of bailiffs, men in black suits and dark glasses and with grim, set expressions on their faces that struck K. as ludicrous. 'You look like extras from the *X-Files!*' he exclaimed, but the bailiffs were silent. They held K.'s arms and pressed him close from both sides, and in this manner K. was guided downstairs and into the street. In silence the bailiffs steered K. through indifferent crowds of rush-hour commuters and midmorning traffic jams of delivery trucks and taxicabs, to the new Marriott in downtown Brooklyn. A sign in the lobby of the Marriott said: 'Welcome Trial of K., Liberty Ballroom A/B,' and in smaller letters underneath: 'A Smoke-Free Building.' K. and the bailiffs moved through the lobby to the entrance of the ballroom which now served as a makeshift court. The ballroom was already packed with spectators, who broke into a chorus of murmurs at K.'s appearance at the back of the room. The bailiffs released K.'s arms and indicated that he should precede them to the front of the court, where judge and jury, as well as prosecuting and defending attorneys, waited. K. moved to the front, holding himself erect to indicate his indifference to the craning necks and goggling eyeballs of the spectators, his deafness to their murmurs. As he approached the bench K.

saw that his defending attorney was none other than the Advertising Pitchman. The Pitchman levered his bulk out of his chair and rose to greet K., offering a hand to shake. K. took his hand, which was surprisingly soft and which retreated almost instantly from K.'s grip. Now K. saw that the prosecuting attorney was the Famous Clown. The Famous Clown was dressed in an impeccable three-piece suit and tremendously wide, pancake-like black shoes which were polished to a high gloss. The Famous Clown remained in his seat, scowling behind bifocal lenses at a sheaf of papers on his desk, pretending not to have noticed K.'s arrival. Seated at the high bench in the place of a judge was the Waif. The Waif sat on a tall stool behind the bench. The Waif wore a heavy black robe, and on its head sat a thickly curled wig which partly concealed its straw-like thatch of hair but did nothing to conceal the infinitely suffering black pools of its eyes. The Waif toyed with its gavel, seemingly preoccupied and indifferent to K.'s arrival in the courtroom. K. was guided by the Pitchman to a seat at the defense table, where he faced the Waif squarely, the Prosecuting Clown at his right. The jurors sat at a dais to K.'s left, and he found himself resistant to turning in their direction. K. wanted no pity, no special dispensation. 'Don't fear,' stage-whispered the Pitchman. He winked and clapped K.'s shoulder, conspiratory and garrulous at once. 'We've practically ended this trial before it's begun,' the Pitchman said. 'I've exonerated you of nearly all of the charges. Incompleteness, for one. It turns out their only witnesses were the Unfinished Chapters and the Passages Deleted by the Author. They were prepared to put them on the stand one after another, but I disqualified them all on grounds of character.' 'Their character was deficient?' asked K. 'I should say so,' boasted the Pitchman, arching an eyebrow dramatically. 'Why, just have a look at them. You've left them woefully underwritten!'

K. hadn't understood himself to be the *author* of the Unfinished Chapters and the Passages Deleted by the Author, but rather a fictional character, one subject to the deprivations of being underwritten himself. However, one glance at the Unfinished Chapters and the Passages Deleted by The Author, all of whom sat crowded together in the spectators' gallery, muttering resentfully and glaring in K.'s direction, told K. that they did not themselves understand this to be the case. The Unfinished Chapters held themselves with a degree of decorum, their ties perhaps a little out-of-fashion and certainly improperly knotted, but they at least wore ties; the Passages Deleted by the Author were hardly better than unwashed rabble. Still, K.'s instinct was for forgiveness. He reflected that for Chapters and Passages alike it must have been bitter indeed to be denied their say in court after so long. 'Additionally,' continued the Pitchman, 'you've been cleared of the various charges of Impersonation, Ventriloquism, Usurpation and the like.' 'How was this achieved?' asked K, a little resentfully. 'Which other witnesses had to be smeared in order that I not need defend myself in this matter in which, incidentally, I am entirely innocent?' The Pitchman was undeterred, and said with a guttural chuckle, 'No, not witnesses. This was a side bargain with my counterpart on the opposite aisle.' K. glanced at the Famous Clown, who just at that moment was staring across at the Advertising Pitchman with poisonous intensity, even as he readjusted his false buck teeth. K. heard a sharp and rhythmic clapping sound and saw that the Famous Clown was slapping his broad, flat shoes against the floor beneath his desk. The Pitchman seemed not to notice or care. He said, 'Let's just say you're not the only one in this room with skeletons in his closet – or perhaps I should say with a dressing room full of masks and putty noses.' The Pitchman groped his own bulbous proboscis, and grew for one moment reflective, even tragic in his aspect. 'I speak even for myself . . .' He seemed about to digress into some reminiscence, then apparently thought better of it, and waved his hand. 'Still, congratulations would be premature. One charge against you remains – a trifle, I'm sure. This charge you can eradicate with a few swift brushstrokes.' 'How with brushstrokes?' asked K. 'You stand charged with Forgery,' said the Pitchman. 'Patently absurd, I know, yet it is the only jeopardy that still remains. A woman has stepped forward and claimed your work as her own. I negotiated with the prosecution a small demonstration before the jury, knowing how this opportunity to clear yourself directly would please you.' 'A demonstration?' asked K. 'Yes,' chuckled the Pitchman. 'One hardly worthy of your talents. A hot-dog eating contest would be more exalted. Regardless, it should provide the flourish these modern show trials require.' K. saw now that the bailiffs had dragged two painting easels to the front of the courtroom and erected them before the Waif's bench. Blank canvases were mounted on each of the easels, and two sets of brushes and two palettes of oils were made available on a table to one side. The Waif was now rolling the handle of its gavel back and forth across the desktop, in an uncharacteristic display of agitation. 'A masterpiece isn't required,' said the Pitchman. 'Merely a display of competence, of facility.' 'But who is this woman?' asked K. 'Here she is now,' whispered the Pitchman, nudging K.'s shoulder. K. turned. The woman who had entered the courtroom was Lilia, Titorelli's art handler. There was a buzz from the jury box, like

a small hive of insects. Lilia wore a prim white smock and a
white painter's hat. Her gaze was fiercely determined, her eyes
never lighting on K.'s. 'Go now,' whispered the Pitchman. 'A
sentimental subject would be best, I think. Something to stir
the hearts of the jurors.' K. stood. He saw now that the jury
box was full of ragged children, much like the Waif who stood
now in its robes and clapped its gavel to urge the painters to
commence the demonstration. Lilia seized a brush and began
immediately to paint, first outlining two huge orbs in the
center of the canvas. K. wondered if they were breasts, then
saw that in fact they were two enormous, bathetic eyes: Lilia
was initiating a portrait of the Waif. K. moved for the table.
As he reached to take hold of a brush he felt a sudden clarifying
pain in the shoulder where the Pitchman had nudged him a
moment before, a pain so vivid that he wondered if he would
be at all able to paint, or even to lift his arm; it now felt heavy
and inert, like a dead limb. Lilia, meanwhile, continued to
work intently at her easel.

*(Note: It is here the fragment ends. Nevertheless, I believe this sequence,
taken in conjunction with the completed chapters which precede it,
reveals its meaning with undeniable clarity.* – Box Dram, Editor)

'I don't like that ending. To me it's a "ballet" written by a Jewish
intellectual before the advent of Hitler. Kafka wouldn't have put
that after the death of six million Jews. It all seems very much
pre-Auschwitz to me. I don't mean that my ending was a particularly good one, but it was the only possible solution.'

Orson Welles, on *The Trial*

See K. awaken one morning from righteous dreams to find himself transformed in his bed into a caped superhero: Holocaust Man!

See Holocaust Man stride forth in the form of the golem, with a marvelously powerful rocklike body and the Star of David chiseled into its chest!

See Holocaust Man and his goofy sidekick, Clown Man, defeat Mister Prejudice, Mister Guilt, Mister Tuberculosis, Mister Irony, Mister Paralysis, and Mister Concentration Camp!

See Holocaust Man and Clown Man lead a streaming river of tattered, orphaned children to safety across the battlefields of Europe!

Laugh on the outside! Cry on the inside!

Banvard's Folly
(Or, How Do You Lose a Three-Mile Painting?)

PAUL COLLINS

> Mister Banvard has done more to elevate the taste for fine arts, among those who little thought on these subjects than any single artist since the discovery of painting and much praise is due him.
>
> *The London Times*

The life of John Banvard is the most perfect crystallization of loss imaginable. In the 1850s, Banvard was the most famous living painter in the world, and possibly the first millionaire artist in history. Acclaimed by millions and by such contemporaries as Dickens, Longfellow, and Queen Victoria, his artistry, wealth, and stature all seemed unassailable. Thirty-five years later, this same man was laid to rest in a pauper's grave in a lonely frontier town in the Dakota Territory. His most famous works were destroyed, and an examination of reference books will not turn up a single mention of his name. John Banvard, the greatest artist of his time, has been utterly obliterated by history.

What happened?

In 1830, a fifteen-year-old schoolboy passed out this handbill to his classmates, complete with its homely omission of a fifth entertainment:

BANVARD'S
ENTERTAINMENTS
(To be seen at No. 68 Centre Street, between
White and Walker.)
Consisting of
1st. Solar Microscope
2nd. Camera Obscura
3rd. Punch & Judy
4th. Sea Scene
6th. Magic Lantern
Admittance (to see the whole) six cents.
The following are the days of performance, viz:
Mondays, Thursdays, and Saturdays.
Performance to commence at half-past 3 p.m.
JOHN BANVARD, Proprietor

Although they were not to know, they were only the first of
over two million to witness the showmanship of John Banvard.
Visiting Banvard's home museum and diorama, they might
have been greeted by his father Daniel, a successful building contractor and a dabbler in art himself. The adventurous
son had acquired a taste for sketching, writing, and science
– the latter pursuit beginning with a bang when an experiment with hydrogen exploded in the young man's face, badly
injuring his eyes.

Worse calamities lay in store. When Daniel Banvard suffered a stroke in 1831, his business partner fled with the
firm's assets. Daniel's subsequent death left the family bank-
rupt. After watching his family's possessions auctioned off,
John 'lit out for the territories' – to Kentucky, to be exact.
Taking up residence in Louisville as a drugstore clerk, he honed

his artistic skills by drawing chalk caricatures of customers in the back of the store. His boss, not interested in patronizing adolescent art, fired him. Banvard soon found himself scrounging for signposting and portrait jobs on the docks.

It was here that he met William Chapman, the owner of the country's first showboat. Chapman offered Banvard work as a scene painter. The craft itself was primitive by the standards of later showboats, as Banvard later recalled:

The boat was not very large, and if the audience collected too much on one side, the water would intrude over the low gunwales into their exhibition room. This kept the company by turns in the un-artist-like employment of pumping, to keep the boat from sinking. Sometimes the swells from a passing steamer would cause the water to rush through the cracks of the weatherboarding and give the audience a bathing . . . They made no extra charge for this part of the exhibition.

The pay proved to be equally unpredictable. But if nothing else, Chapman's showboat gave Banvard ample practice in the rapid sketching and painting of vast scenery – a skill that would prove invaluable later in life.

Deciding that he'd rather starve on his own payroll than on someone else's, Banvard left the following season. He disembarked in New Harmony, Ohio, where he set about assembling a theater company. Banvard himself would serve as an actor, scene painter, and director; occasionally, he'd dash onstage to perform as a magician. He funded the venture by suckering a backer out of his life savings, a pattern of arts financing that would haunt him later in life.

The river back then was still unspoilt – and unsafe. But the crew did last for two seasons, performing Shakespeare and popular plays while they floated from port to port. Few towns could then support their own theater, but they could afford to splurge when the floating dramatists tied up at the docks. Customers sometimes bartered their way aboard with chickens and sacks of potatoes, and this helped fill in the many gaps in the crew's menu. But eventually food, money, and tempers ran so short that Banvard, broke and exhausted from bouts with malarial ague, was reduced to begging on the docks of Paducah, Kentucky. While Banvard was now a toughened showman with years of experience, he was also still a bright, intelligent, and sympathetic teenager. A local theater impresario took pity on the bedraggled boy and hired him as a scene painter. Banvard, relieved, quit the showboat.

It was a good thing that he did quit – farther downriver, a bloody knife fight broke out between the desperate thespians. The law showed up in the form of a hapless constable, who promptly stumbled through a trap door in the stage and died of a broken neck. With a dead cop on the their hands, the company panicked and abandoned ship; Banvard never heard from any of them again.

While in Paducah, Banvard made his first attempts at crafting 'moving panoramas.' The panorama – a circular artwork that surrounded the viewer – was a relatively new invention, a clever use of perspective that emerged in the late 1700s. By 1800, it was declared an official art form by the Institut de France. Photographic inventor L. J. Daguerre went on to pioneer the 'diorama,' which was a panorama of moving canvas panels viewed through atmospheric effects. When Banvard was growing up in Manhattan, he could walk a few blocks to gape at these continuous rolls of painted canvas depicting seaports and 'A Trip to Niagara Falls.'

Moving into his twenties with the memories of his years of desperate illness and hunger behind him, Banvard spent his spare time in Paducah painting landscapes and creating his own moving panoramas of Venice and Jerusalem; stretched between two rollers and operated on one side by a crank, they allowed audiences to stand in front and watch exotic scenery roll by. Banvard could not stay away from the river for long, though. He began plying the Mississippi, Ohio, and Missouri Rivers again, working as a dry-goods trader and an itinerant painter. He also had his eye on greater projects: a diorama of the 'infernal regions' had been touring the frontier successfully, and Banvard thought he could improve upon it. During a stint in Louisville, he executed a moving panorama that he described as 'INFERNAL REGIONS, nearly 100 feet in length.' He completed and sold this in 1841, and it came as a crowning success atop the sale of his Venice and Jerusalem panoramas.

It is not easy to imagine the effect that panoramas had upon their viewers. It was the birth of motion pictures – the first true marriage of the reality of vision with the reality of physical movement. The public was enthralled, and so was Banvard: he had the heady rush of an artist working at the dawn of a new media. Emboldened by his early successes, the 27-year-old painter began preparations for a painting so enormous and so absurdly ambitious that it would dwarf any attempted before or since: a portrait of the Mississippi River.

When we read of the frontier today, we are apt to envision California and Nevada. In Banvard's time, though, 'the frontier' still meant the Mississippi River. A man setting off into its wilds and tributaries would only occasionally find the friendly respite of a town; in between he faced exposure, mosquitoes, and if he ventured ashore, bears. But Banvard had been up and down the river many times now, and had taken at least one trip solo as a traveling salesman. The idylls of river life had its charms and hazards, as he later recalled:

All the toil, and its dangers, and exposure, and moving accidents of this long and perilous voyage, are hidden, however, from the inhabitants, who contemplate the boats floating by their dwellings and beautiful spring mornings, when the verdant forest, the mild and delicious temperature of the air, the delightful azure of the sky of this country, the fine bottom on one hand, and the romantic bluff on the other, the broad and the smooth stream rolling calmly down the forest, and floating the boat gently forward, present delightful images and associations to the beholders. At this time, there is no visible danger or call for labor. The boat takes care of itself; and little do the beholders imagine how different a scene may be presented in half an hour. Meantime, one of the hands scrapes a violin, and others dance. Greetings, or rude defiances, or trials of wit, or proffers of love to the girls on shore, or saucy messages, are scattered between them and the spectators along the banks.

Banvard knew the physical challenge that he faced and was prepared for it. But the challenge to his artistry was scarcely imaginable. In the spring of 1842, after buying a skiff, provisions, and a portmanteau filled with pencils and sketch pads, he set off down the Mississippi River. His goal was to sketch the river from St Louis all the way to New Orleans.

For the next two years, he spent his nights with his portmanteau as a pillow, and his days gliding down the river, filling his sketch pads with river views. Occasionally, he'd pull into port to hawk cigars, meats, household goods, and anything else he could to sell to river folk. Banvard prospered at this, at one point trading up to a larger boat so as to sell more goods. Recalling those days to audiences a few years later – with a flair for drama, of course – he remembered the trying times in between, when he was alone on the river:

His hands became hardened with constantly plying the oars, and his skin as tawny as an Indian's, from exposure to the sun and the vicissitudes of the weather. He would be weeks altogether without speaking to a human being, having no other company than his rifle, which furnished him with his meat from the game of the woods or the fowl of the river . . . In the latter part of the summer he reached New Orleans. The yellow fever was raging in that city, but unmindful of that, he made his drawing of the place. The sun the while was so intensely hot, that his skin became so burnt that it peeled from off the back of his hands, and from his face. His eyes became inflamed by such constant and extraordinary efforts, from which unhappy effects he has not recovered to this day.

But in his unpublished autobiography, he recalled his travels a bit more benignly:

The river's current was averaging from four to six miles per hour. So I made fair progress along down the stream and began to fill my portfolio with sketches of the river shores. At first it appeared lonesome to me drifting all day in my little boat, but I finally got used to this.'

By the time he arrived back in Louisville in 1844, this adventurer had acquired the sketches, the tall tales, and the funds to realize his fantastic vision of the river he had traveled. It would be the largest painting the world had ever known.

Banvard was attempting to paint three thousand miles of the Mississippi from its Missouri and Ohio sources. But if his project was grander than any before, so were the ambitions of his era. Ralph Waldo Emerson, working the New England public lecture circuit, had already urged that 'Our fisheries, our Negroes, and Indians, our boasts . . . the northern trade, the southern planting, the Western clearing, Oregon, and Texas, are yet unsung. Yet America is a poem in our eyes, its ample geography dazzles the imagination . . .' The idea had been voiced by novelists like Cooper before him, and later on by such poets as Walt Whitman. When Banvard built a barn on the outskirts of Louisville in 1844 to house the huge bolts of canvas that he had custom-ordered, he was sharing in this grand vision of American art.

His first step was to devise a tracked system of grommets to keep the huge panorama canvas from sagging. It was ingenious enough to be patented and featured in a *Scientific American* article a few years later. And then, for month after month, Banvard worked feverishly on his creation, painting in broad strokes. Trained in background painting, he specialized in conveying the impression of vast landscapes. Looked at closely, this work held little for the connoisseur trained in conventions of detail and perspective. But motion worked magic upon the rough hewn cabins, muddy banks, blooming cottonwoods, frontier towns, and medicine show flatboats.

During this time he also worked in town on odd jobs, but if he told anyone of his own painting, we have no record of it. Fortunately, though, we have a letter from an unexpected visitor to Banvard's barn. Lieutenant Selin Woodworth had grown up a few houses away from Banvard and hadn't seen him in 16 years, and he could hardly pass by in the vast frontier without saying hello. When he showed up unannounced at the barn, he was amazed by what maturity had wrought in his childhood friend:

I called at the artist's studio, an immense wooden building . . . the artist himself, in his working cap and blouse, pallet and pencil in hand, came to the door to admit us . . . Within the studio, all seemed chaos and confusion, but the lifelike and natural appearance of a portion of his great picture, displayed on one of the walls in a yet unfinished state . . . A portion of this canvas was wound upon a upright roller, or drum, standing on one end of the building, and as the artist completes his painting he thus disposes of it.

Any description of this gigantic undertaking . . . would convey but a faint idea of what it will be when completed. The remarkable truthfulness of the minutest objects upon the shores of the rivers, independent of the masterly and artistical execution of the work will make it the most valuable historical painting in the world, and unequaled for magnitude and variety of interest, by any work that has been heard of since the art of painting was discovered.

This was the creation that Banvard was ready to unveil to the world.

Banvard approached his opening day with the highest of hopes. Residents reading the *Louisville Morning Courier* discovered on June 29, 1846, that their local painter had rented out a hall to show off his work: 'Banvard's Grand Moving Panorama of the Mississippi will open at the Apollo Rooms, on Monday evening, June 29, 1846, and continue every evening till Saturday, July 4.' A review in the same paper declared that 'The great three-mile painting is destined to be one of the most celebrated paintings of the age.' Little did the writer of this review know how true this first glimpse was to prove: while it was to be the most celebrated painting of the age, it did not last for the ages.

Opening night certainly proved to be inauspicious. Banvard paced around his exhibition hall waiting for the crowds and the fifty cent admission fees to come pouring in. Darkness slowly fell, and a rain settled in. The panorama stood upon the lighted stage, fully wound and awaiting the first turn of the crank. And as the sun set and rain drummed on the roof, John Banvard waited and waited.

Not a single person showed up.

It was a humiliating debut, and it should have been enough to make him pack up and leave. But the next day saw John Banvard move from being a genius of artistry to a genius of promotion. He spent the morning of the thirtieth working the Louisville docks, chatting to steamboat crews with the assured air of one who'd navigated the river many times himself. Moving from boat to boat, he passed out free tickets to a special afternoon matinee.

Even if they had paid the full fee, the sailors would have got their money's worth that afternoon. As the painted landscape glided by behind him, Banvard described his travels upon the river – a tall tale of pirates, colorful frontier eccentrics, hair's-breadth escapes, and wondrous vistas – a tad exaggerated, perhaps, but it still convinced a hall full of sailors that could have punctured his veracity with a single catcall. When he gave his evening performance, crew recommendations to passengers boosted his take to ten dollars – not bad for an evening's work in 1846. With each performance the audience grew, and within a few days he was playing to a packed house.

Flush with money and a successful debut, Banvard returned to his studio and added more sections to the painting and moved it to a larger venue. The crowds continued to pour in, and nearby towns chartered steamboats to see the show. With the added sections, the show stretched to over two hours in length; the canvas would be cranked faster or slower depending on audience response. Each performance was unique, even for a customer who sat through two in a row. The canvas wasn't rewound at the end of the show, so the performances alternated between upriver and downriver journeys.

After a successful shakedown cruise, Banvard was ready to take his 'Three-Mile Painting' to the big city. He held his last Louisville show on October 31st and then headed for the epicenter of American intellectual culture: Boston.

Banvard installed his panorama in Boston's Armory Hall in time for the Christmas season. He had honed his delivery to a perfect blend of racy improvisation, reminiscences, and tall tales about infamous frontier brigands. The crank machinery was now hidden from the audience, and Banvard had commissioned a series of piano waltzes to accompany his narration. With creative lighting and the unfurling American landscape behind him, Banvard had created a seemingly perfect synthesis of media.

Audiences loved it. By Banvard's account, in six months 251,702 Bostonians viewed his extraordinary show; at fifty cents a head, he'd made about $100,000 in clear profit. In just one year, he'd gone from a modest frontier sign painter to a famous and wealthy man – and probably the country's richest artist. When he published the biographical pamphlet *Description of Banvard's Panorama of the Mississippi River* (1847) and a transcription of his show's music, it brought in even more money. But there was an even happier result to his inclusion of piano music – the young pianist he'd hired, Elizabeth Goodman, soon became his fiancée, and then his wife.

Accolades continued to pour in, culminating in a final Boston performance that saw the Governor, the Speaker of the House, and state representatives in the audience unanimously passing a resolution to honor Banvard. His success was also the talk of Boston's intellectual elite. John Greenleaf Whittier titled a book after it (*The Panorama and Other Poems*) in 1856, and Henry Wadsworth Longfellow wrote about the Mississippi in his epic *Evangeline* after seeing one of Banvard's first Boston performances. Longfellow had never seen the river himself – to him, the painting was real enough to suffice. In fact, Longfellow was to invoke Banvard again in his novel *Kavanaugh*, using him as the standard by which future American literature was to be judged: 'We want a national epic that shall correspond to the size of the country; that shall be to all other epics what Banvard's panorama of the Mississippi is to all other paintings – the largest in the world.'

There is little doubt that Banvard's 'Three-Mile Painting' was the longest ever produced. But it was a misleading appellation. John Hanners – the scholar who has almost single-handedly kept Banvard's memory alive in our time – points out that: 'Banvard always carefully pointed out that others called it three miles of canvas . . . Since the area in its original form was 15,840 square feet, not three miles in linear measurement.'

But perhaps Banvard was in no hurry to correct the public's

inflated perceptions of his painting. His fame was now preceding him, and he moved his show to New York City in 1847 to even bigger crowds and greater enrichment; it was hailed there as 'a monument of native talent and American genius.' Each night's receipts were carted to the bank in locked strong boxes; rather than count the massive deposits, the banks simply started weighing Banvard's haul.

With acclaim and riches came the less sincere flattery of his fellow artists. The artist closest upon Banvard's heels was John Rowson Smith, who had painted a supposed 'Four-Mile Painting.' For all Banvard's tendencies toward exaggeration, there is even less reason or evidence to believe that his opportunistic rivals produced panoramas larger than his. Still, it was a worrisome trend. Banvard had been hearing for some time of plans by unscrupulous promoters to copy his painting and to then show the pirated work in Europe as the 'genuine Banvard panorama.' With the US successfully behind him, Banvard closed his New York show and booked a passage to Liverpool.

Banvard spent the summer of 1848 warming up for his London shows with short runs in Liverpool, Manchester, and other smaller cities. Reaching London, the enormous Egyptian Hall was booked for his show. He began by suitably impressing the denizens of Fleet Street papers with a special showing. 'It is impossible,' the *Morning Advertiser* marveled, 'to convey an adequate idea of this magnificent [exhibition.]' The *London Observer* was equally impressed in its review of November 27, 1848: 'This is truly an extraordinary work. We have never seen a work . . . so grand in its whole character.' Banvard was rapidly achieving a sort of artistic beatification in the press.

The crowds and the money flowed in yet again. But to truly bring in the chattering classes, Banvard needed something that he'd never had in the United States: the imprimatur of royalty. After much finagling and plotting by Banvard, he was summoned to Windsor Castle on April 11, 1849 for a special performance to Queen Victoria and the royal family. Banvard was already a rich man, but royal approval could make the difference being a mere artistic showman and an officially respected painter. Banvard gave the performance of his life, delivering his anecdotes in perfect combination with his wife at the piano; at the end, when he gave his final bow to the family assembled at St George's Hall, Banvard knew that he had made it as an artist. For the rest of his life, he was to look back upon this as his finest hour.

His panorama show was now a sensation, running for a solid twenty months in London to over 600,000 spectators. An enlarged and embellished reprint of his autobiographical pamphlet, now titled *Banvard, or the Adventures of an Artist* (1849), also sold well to Londoners, and his show's waltzes could be heard in many a parlor. He penetrated every level of society; after attending one show, Charles Dickens wrote to him in an admiring letter: 'I was in the highest degree interested and pleased by your picture.' To the other dwellers of this island nation, whose experience of sailing was often that of stormy seas, Banvard offered the spice of frontier danger blended with the honeyed idylls of riverboat life:

Certainly, there can be no comparison between the comfort of the passage from Cincinnati, New Orleans, in such a steamboat, and to a voyage at sea. The barren and boundless expanse of waters soon tires upon every eye but a seaman's. And then there are storms, and the necessity of fastening the tables, and of holding onto something to keep in bed. There is the insupportable nausea of sea sickness, and there is danger. Here you are always near the shore, always see green earth, can always eat, write and study, undisturbed. You can always obtain cream, fowls, vegetables, fruit, fresh meat, and wild game, in their season, from the shore.

Toward the end of these London shows, Banvard found himself increasingly dogged by imitators – there were fifty competing panoramas in the 1849–50 season alone. In addition to longtime rival John Rowson Smith, Banvard now had scurrilous accusations of plagiarism flung at him by fellow expatriate portraitist George Caitlin, a jealous painter who had 'befriended' Banvard in order to borrow money. Banvard also found his shows being set upon by the spies of his rivals, who hired art students to sit in the audience and sketch his work as it rolled by.

We know that a form of art has permeated a culture when such cheap imitations appear, and even more so when parodies of these imitations emerge. There is a long-forgotten work in this vein by American humorist Artemus Ward, which was published posthumously as *Artemus Ward, His Panorama* (1869). Ward spent the last years of his life working in London, and had probably attended some of the numerous panoramic travelogues and travesties that darted about in Banvard's wake. His panorama, as shown by illustrations of the supposed stage (which, as often as not, is obscured by a faulty curtain), consists of a discourse on San Francisco and Salt Lake City, often interrupted by crapulous bits of tangential mumbling in small type:

If you should be dissatisfied with anything here to-night – I will admit you all free in New Zealand – if you will come to me there for the orders.

This story hasn't anything to do with my Entertainment, I know – but one of the principle features of my Entertainment is that it contains so many things that don't have anything to do with it.

For ads reproduced in the book, Ward munificently assures his audiences that his lecture hall has been lavishly equipped with 'new doorknobs.' But Banvard's most serious rivals were not such bumblers, and so he had to swing back into action. Locking himself in the studio again, he created another Mississippi panorama. Where the first panorama had been a view of the eastern bank, this new painting depicted the western bank. He then placed the London show in the hands of a new narrator, and toured Britain himself with the second painting for two years, bringing in nearly 100,000 more viewers.

What might Banvard have done with these two paintings had he placed them on stage together? Angled in diagonally from each side to terminate just behind the podium, moving in unison, they would have provided a sort of stereo-optical effect to the audience of floating down the center of the Mississippi River. It would have been the first 'surround multimedia.' For all of Banvard's innovation, though, there is no record of such an experiment.

Not all of Banvard's time in London was spent on his own art. In his spare hours, he haunted the Royal Museum; he was fascinated by its massive collection of Egyptian artifacts. He soon became a protégé of the resident Egyptologists, and under their tutelage he learned to decipher hieroglyphics – the only American of his time, by some accounts, to learn this skill. For decades afterward, he was able to pull sizable crowds to his lectures on the reading of hieroglyphics.

Banvard moved his show to Paris, where his success continued unabated for another two years. He was now also a family man: a daughter, Gertrude, was born in London, and a son, John Jr., was born in Paris. Having children scarcely slowed down his travels; on the contrary, he left the family to spend the next year on an artistic pilgrimage to the Holy Land. In a reprise of his American journey, he sailed down the Nile and filled up notebooks with sketches. But he no longer had to sleep with these notebooks as a pillow. He was now wealthy enough to travel in comfort, and he bought thousands of artifacts along the way – a task assisted by his unusual ability at translating hieroglyphics.

These travels were to become the basis for yet two more panoramas: one of the Palestine, and the other of a trip down the Nile. Neither were to earn him as much as his Mississippi panorama; the market was now flooded with imitations, and the public was beginning to weary of the panoramic lecture. Even so, Banvard's abilities were greater than ever. As one American reviewer commented in 1854 in *Ballou's Pictorial Drawing Room Companion*:

Mr Banvard made a name and fortune by his three mile panorama of the Mississippi. It was one of those cases in which contemporary justice is bestowed upon true merit . . . His sole teacher in his art is Nature; there are few conventionalisms in his style. His present great work is far superior in artistic merit to his Mississippi – showing his rapid improvement; its effect is enhanced by its great height.

Just eight years after his voyage down the Mississippi, he had become both the most famous living artist in the world and the richest artist in history.

Banvard returned to the US with his family in the spring of 1852. He was a fantastically wealthy man, enough so that he could retire to a castle and casually dabble in the arts for the rest of his life. And at first that's exactly what he did.

The world's most famous artist needed an equally imposing home to live in: accordingly, he bought a sixty-acre lot on Long Island and proceeded to build a replica of Windsor Castle. When the local roads didn't meet the needs of his castle, he simply built one of his own. He dubbed the castle 'Glenada' in honor of his daughter, Ada; neighbors, who were alternately aghast and awed by the unheard-of construction expenses being incurred, simply dubbed it 'Banvard's Folly.'

A reporter touring the site was kinder in his appraisal of Banvard's castle:

It has a magnificent appearance, reminding you forcibly of some of the quaint old castles nestled among the glens of old Scotland . . . There are nine offices on the first floor, as you enter from the esplanade, viz., the drawing room, parlors, conservatory, ante room, servant's room, and several chambers. The second story contains the nursery, school room, guest chambers, bath, library, study, etc., with the servants' rooms in the towers. The basement is occupied with the offices, store rooms, etc. Although the facade extends in front one hundred and fifteen feet, still Mr Banvard says his castle is not completed, as he has plans arranged for adding a large donjon, or keep, to be occupied by his studio, painting-room, and a museum for the reception of the large collection of curiosities which he has gathered in all parts of the world ... it has been proposed to change the name of the place [Cold Spring Harbor] and call it BANVARD ...

Not surprisingly, the residents of the town failed to see the charm of this last proposal.

Still, Banvard spent the next decade in relative prosperity and modest continued artistic success. Indeed, his artistic horizons broadened each year. In 1861, he provided the Union military with his own hydrographic charts of the Mississippi River. General Fremont wrote back personally to thank him for his expert assistance. That same year, Banvard provided the illustration for the first successful chromolithograph in America. The process was unique in duplicating both the color and the canvas texture of the original illustration, which Banvard had titled 'The Orison.' The result was a tremendous success, and helped assure his continued reputation as a technically innovative artist.

Banvard then turned his attention back to his first love: the theater. 'Amasis, Or, The Last of the Pharaohs' was a massively staged 'biblical-historical' drama that ran in Boston in 1864. Banvard had both written the play and painted its enormous scenery, and was gratified by its warm reception among critics. It seemed to him that there was nothing that he could not succeed at.

Even as Banvard displayed his Egyptian artifacts to guests at Glenada, the role of museum was changing rapidly in America. By 1780, the 'cabinet of wonder' kept by wealthy dilettantes had evolved into the first recognizable museum, operated by Charles Peale in Philadelphia. Joined by John Scudder's American Museum in New York, these museums focused on educational lectures and displays – illustrations and examples of unusual natural objects, as well as the occasional memento.

This all changed when P. T. Barnum bought out Scudder's American Museum in 1841. Barnum brought in a carnivalesque element of equal parts spectacle and half-believable fraud – a potent and highly salable concoction of freak shows, dioramas, magic acts, natural history, and the sheer unrepentant bravado of acts like Tom Thumb and 'George Washington's nursemaid.' Barnum was not an infallible entrepreneur, but he was the shrewdest showman that the country had ever produced. Imitators attracted by Barnum's success soon found themselves crushed under the weight of Barnum's one-upmanship and his endless capacity for hyperbolic advertising.

By 1866, Barnum's total ticket sales were greater than the country's population of thirty-five million. John Banvard, with a castle full of actual artifacts, could scarcely ignore the fortune Barnum was making just a few miles away with objects of much more questionable provenance. Goaded by this, he paid a visit to his old sailing partner William Lillienthal. It had been over 15 years since the two had floated down the Nile, collecting the artifacts that now formed the core of Banvard's collection.

With Lillienthal's help – and a lot of investors' money – Banvard was going to take on P. T. Barnum. Their venture was precarious from the start. Aside from the daunting task of taking on America's greatest showman, Banvard was hampered by his own inexperience. Years of panoramic touring and a successful play had convinced Banvard that he could run a museum, but he had never really run a conventional business with a staff and a building to maintain. In all his years as a showman, he'd earned millions with the help of only one assistant, a secretary who he eventually fired for stealing a few dollars.

Lillienthal and Banvard financed the Banvard Museum by floating a stock offering worth $300,000. In lieu of cash, they paid contractors and artisans with shares of this stock; other shares were bought by some of the most prominent families in Manhattan. There was one problem, though; Banvard had never registered his business or its stock with the state of New York. No share certificates existed for the stock. Unbeknownst to Banvard's backers, and perhaps to Banvard himself, the shares were utterly worthless.

Flush with the money of the unwary, Banvard's Museum raced toward completion.

When the massive 40,000 square-foot building opened on June 17, 1867, it was simply the best museum in Manhattan. The famous Mississippi panorama was on stage in a central auditorium that seated 2,000 spectators, and there were a number of smaller lecture rooms and displays of Banvard's hand-picked collection of antiquities. The lecture rooms were important, as Banvard had invited in student groups for free to emphasize the family-friendly educational qualities of his museum, as opposed to Barnum's sensationalism. The museum also had one genuine crowd-pleaser built right in: ventilation. Poor auditorium ventilation was a constant complaint dogging panoramist shows, and Banvard took the initiative to install louvres and windows all the way around his auditorium.

P. T. Barnum had met a serious challenger in John Banvard. One week after Banvard's opening, Barnum ran ads in *The New York Times*, crowing that his own museum was 'THOROUGHLY

VENTILATED! COOL! Delightful!! Cool!!! Elegant, Spacious, and Airy Halls.' This was hardly true, of course; Banvard's building was far superior, and Barnum knew it. But Barnum had a grasp of advertising that not even Banvard could match. The rest of the summer was to see America's greatest showmen – and its first entertainment millionaires – locked in an economic struggle to the death.

With each stab at innovation by Banvard, Barnum would parry with inferior copies but superior advertising. Banvard had the Mississippi panorama; Barnum had a Nile panorama, probably copied from Banvard's. Banvard had the real Cardiff Man skeleton; Barnum had a fake. On and on the showmen battled throughout the summer, with the stage and the newspapers as their respective weapons of choice.

The struggle ended with shocking speed. Banvard was in far over his head; creditors were dunning him for payments, and shareholders were furious over the discovery that their stock had been worthless all along. On September 1st – scarcely ten weeks after opening – Banvard's Museum padlocked its doors shut.

Banvard improvised furiously. The building reopened one month later as Banvard's Grand Opera House and Museum. Productions dropped in and out over the next six months – first a leering dance production, then adaptations of *Our Mutual Friend* and *Uncle Tom's Cabin*. None were successful. Unable to make anything work, Banvard finally leased out the building to a group of promoters that included – perhaps to his chagrin – P. T. Barnum.

Banvard spent the next decade with the barest grasp on solvency, and then only by quietly appropriating lease money that should have been going to shareholders and other creditors. He and his wife lived virtually alone on their rambling sixty-acre estate; they were down to one servant for the whole property. After his shoddy treatment of the museum backers, no New Yorker would want to invest in a Banvard enterprise now; he wrote two more plays only to find that no producer would take them.

If his financial ethics were suspect, Banvard's artistic integrity was suffering even more. The innovator had been reduced to plagiarism: first in his history book, *The Court and Times of George IV, King of England* (1875), which was lifted from a book written in 1831; and then again the next year, when he finally managed to write a play that opened in his old museum, now named the New Broadway Theatre. *Corrina, A Tale of Sicily* was not only plagiarized, but it was plagiarized from a living and thoroughly annoyed playwright.

Humiliated and surrounded by creditors, Banvard desperately sought a buyer for his theater. P. T. Barnum, when approached, sent a crushing reply back to his old rival: 'No sir!! I would not take the Broadway Theatre as a gift if I had to run it.' When Banvard finally did unload his decrepit building in 1879, he had to watch its new owners achieve exactly where he had failed. As Daly's Theatre, the building thrived for decades before finally being torn down in 1920.

Banvard's castle was not to be as long-lived as his museum. Banvard and his wife clung to Glenada for as long as they could, but by 1883, their deep entanglement in bankruptcy forced them to sell it off. It eventually fell to the wrecking ball, and virtually all their other possessions were sold off to meet the demands of creditors. But the Mississippi panorama was spared from the auction block – now worn from nearly 40 years of use, and nearly forgotten by the public, perhaps it was judged to be worthless anyway.

Banvard and his wife were now both well into their sixties, and with scarcely any money to their name. They packed their few remaining belongings and quietly left New York. The only place left for them was what Banvard had left so long ago: the lonely, far-off American frontier. He was returning as he had left, a poor and forgotten painter.

It was a deeply humbled and aged John Banvard that arrived in the frontier town of Watertown, in present-day South Dakota. He and his wife, the recent proprietors of a castle, had been reduced to living in a spare room of their son's house. Eugene Banvard was an attorney with some interest in local public works and construction projects, and occasionally the elder Banvard renewed his energies of yore by pitching in with his son on these projects.

For the most part, though, Banvard retreated into his writing. He was to write about 1,700 poems in his life – as many as Emily Dickinson – and like her, he only ever published a few of them. Unlike the more dubious plays and histories that he had 'authored,' his poems appear to be original to Banvard, and sincere if not particularly innovative efforts. Taking up the pen name of 'Peter Pallette,' Banvard wrote hundreds of poems during his years in Watertown, becoming the state's first published poet. One of Banvard's more sustained efforts, published in Boston back in 1880 as 'The Origin of the Building of Solomon's Temple,' centered on the biblical brothers Ornan and Araunah. It opens with a standard Romantic invocation:

I'll tell you a legend, a beautiful legend;
A legend an Arab related to me.
We sat by a fountain beneath a high mountain,
A mountain that soar'd by the Syrian sea:
When a harvest moon shewed its silvery sheen,
Which called into thought the Arabian's theme.

The book's epilogue descends into a miscellany of details about English church building, Egyptian obelisks, and loony speculations about Masonic oaths, a subject of apparently inexhaustible interest to the author.

On a more practical note, Banvard also authored a pocket-sized treatise on *Banvard's System of Short-Hand* (1886) – one of the first books published in the Dakota Territories. He claimed it could it be learned within a week, and that he had been using it for years, keeping in practice by surreptitiously transcribing conversations on buses and ferry boats: 'The author acquired the knowledge of shorthand precisely in this manner when he was but a youth . . . He has many of these little volumes now in his possession and they have become quite of value as forming a daily journal of these times.'

For transcription practice, Banvard included his own poems and pithy maxims, such as 'He jests at scars who never felt a wound.' Banvard had felt some wounds himself of late, and more were to come before his strange journey came to an end. But that same year, now into his seventies, he locked himself in his studio one last time, ready to produce a final masterpiece.

Dioramas and panoramas were no longer a novelty by 1886, and Edison's miraculous work in motion pictures was just over the horizon. If the art form hadn't aged well, neither had its greatest proponent – along with the usual infirmities of age and his ruined finances, Banvard's eyesight had worsened with age. His eyes had never been terribly strong since his childhood laboratory mishap. Still, even now he could muster a certain heartiness. 'In his mature years his appearance was like that of many Mississippi River pilots,' said one contemporary. 'A thickset figure, with heavy features, bushy dark hair, and rounded beard.'

Nonetheless, Banvard's family was uneasy with his notions of taking the show on the road one last time, as his daughter later recalled: 'My mother and the older members of the family were quite averse to his giving [the performance], as they felt his health was too impaired for him to attempt it.' If the older members of the family were against it, one can imagine the solace Banvard took in his grandchildren, who were only now seeing the family patriarch revive the art that had made him rich and famous long before they were even born.

For his diorama, Banvard had chosen a cataclysm still in the living memory of many Americans: 'The Burning of Columbia.' Most of the capital city of South Carolina was burnt to the ground by General Sherman's troops in a day-long conflagration on February 17, 1865. Banvard's rendition of it was by all accounts a magnificent performance. Even more impressively – in an echo of his humble beginnings – Banvard ran the diorama and a massed array of special effects as a one-man show. As one audience member recalled:

Painted canvases, ropes, windlasses, kerosene drums, lycopodium, screens, shutters, and revolving drums were his accessories. Marching battalions, dashing cavalry, roaring cannon, blazing buildings, the rattle of musketry, and the din of battle were the products, resulting in a final spectacle beyond belief, when one considers it was a one man show.

I have read of the millions expended in the production of a single modern movie, but when I remember what John Banvard did and accomplished in a spectacular illusion in Watertown, Dakota Territory, more than fifty years ago for an outlay of ten dollars, I am rather ashamed of Hollywood.

For all the spectacle, though, Banvard's day had long passed. Dakota was simply too sparsely populated to support much of a traveling show, and the artist found himself packing away the scrims, drums, and screens for one last time, never to be used again.

A few years later, in 1889, his wife Elizabeth died. They had been married for over 40 years; as is so often the case in a long companionship, the spouse followed not long afterward. A visitor to his Watertown grave will scarcely guess from the simple inscription that this had once been the world's richest artist:

JOHN BANVARD
Born
Nov. 15, 1815
Died
May 16, 1891

As word of his death reached newspapers back east and in Europe, editors and columnists expressed amazement: How could this millionaire have died penniless on a lonely frontier? Had they sought to get any answers from his family, though, they would have come up empty-handed. Unable to pay their bills, the Banvards all fled town after the funeral.

In their haste to evacuate their house on 513 Northwest 2nd St, they had left much behind, and an auction was held by creditors. Among John Banvard's remaining possessions was a yellowed scrap of paper listing his unpaid $15.51 bill for his own father's funeral service in 1831. Young John had spent his life haunted by his father's lonely death and humiliating bankruptcy. Sixty years later, still clutching the shameful funeral bill, he had met the same fate.

So where are his paintings?

His early panoramas of the Inferno, Venice, and Jerusalem were lost in a steamboat wreck in the 1840s. A few small panels are scattered across South Dakota; The Robinson Museum, in Pierre, has three. Two more are in Watertown; the Kampeska Heritage Museum has 'River Scene with Glenada,' while the Mellette Memorial Association has a hint of the 'Three-Mile Painting' with 'Riverboats in Fog.'

And what of the paintings that made his fame and fortune, the ingenious moving panoramas? One grandson, interviewed many years later, remembered playing on the massive rolls when he was little. But after the elder Banvard's death, they lay abandoned to the auctioneer. As Edith Banvard recalled in a 1948 interview: 'I understood that part of it was used for scenery ... in the Watertown opera house.' From there, she conjectured, the rolls may have been cut into pieces and sold as theater backdrops. Worn from decades of touring, and torn from their original context as moving pictures, they might have seemed little more than old rags. Not surprisingly, no record is known of what theaters might have done with them.

One persistent account, however, holds that Banvard's masterpieces never left Watertown at all. They were shredded to insulate local houses – and there, imprisoned in the walls, they remain to this day.

The Man From Out Of Town

SHEILA HETI

Since his first day in town the man had been looking for a nice girl to spend good times with, but none of the girls would have him. He wasn't sure why but suspected it had to do with his status. The waitress who served him corroborated this when she called him a bum, even though he was not living on the street and he had two suits.

Not until his roommate found out the cause of his sorrowful mood did he call up a girl he had known from the park, and invite her over for a dinner of pork and mashed potatoes with nutmeg.

It was her high ass that mysteriously lifted itself up to her waist that caused the man to see what a nice girl she was, and how pleasant she could be to spend good times with. She also had a sweet smile and some pretty funny things to say, and whenever she laughed the sun would stream a last dying ray in through the window. Noticing all this, the roommate kept playing good tunes, and by the end of the night the man and the girl were dancing together and she was laughing into his shoulder; a good sign.

In the morning she sat on his couch in a denim shirt and yesterday's underwear, and her voice seemed deep when she said, 'I'm going to be late for work.'

'It's Sunday though.'

'Still,' and she looked out the window and the greyness of the day convinced her. Wandering into his room she found her suit and zipped it up, and left his apartment with a good-bye shrug. Following her with his eyes as she walked to the bus stop, the man knew that this was not the girl who would be agreeable to spending good times with him. It was not easy to explain.

In the afternoon he walked down the boardwalk, drinking warm soda from a red-and-white cup that was waxy on the outside and was gradually melting, when a man with a dog caught up to him and threw his arm around his shoulder and asked in a jaunty voice what the matter was.

The man who was new in town was startled because he did not expect city people to care about each other, but he answered saying, 'It's that the woman who came over last night seemed to really like me but she left this morning without making plans to see me again.'

'I know what it's like. I thought it must be women that were troubling you because of that troubling look on your face. You ought to come to where I work tonight, because there are plenty of pretty ladies where I work.'

'Where do you work?'

'A dance club.'

'Oh no,' said the man who was from a small town. 'I don't mean that I want to pay a woman to take off her clothes.'

That night as he sat in a booth by the wall, a tall voluptuous woman with red hair came and sat across from him. When she spoke her voice was tiny and girlish, and when he spoke back her eyes lit up, knowing a good man when she saw one. If he found her interest in him any consolation he did not show it, and continued to order drinks which cost seven dollars.

'Let me put that next one on my tab,' she said, and adjusted her body in such a way that her breasts raised themselves parallel to the table. The man did not fail to notice this.

'Would you like to come home with me tonight?' he asked.

Growing suspicious, she said, 'I thought you were a different sort of man, that's what Henry told me, and now you ask me the question everyone asks.'

'I'm so ashamed,' he responded sincerely. 'I didn't mean it that way, but I don't like being alone, and you seem like a kind woman who would be a pleasure to spend good times with, even just talking.'

She found this genuine enough, and was touched that there was nothing of the brute in him; perhaps Henry was right. Even her so-called sisters, whom she hastily consulted in the back room, gave approving nods when they saw his modest eyes looking mainly at the fixtures.

The apartment was sticky because of the heat, and it wasn't long before they were lying in their underwear on his bed, and he was telling how he had become a widower so young, which was a lie for he had never been married, or even in a real relationship twice. Since she had noticed him not noticing the dancers when she returned to the back room to get her regular clothes, she believed what he was saying; every word of it. There were simple ways some ladies had of telling a good guy from a bad, and her way was as stupid as any.

Quite soon she found herself giving him head, and was trying her hardest because he seemed so patently not to be enjoying it. When he laid her he did so with great care and the air of a depressive, which made her trust him all the more.

It wasn't three weeks before they decided to live in a new apartment together, which caused tension between the man and his roommate until a replacement was found.

Their life together was a gentle life of great delicacy and consideration, as they both felt sorry for the man, and he was also harbouring a great confusion at his sorrowful mood not being alleviated by the presence of this woman with the red hair.

Since in their hearts they both expected her to become pregnant, when she eventually did it was no great surprise. He merely stroked her arm as she lay at the base of the bed and cried about money. 'I must go live with my sister,' she told him. There was no part of her that was enthusiastic about living the life of a dancer with a young child. 'Do you want to come with me?' she asked.

He grew anxious at this request and took a long stroll. Her sister lived in a small town with a husband and three children, and the man who was from out of town had deliberately moved out of his town and had barely been in the city a year. When he thought about it now, the woman with the red hair hadn't been so difficult a catch; not so terribly hard to find a girl to spend good times with in a metropolis; he didn't know why he hadn't thought of it sooner. He declined and she ran away with her bags and her tears.

But it wasn't so easy the second time around to get a nice girl, and the man soon grew lonely. After two months he was forced to take in a roommate, but the only one he could find was smelly and young with a belly that hung out without discretion. This situation made the man even more lonesome than before, and one day at one o'clock in the afternoon he decided to visit the woman with the red hair. Walking past a fountain on his way to the train station, he passed a girl of late teenage years who was blonde and who he supposed would like the companionship of a man like him. Dragging her into the park he tore out two-thirds of her hair.

Do Not Disturb

A. M. HOMES

My wife, the doctor, is not well. In the end she could be dead. It started suddenly, on a country weekend, a movie with friends, a pizza, and then pain.

'I liked the part where he lunged at the woman with a knife,' Eric says.

'She deserved it,' Enid says.

'Excuse me,' my wife says, getting up from the table.

A few minutes later I find her doubled over on the sidewalk. 'Something is ripping me from the inside out.'

'Should I get the check?' She looks at me like I am an idiot.

'My wife is not well,' I announce, returning to the table. 'We have to go.'

'What do you mean – is she all right?'

Eric and Enid hurry out while I wait for the check. They drive us home. As I open the front door, my wife pushes past me and goes running for the bathroom. Eric, Enid and I stand in the living room, waiting.

'Are you all right in there?' I call out.

'No,' she says.

'Maybe she should go to the hospital,' Enid says.

'Doctors don't go to the hospital,' I say.

She is a specialist in emergency medicine. All day she is at the hospital putting the pieces back together and then she comes home to me. I am not the one who takes care. I am the one who is always on the verge.

'Call us if you need us,' Eric and Enid say, leaving.

She lies on the bathroom floor, her cheek against the white tile. 'I keep thinking it will pass.'

I tuck the bath mat under her head and sneak away. From the kitchen I call a doctor friend. I stand in the dark, whispering, 'She's just lying there on the floor, what do I do?'

'Don't do anything,' the doctor says, half-insulted by the thought that there is something to do. 'Observe her. Either it will go away, or something more will happen. You watch and you wait.'

Watch and wait. I'm thinking about our relationship. We haven't been getting along. The situation has become oxygenless and addictive, a suffocating annihilation, each staying to see how far it will go.

I sit on the edge of the tub, looking at her. 'I'm worried.'

'Don't worry,' she says. 'And don't just sit there staring.'

Earlier in the afternoon we were fighting, I don't remember about what. I only know – I called her a bitch.

'I was a bitch before I met you and I'll be a bitch long after you're gone. Surprise me,' she said, 'tell me something new.'

I wanted to say I'm leaving. I wanted to say, I know you think I never will and that's why you treat me like you do. But I'm going. I wanted to get in the car, drive off and call it a day.

The fight ended with the clock. She glanced at it. 'It's six thirty, we're meeting Eric and Enid at seven; put on a clean shirt.'

She is lying on the bathroom floor, the print of the bathmat making an impression on her cheek. 'Are you comfortable?' I ask.

She looks surprised, as though she's just realized she's on the floor.

'Help me,' she says, struggling to get up.

Her lips are white and thin.

'Bring me a trash can, a plastic bag, a thermometer, some Tylenol and a glass of water.'

'Are you going to throw up?'

'I want to be prepared,' she says.

We are always prepared. The ongoing potential for things to go wrong is our bond, a fascination with crisis, with control. We have flare guns and fire extinguishers, walkie talkies, a rubber raft, a small generator, a hundred batteries in assorted shapes and sizes, a thousand bucks in dollar bills, enough toilet paper and bottled water to get us through six months. When we travel we have smoke hoods in our carry-on bags, protein bars, water purification tablets and a king-sized bag of M&Ms.

She slips the digital thermometer under her tongue; the numbers move up the scale – each beep is a tenth of a degree.

'A hundred and one point four,' I announce.

'I have a fever?' she says in disbelief.

'I wish things between us weren't so bad.'

'It not as bad as you think,' she says. 'Expect less and you won't be disappointed.'

We try to sleep; she is hot, she is cold, she is mumbling something about having 'a surgical belly,' something about 'guarding and rebound.' I don't know if she's talking about herself or the NBA.

'This is incredible,' she sits bolt upright and folds over again, writhing. 'Something is struggling inside me. It's like one of those alien movies, like I'm going to burst open and something is going to spew out, like I'm erupting.' She pauses, takes a breath. 'And then it stops. Who would ever have thought this would happen to me – and on a Saturday night?'

'Is it your appendix?'

'That's the one thought I have, but I'm not sure. I don't have the classic symptoms. I don't have anorexia or diarrhea. When I was eating that pizza, I was hungry.'

'Is it an ovary? Women have lots of ovaries.'

'Women have two ovaries,' she says. 'It did occur to me that it could be Mittelschmertz.'

'Mittelschmertz?'

'The launching of the egg, the middle of the cycle.'

At five in the morning her temperature is one hundred and three. She is alternately sweating and shivering.

'Should I drive you back to the city or to the hospital out here?'

'I don't want to be the doctor who goes to the ER with gas.'

'Fine.'

I'm dressing myself, packing, thinking of what I'll need: cell phone, note book, pen, something to read, something to eat, wallet, insurance card.

We are in the car, hurrying. There's an urgency to the situation, the unmistakable sense that something bad is happening. I am driving seventy miles an hour.

'I think I'm dying,' she says.

I pull up to the emergency entrance and half-carry her in, leaving the car doors open, the engine running; I have the impulse to drop her off and walk away.

The emergency room is empty. There is a bell on the check-in desk. I ring it twice.

A woman appears. 'Can I help you?'

'My wife is not well,' I say. 'She's a doctor.'

The woman sits at her computer. She takes my wife's name and number. She takes her insurance card and then her temperature and blood pressure. 'Are you in a lot of pain?'

'Yes,' my wife says.

Within minutes a doctor is there, pressing on my wife. 'It's got to come out,' he says.

'What?' I ask.

'Appendix. Do you want some Demerol?'

She shakes her head. 'I'm working tomorrow and I'm on call.'

'What kind of doctor are you?'

'Emergency medicine.'

In the cubicle next to her, someone vomits.

The nurse comes to take blood. 'They called Barry Manilow, he's a very good surgeon.' She ties off my wife's arm. 'We call him Barry Manilow because he looks like Barry Manilow.'

'I want to do right by you,' Barry Manilow says, as he's feeling my wife's belly. 'I'm not sure it's your appendix, not sure it's your gall bladder either. I'm going to call the radiologist and let him scan it. How's that sound?'

She nods.

I take the surgeon aside. 'Should she be staying here? Is this the place to do this?'

'It's not a kidney transplant,' he says.

The nurse brings me a cold drink. She offers me a chair. I sit close to the gurney where my wife lies. 'Do you want me to get you out of here? I could hire a car and have us driven to the city. I could have you MedEvaced home.'

'I don't want to go anywhere,' she says.

Back in the cubicle, Barry Manilow is talking to her. 'It's

not your appendix. It's your ovary. It's a hemorhagic cyst; you're bleeding and your hematicrit is falling. We have to operate. I've called a gynecologist and the anesthesiologist – I'm just waiting for them to arrive. We're going to take you upstairs very soon.'

'Just do it,' she says.

I stop Barry Manilow in the hall. 'Can you try and save the ovary? She very much wants to have children. It's just something she hasn't gotten around to yet – first she had her career, then me, and now this.'

'We'll do everything we can,' he says, disappearing through the door marked Authorized Personnel Only.

I am the only one in the surgical waiting room, flipping through copies of *Field and Stream*, *Highlights for Children*, a pamphlet on colon cancer. Less than an hour later, Barry Manilow comes to find me. 'We saved the ovary. We took out something the size of a lemon.'

'The size of a lemon?'

He makes a fist and holds it up. 'A lemon,' he says. 'It looked a little funny. We sent it to Pathology.' He shrugs.

A lemon, a bleeding lemon, like a blood orange, a lemon souring in her. Why is fruit used as the universal medical measurement?

'She should be upstairs in about an hour.'

When I get to her room she is asleep. A tube poking out from under the covers drains urine into a bag. She is hooked up to oxygen and an IV.

I put my hand on her forehead. Her eyes open.

'A little fresh air,' she says, pulling at the oxygen tube. 'I always wondered what all this felt like.'

She has a morphine drip, the kind she can control herself.

She keeps the clicker in hand. She never pushes the button.

I feed her ice chips and climb into the bed next to her. In the middle of the night I go home. In the morning she calls, waking me up.

'Flowers have been arriving like crazy,' she says, 'from the hospital, from the ER, from the clinic.'

Doctors are like firemen; when one of their own is down they go crazy.

'They took the catheter out, I'm sitting up in a chair. I already had some juice and took myself to the bathroom,' she says, proudly. 'They couldn't be nicer. But of course, I'm a very good patient.'

I interrupt her. 'Do you want anything from the house?'

'Clean socks, a pair of sweat pants, my hair brush, some toothpaste, my face soap, a radio, maybe a can of Diet Coke.'

'You're only going to be there a couple of days.'

'You asked if I needed anything. Don't forget to feed the dog.'

Five minutes later she calls back – crying. 'Guess what, I have ovarian cancer.'

I run out the door. When I get there the room is empty. I'm expecting a big romantic crying scene, expecting her to cling to me, to tell me how much she loves me, how she's sorry we've been having such a hard time, how much she needs me, wants me, now more than ever. The bed is empty. For a moment I think she's died, jumped out the window, escaped.

In the bathroom, the toilet flushes. 'I want to go home,' she says, stepping out, fully dressed.

'Do you want to take the flowers?'

'They're mine, aren't they? Do you think all the nurses know I have cancer? I don't want anyone to know.'

The nurse comes with a wheelchair; she takes us down to the lobby. 'Good luck,' she says, loading the flowers into the car.

'She knows,' my wife says.

We're on the Long Island Expressway. I am dialing and driving. I call my wife's doctor in New York.

'She has to see Kibbowitz immediately,' the doctor says.

'Do you think I'll lose my ovary?'

She will lose everything. Instinctively I know that.

We are home. She is on the bed with the dog on her lap. She peaks beneath the gauze; her incision is crooked, the lack of precision an incredible insult. 'Do you think they can fix it?' she asks.

In the morning we go to Kibbowitz. She is again on a table, her feet in the stirrups, in launch position, waiting. Before the doctor arrives she is interviewed and examined by seven medical students. I hate them. I hate them for talking to her, for touching her, for wasting her time. I hate Kibbowitz for keeping her on the table for more than an hour, waiting.

She is angry with me for being annoyed. 'They're just doing their job.'

Kibbowitz arrives. He is enormous, like a hockey player, a brute and a bully. I can tell immediately that she likes him. She will do anything he says.

'Scooch down a little closer to me,' he says settling himself on a stool between her legs. She lifts her ass and slides down. He examines her. He peeks under the gauze. 'Crooked,' he says. 'Get dressed and meet me in my office.'

'I want a number,' she says. 'A survival rate.'

'I don't deal in numbers,' he says.

'I need a number.'

He shrugs. 'How's seventy percent.'

'Seventy percent what?'

'Seventy percent live five years.'

'And then what?' I ask.

'And then some don't,' he says.

'What has to come out?' she asks.

'What do you want to keep?'

'I wanted to have a child.'

This is a delicate negotiation; they talk parts. 'I could take just the one ovary,' he says. 'And then after the chemo you could try and get pregnant and then after you had a child we could go in and get the rest.'

'Can you really get pregnant after chemo?' I ask.

The doctor shrugs. 'Miracles happen all the time,' he says. 'The problem is you can't raise a child if you're dead. You don't have to decide now, let me know in a day or two. Meanwhile I'm going to book the operating room for Friday morning. Nice meeting you,' he says, shaking my hand.

'I want to have a baby,' she says.

'I want to have you,' I say.

Beyond that I say nothing. Whatever I say she will do the opposite. We are at that point – spite, blame and fault. I don't want to be held responsible.

She opens the door of the consulting room. 'Doctor,' she shouts, hurrying down the hall after him, clutching her belly, her incision, her wound. 'Take it,' she screams. 'Take it all the hell out.'

He is standing outside another examining room, chart in hand.

He nods. 'We'll take it though your vagina. We'll take the ovaries, the uterus, cervix, omentum and your appendix if they didn't already get it in Southampton. And then we'll put a port in your neck and sign you up for chemotherapy, eight rounds should do it.'

She nods.

'See you Friday.'

We leave. I'm holding her hand, holding her pocketbook on my shoulder trying to be as good as anyone can be. She is growling and scratching; it's like taking a cat to the vet.

'Why don't they just say eviscerate? Why don't they just come out and say on Friday at nine we're going to eviscerate you – be ready.'

'Do you want a little lunch?' I ask as we are walking down the street. 'Some soup? There's a lovely restaurant near here.'

She looks flushed. I put my hand to her forehead. She's burning up. 'You have a fever. Did you mention that to the doctor?'

'It's not relevant.'

Later when we are home, I ask. 'Do you remember our third date? Do you remember asking me – how would you kill yourself if you had to do it with bare hands? I said I would break my nose and shove it up into my brain and you said you would reach up with your bare hands and rip your uterus out through your vagina and throw it across the room.'

'What's your point?'

'No point, I just suddenly remembered it. Isn't Kibbowitz taking your uterus out through your vagina?'

'I doubt he's going to throw it across the room,' she says. There is a pause. 'You don't have to stay with me now that I have cancer. I don't need you. I don't need anyone. I don't need anything.'

'If I left, I wouldn't be leaving because you have cancer.

But I would look like an ass, everyone would think I couldn't take it.'

'I would make sure they knew it was me, that I was a monster, a cold steely monster, that I drove you away.'

'They wouldn't believe you.'

She suddenly farts and runs embarrassed into the bathroom – as though this is the first time she's farted in her life. 'My life is ruined,' she yells, slamming the door.

'Farting is the least of it,' I say.

When she comes out she is calmer. She crawls into bed next to me, wrung out, shivering.

I hold her. 'Do you want to make love?'

'You mean one last time before I'm not a woman, before I'm a dried old husk?'

Instead of fucking we fight. It's the same sort of thing, dramatic, draining. When we're done, I roll over and sleep in a tight knot on my side of the bed.

'Surgical menopause,' she says. 'That sounds so final.'

I turn toward her. She runs her hand over her pubic hair. 'Do you think they'll shave me?'

I'm not going to be able to leave the woman with cancer. I'm not the kind of person who leaves the woman with cancer, but I don't know what you do when the woman with cancer is a bitch. Do you hope that the cancer prompts the woman to reevaluate herself, to take it as an opportunity, a signal for change? As far as she's concerned there is no such thing as the mind/body connection, there is science and there is law. There is fact and everything else is bullshit.

Friday morning, while she's in the hospital registration area waiting for her number to be called, she makes another list out loud: 'My will is in the top left drawer of the dresser. If anything goes wrong pull the plug. No heroic measures. I want to be cremated. Donate my organs. Give it away, all of it, every last drop.' She stops. 'I guess no one will want me now that I'm contaminated.' She says the word contaminated, filled with disgust, disappointment, as though she has soiled herself.

It is nearly eight p.m. when Kibbowitz comes out to tell me he's done. 'Everything was stuck together like macaroni and cheese. It took longer than I expected. I found some in the fallopian tube and some on the wall of her abdomen. We cleaned everything out.'

She is wheeled back to her room, sad, agitated, angry.

'Why didn't you come and see me?' she asks, accusitorily.

'I was right there the whole time, on the other side of the door waiting for word.'

She acts as though she doesn't believe me, as though I went off and screwed a secretary from the patient services office while she was on the table.

'How're you feeling?'

'As though I've taken a trip to another country and my suitcases are lost.'

She is writhing. I adjust her pillow, the position of the bed. 'What hurts?'

'What doesn't hurt? Everything hurts. Breathing hurts.'

Because she is a doctor, because she did her residency at this hospital, they give me a small folding cot to set up in the corner of the room. Bending to unfold it, something happens in my back, a hot searing pain spreads across and down. I lower myself to the floor, grabbing the blanket as I go.

Luckily, she is sleeping.

The nurse coming in to check her vital signs sees me. 'Are you in trouble?' she asks.

'It's happened before,' I say. 'I'll just lie here and see what happens.'

She brings me a pillow and covers me with the blanket.

Eric and Enid arrive. My wife is asleep and I am still on the floor. Eric stands over me.

'We're sorry,' Eric whispers. 'We didn't get your message until today. We were at Enid's parents – upstate.'

'It's shocking, it's sudden, it's so out of the blue.' Enid moves to look at my wife. 'She looks like she's in a really bad mood, her brow is furrowed. Is she in pain?'

'I assume so.'

'If there's anything we can do, let us know,' Eric says.

'Actually, could you walk the dog?' I pull the keys out of my pocket and hold them in the air. 'He's been home alone all day and all night.'

'Walk the dog, I think we can do that,' Eric says, looking at Enid for confirmation.

'We'll check on you in the morning,' Enid says.

'Before you go; there's a bottle of Percoset in her purse – give me two.'

During the night she wakes up. 'Where are you?' she asks.

'I'm right here.'

She is sufficiently drugged that she doesn't ask for details. At around six she opens her eyes and sees me on the floor.

'Your back?'

'Yep.'

'Cancer beats back,' she says and falls back to sleep.

When the cleaning man comes with the damp mop, I prise myself off the floor. I'm fine as long as I'm standing.

'You're walking like you have a rod up your ass,' my wife says.

'Is there anything I can do for you?' I ask, trying to be solicitous.

'Can you have cancer for me?'

The pain management team arrives to check on my wife's level of comfort.

'On a scale of one to ten how do you feel?' the pain fellow asks.

'Five,' my wife says.

'She lies,' I say.

'Are you lying?'

'How can you tell?'

The specialist arrives. 'I know you,' he says, seeing my wife in the bed. 'We went to school together.'

My wife tries to smile.

'You were the smartest one in the class and now look,' he reads my wife's chart. 'Ovarian cancer and you, that's horrible.'

My wife is sitting up high in her hospital bed, puking her guts into a metal bucket, like a poisoned pet monkey. She is throwing up bright green like an alien, like nothing anyone has seen before. Ted, her boss, stares at her, mesmerized.

The room is filled with people – people I don't know, medical people, people she went to school with, people she did her residency with, a man whose fingers she sewed back on, relatives I've not met. I don't understand why they don't excuse themselves, why they don't step out of the room. They're all watching her like they've never seen anyone throw up before – riveted.

She is not sleeping. She is not eating. She is not getting up and walking around. She is afraid to leave her bed, afraid to leave her bucket.

I make a sign for the door. I borrow a black magic marker from the charge nurse and print in large black letters: Do Not Disturb.

They push the door open. They come bearing gifts, flowers, food, books. 'I saw the sign, I assumed it was for someone else.'

I am wiping green spittle from her lips.

'Do you want me to get rid of everyone?' I ask.

I want to get rid of everyone. The idea that these people have some claim to her, some right to entertain, distract, bother her more than me, drives me up the wall. 'Should I tell them to go?'

She shakes her head. 'Just the flowers, the flowers nauseate me.'

An hour later, I empty the bucket again. The room remains overcrowded. I am on my knees by the side of her hospital bed, whispering 'I'm leaving.'

'Are you coming back?' she whispers.

'No.'

She looks at me strangely. 'Where are you going?'

'Away.'

'Bring me a Diet Coke.'

She has missed the point.

It is heartbreaking seeing her in a stained gown, in the middle of a bed, unable to tell everyone to go home, unable to turn it off. Her pager is clipped to her hospital gown, several times it goes off. She returns the calls. She always returns the calls. I imagine her saying, 'What the hell are you bothering me for – I'm busy, I'm having cancer.'

Later, I'm on the edge of the bed, looking at her. She is increasingly beautiful, more vulnerable, female.

'Honey?'

'What?' Her intonation is like a pissy caged bird – cawww. 'What? What are you looking at? What do you want?' Cawww.

'Nothing.'

I am washing her with a cool washcloth.

'You're tickling me,' she complains.

'Make sure you tell her you still find her attractive,' a man in the hall tells me. 'Husbands of women who have mastectomies need to keep reminding their wives that they are beautiful.'

'She had a hysterectomy,' I say.

'Same thing.'

Two days later, they remove the packing. I am in the room when the resident comes with long tweezers like tongs and pulls yards of material from her vagina, wads of cotton, gauze, stained battlefield red. It's like a magic trick gone awry, one of those jokes about how many people you can fit in a telephone booth; more and more keeps coming out.

'Is there anything left in there?' she asks.

The resident shakes his head. 'Your vagina now just comes to a stop, it's a stump, an unconnected sleeve. Don't be surprised if you bleed, if you pop a stitch or two.' He checks her chart and signs her out. 'Kibbowitz has you on pelvic rest for six weeks.'

'Pelvic rest?' I ask.

'No fucking,' she says.

Not a problem.

Home. She watches forty-eight hours of Holocaust films on cable TV. Although she claims to compartmentalize everything, suddenly she identifies with the bald, starving, prisoners of war. She sees herself as a victim. She points to the naked corpse of a woman, 'That's me,' she says. 'That's exactly how I feel.'

'She's dead,' I say.

'Exactly.'

Her notorious vigilance is gone. As I'm fluffing her pillows, her billy club rolls out from under the bed. 'Put it in the closet,' she says.

'Why?' I ask, rolling it back under the bed.

'Why sleep with a billy club under the bed? Why do anything when you have cancer?'

During a break between *Schindler's List*, *Shoah*, and *The Sorrow and the Pity* she taps me, 'I'm missing my parts,' she says. 'Maybe one of those lost eggs was someone special, someone who would have cured something, someone who would have invented something wonderful. You never know who was in there. They're my lost children.'

'I'm sorry.'

'For what?' she looks at me accusingly.

'Everything.'

'Thirty-eight-year-olds don't get cancer, they get Lyme disease, maybe they have appendicitis, on rare occasions in some other parts of the world they have Siamese twins, but that's it.'

In the middle of the night she wakes up, throws the covers off, 'I can't breathe, I'm burning up. Open the window, I'm hot, I'm so hot.'

'Do you know what's happening to you?'

'What are you talking about?'

'You're having hot flashes.'

'I am not,' she says as though I've insulted her. 'They don't start so soon.'

They do.

'Get away from me, get away,' she yells. 'Just being near you makes me uncomfortable, it makes my temperature unstable.'

On Monday she starts chemotherapy.

'Will I go bald?' she asks the nurse.

'Most women buy a wig before it happens,' the nurse says, plugging her into the magic potion.

I am afraid that when she's bald I won't love her anymore. I can not imagine my wife bald.

One of the other women, her head wrapped in a red turban, leans over and whispers, 'My husband says I look like a porno star.' She winks. She has no eyebrows, no eyelashes, nothing.

We shop for a wig. She tries on every style, every shape and color. She looks like a man in drag, like it's all a horrible joke.

'Maybe my hair won't fall out?' she says.

'It's okay,' the woman in the wig shop says. 'Insurance covers it. Ask your doctor to write a prescription for a cranial prosthesis.'

'I'm a doctor,' my wife says.

The wig woman looks confused. 'It's okay,' she says, putting another wig on my wife's head.

She buys a wig. I never see it. She brings it home and immediately puts it in the closet. 'It looks like Linda Evans, like someone on *Dynasty*. I just can't do it,' she says.

Her scalp begins to tingle. Her hair hurts. 'It's like someone grabbed my hair and is pulling as hard as they can.'

'It's getting ready to go. It's like a time bomb. It ticks and then it blows.'

'What are you, a doctor? Suddenly you know everything about cancer, about menopause, about everything?'

In the morning her hair is falling out. It's all over the pillow, all over the shower floor.

'Your hair's not really falling out,' Enid says when we meet them for dinner. Enid reaches and touches her hair, sweeps her hand through it, as if to be comforting. She ends up with a hand full of hair; she has pulled my wife's hair out. She tries to put it back, she furiously pats it back in place.

'Forget that I was worried about them shaving my pubic hair, how 'bout it all just went down the drain?'

She looks like a rat, like something that's been chewed on and spit out, like something that someone tried to electrocute and failed. In four days she is eighty per cent bald.

She stands before me naked. 'Document me.'

I take pictures. I take the film to one of those special stores that has a sign in the window – we don't censor.

I give her a baseball cap to wear to work. Every day she goes to work; she will not miss a day, no matter what.

I, on the other hand, can't work. Since this happened, my work has been non-existent. I spend my day as the holder of the feelings, the keeper of sensation.

'It's not my fault,' she says. 'What the hell do you do all day while I'm at the hospital?'

Recuperate.

She wears the baseball cap for a week and then takes a razor, shaves the few scraggly hairs that remain and goes to work bald, without a hat, without a wig – starkers.

There's something aggressive about her baldness.

'How do you feel?' I ask at night when she comes home from the hospital.

'I feel nothing.'

'How can you feel nothing? What are you made of?'

'I am made of steel and wood,' she says, happily.

As we're falling asleep she tells me a story, 'It's true, it happened as I was walking into the hospital. I accidentally bumped into someone on the sidewalk. Excuse me, I said and continued on. He ran after me, "Excuse me, Excuse me. You knocked my comb out of my hand and I want you to go back and pick it up." What? We bumped into each other, I said excuse me, that will have to suffice. "You knocked it out of my hand on purpose. You're just a bald bitch. A fucking bald bitch." I wheeled around and chased him. "You fucking crazy ass," I screamed. "You fucking crazy ass," I screamed it about four times. "He's lucky I didn't fucking kill him," she says.

I am thinking she's lost her mind. I'm thinking she's lucky he didn't kill her.

She gets up and stands on the bed – naked. She strikes a pose like a body builder. 'Cancer Man,' she says, flexing her muscles, creating a new superhero. 'Cancer Man!'

Luckily she has good insurance. The bill for the surgery comes – it's itemized. They charge per part removed. Ovary $7,000, appendix $5,000. The total is $72,000 dollars. 'It's all in a day's work,' she says.

We are lying in bed. I am lying next to her, reading the paper.

'I want to go to a desert island, alone. I don't want to come back until this is finished,' she says and then looks at me. 'It will never be finished – do you know that? I'm not going to have children and I'm going to die.'

'Do you really think you're going to die?'

'Yes.'

I reach for her.

'Don't,' she says, 'Don't go looking for trouble.'

'I wasn't. I was trying to be loving.'

'I don't feel loving,' she says. 'I don't feel physically bonded to anyone right now, including myself.'

'Will we ever again?'

'I don't know.'

'You're pushing me away.'

'I'm recovering,' she says.

'It's been eighteen weeks.'

Her blood counts are low. Every night for five nights, I inject her with Nupagen to increase the white blood cells. She teaches me how to prepare the injection, how to push the needle into the muscle of her leg. Every time I inject her, I apologize.

'For what?' she asks.

'Hurting you.'

'Forget it,' she says, disposing of the needle.

She rolls far away from me in her sleep. She dreams of strange things.

'I dreamed I was with my former boyfriend and he turned into a black woman slave and she was on top of me, between my legs, a lesbian slave fantasy.'

'Could I have a hug?' I ask.

She glares at me. 'Why do you persist? Why do you keep asking me for things I can't do, things I can't give?'

'A hug?'

'I can't give you one.'

'Anyone can give a hug. I can get a hug from the doorman.'

'Then do,' she says. 'I need to be married to someone who is like a potted plant, someone who needs nothing.'

'Water?'

'Very little, someone who's like a cactus or an orchid.'

'It's like you're refusing to be human,' I tell her.

'I have no interest in being human.'

This is information I should be paying attention to. She is

telling me something and I'm not listening. I don't believe what she is saying.

I go to dinner with Eric and Enid alone.

'It's strange,' they say. 'You'd think the cancer would soften her, make her more appreciative. You'd think it would make her stop and think about what she wants to do with the rest of her life. When you ask her, what does she say?' Eric and Enid want to know.

'Nothing. She says she wants nothing, she has no needs or desires. She says she has nothing to give.'

Eric and Enid shake their heads. 'What are you going to do?'

I shrug. None of this is new, none of this is just because she has cancer – that's important to keep in mind, this is exactly the way she always was, only more so.

A few days later a woman calls; she and her husband are people we see occasionally.

'Hi, how are you, how's Tom?' I ask.

'He's a fucking asshole,' she says. 'Haven't you heard? He left me.'

'When?'

'About two weeks ago. I thought you would have known.'

'I'm a little out of it.'

'Anyway, I'm calling to see if you'd like to have lunch.'

'Lunch, sure. Lunch would be good.'

At lunch she is a little flirty, which is fine, it's nice actually, it's been a long time since someone flirted with me. In the end, when we're having coffee, she spills the beans, 'So I guess, you're wondering why I called you?'

'I guess,' I say, although I'm perfectly pleased to be having lunch, to be listening to someone else's troubles.

'I heard your wife was sick, I figured you're not getting a lot of sex and I thought we could have an affair.'

I don't know which part is worse, the complete lack of seduction, the fact that she mentions my wife not being well, the idea that my wife's illness would make me want to sleep with her, her stun-gun bluntness – it's all too much.

'What do you think? Am I repulsive? Thoroughly disgusting? Is it the craziest thing you ever heard?'

'I'm very busy,' I say, not knowing what to say, not wanting to be offensive, or seem to have taken offense. 'I'm just very busy.'

My wife comes home from work. 'Someone came in today – he reminded me of you.'

'What was his problem?'

'He jumped out the window.'

'Dead?'

'Yes,' she says, washing her hands in the kitchen sink.

'Was he dead when he got to you?' There's something in her tone that makes me wonder, did she kill him?

'Pretty much.'

'What part reminded you of me?'

'He was having an argument with his wife.'

'Oh?'

'Imagine her standing in the living room, in the middle of a sentence and out the window he goes. Imagine her not having a chance to finish her thought?'

'Yes, imagine, not being able to have the last word?'

'Did she try and stop him?' I ask.

'I don't know,' my wife says. 'I didn't get to read the police report. I just thought you'd find it interesting.'

'What do you want for dinner?'

'Nothing,' she says. 'I'm not hungry.'

'You have to eat something.'

'Why? I have cancer. I can do whatever I want.'

Something has to happen.

I buy tickets to Paris. 'We have to go.' I invoke the magic word, 'It's an emergency.'

'It's not like I get a day off. It's not like I come home at the end of the day and I don't have cancer. It goes everywhere with me. It doesn't matter where I am, it's still me – it's me with cancer. In Paris I'll have cancer.'

I dig out the maps, the guide books, everything we did on our last trip is marked with fluorescent highlighter. I am acting as though I believe that if we retrace our steps, if we return to a place where things were good, there will be an automatic correction, an psychic chiropractic event, which will put everything into alignment.

I gather provisions for the plane: smoke hoods, fresh water, fruit, M&Ms, magazines.

'What's the point?' she says, throwing a few things into a suitcase. 'You can do everything and think you're prepared, but you don't know what's going to happen. You don't see what's coming until it hits you in the face.'

She points at someone outside. 'See that idiot crossing the street in front of the truck, why doesn't he have cancer? He deserves to die.'

She lifts her suitcase – too heavy. She takes things out. She leaves her smoke hood on the bed. 'If the plane fills with smoke, I'm going to be so happy,' she says. 'I'm going to breathe deeply, I'm going to be the first to die.'

I stuff the smoke hood into my suitcase, along with her rain coat, her extra shoes, ace bandages for her bad ankle, reusable ice packs just in case, Vitamin C drops. I lift the suitcases, feeling like a pack animal, a sherpa.

In France, the customs people are not used to seeing bald women. They call her 'Sir.'

'Sir, you're next, Sir. Sir, please step over here, Sir.'

My wife is my husband. She loves it. She smiles. She catches my eye and strikes a subdued version of the superhero/body-builder pose, flexing. 'Cancer Man,' she says.

'And what is the purpose of your visit to France?' the inspector asks. 'Business or pleasure?'

'Reconciliation,' I say, watching her – Cancer Man.

'Business or pleasure?'

'Pleasure.'

Paris is my fantasy, my last-ditch effort to reclaim my marriage, myself, my wife.

As we're checking in to the hotel, I remind her of our previous visit – the chef cut himself, his hand was severed, she saved it and they were able to reattach it. 'You made medical history. Remember the beautiful dinner they threw in your honor.'

'It was supposed to be a vacation,' she says.

The bellman takes us to our room – there's a big basket of fruit, bottles of champagne and Evian with a note from the concierge welcoming us.

'It's not as nice as it used to be,' she says, already disappointed. She opens the Evian and drinks. Her lips curl. 'Even the water tastes bad.'

'Maybe it's you. Maybe the water is fine. Is it possible you're wrong?'

'We see things differently,' she says, meaning she's right, I'm wrong.

'Are you in an especially bad mood, or is it just the cancer?' I ask.

'Maybe it's you?' she says.

We go for a walk, across the river and down by the Louvre. There could be nothing better, nothing more perfect and yet I am suddenly hating Paris, hating it more than anything, the beauty, the fineness of it is dwarfed by her foul humor. I realize there is no saving it, no moment of reconciliation, redemption. Everything sucks. It is irredeemably awful and getting worse.

'If you're so unhappy, why don't you leave?' I ask her.

'I keep thinking you'll change.'

'If I changed anymore I can't imagine who I'd be.'

'Well if I'm such a bitch, why do you stay?'

'It's my job, it's my calling to stay with you, to soften you.'

'I absolutely do not want to be softer, I don't want to give another inch.'

'Well, I am not a leaver, I worked hard to get here, to be able to stay.'

She trips on a cobblestone, I reach for her elbow, to steady her and instead unbalance myself. She fails to catch me. I fall and recover quickly.

'Imagine how I feel,' she says. 'I'm a doctor and I can't fix it. I can't fix me, I can't fix you – what a lousy doctor.'

'I'm losing you,' I say.

'I've lost myself. Look at me – do I look like me?'

'You act like yourself.'

'I act like myself because I have to, because people are counting on me.'

'I'm counting on you.'

'Stop counting.'

All along the Tuileries there are Ferris wheels, the world's largest Ferris wheel is set up in the middle.

'Let's go,' I say, taking her hand, pulling her towards them.

'I don't like rides.'

'It's not much of a ride. It's like a carousel, only vertical. Live a little.'

She gets on. There are no seat belts, no safety bars. I say nothing. I am hoping she won't notice.

'How is it going to end?' I ask while we're waiting for the wheel to spin.

'I die in the end.'

The ride takes off, climbing, pulling us up and over. We are flying, soaring; the city unfolds. It is breathtaking and higher than I thought. And faster. There is always a moment on any ride where you think it is too fast, too high, too far, too wide, and that you will not survive.

'I have never been so unhappy in my life,' my wife says when we're near the top. 'It's not just the cancer, I was unhappy before the cancer. We were having a very hard time. We don't get along, we're a bad match. Do you believe me?'

'Yes,' I say, 'We're a really bad match. We're such a good bad match it seems impossible to let it go.'

'We're stuck,' she says.

'You bet,' I say.

'No. I mean the ride, the ride isn't moving.'

'It's not stuck, it's just stopped. It stops along the way.'

She begins to cry. 'It's all your fault. I hate you. And I still have to deal with you. Every day I have to look at you.'

'No, you don't. You don't have to deal with me if you don't want to.'

She stops crying and looks at me. 'What are you going to do, jump?'

'The rest of your life, or my life, however long or short, should not be miserable. It can't go on this way.'

'We could both kill ourselves,' she says.

'How about we separate?'

I am being more grown up than I am capable of being. I am terrified of being without her but either way, it's death. The ride lurches forward.

I came to Paris wanting to pull things together and suddenly I am desperate to be away from her, to never have this conversation again. She will be dying and we will still be fighting. I begin to panic, to feel I can't breathe. I have to get away.

'Where does it end?'

'How about we say goodbye?'

'And then what? We have opera tickets.'

I can't tell her I'm going. I have to sneak away, to tiptoe out backwards. I have to make my own arrangements.

We stop talking. We're hanging in mid-air, suspended. We have run out of things to say. When the ride circles down, the silence becomes more definitive.

I begin to make my plan. In truth, I have no idea what I am doing. All afternoon, everywhere we go, I cash travelers checks, I get cash advances, I have about five thousand dollars worth of francs stuffed in my pocket. I want to be able to leave without a trace, I want to be able to buy myself out of whatever trouble I get into. I am hysterical and giddy all at once.

We are having an early dinner on our way to the opera.

I time my break for just after the coffee comes. 'Oops,' I say, feeling my pockets, 'I forgot my opera glasses.'

'Really?' she says, 'I thought you had them when we went out.'

'They must be at the hotel. You go on ahead, I'll run back. You know I hate not being able to see.'

She takes her ticket. 'Hurry,' she says. 'I hate it when you're late.'

This is the bravest thing I have ever done. I go back to the hotel and pack my bag. I'm going to get out. I'm going to fly away. I may never come back. I will begin again, as someone else, someone who wants to live, I will be unrecognizable.

I move to lift the bag off the bed, I pull it up and my knee goes out. I start to fall but catch myself. I pull at the bag and take a step – too heavy. I'll have to go without it. I'll have to leave everything behind. I drop the bag, but still I am falling, folding, collapsing. There is pain, spreading, pouring, hot and cold, like water down my back, down my legs.

I am lying on the floor, thinking that if I stay calm, if I can just find my breath, and follow my breath, it will pass. I lie there waiting for the paralysis to recede.

I am afraid of it being over and yet she has given me no choice, she has systematically withdrawn life support: sex and conversation. The problem is that despite this, she is the one I want.

There is a knock at the door. I know it is not her, it is too soon for it to be her.

'*Entrez*,' I call out.

The maid opens the door, she holds the Do Not Disturb sign in her hand.

'Oooff,' she says, seeing me on the floor. 'Do you need the doctor?'

I am not sure if she means my wife or a doctor, a doctor other than my wife.

'No.'

She takes a towel from her cart and props it under my head, she takes a spare blanket from the closet and covers me with it. She opens the champagne and pours me a glass, tilting my head up so I can sip. She goes to her cart and gets a stack of night chocolates and sits beside me, feeding me champagne and chocolate, stroking my forehead.

The phone in the room rings; we ignore it. She refills my glass. She takes my socks off and rubs my feet. She unbuttons my shirt and rubs my chest. I am getting a little drunk. I am just beginning to relax and then there is another knock, a knock my body recognizes before I am fully awake. Everything tightens. My back pulls tighter still, any sensation below my knees drops off.

'I thought something horrible happened to you. I've been calling and calling the room, why haven't you answered? I thought you'd killed yourself.'

The maid excuses herself. She goes into the bathroom and refreshes my cool washcloth.

'What are you doing?' my wife asks.

There is nothing I can say.

'Knock off the mummy routine. What exactly are you doing? Were you trying to run away and then you chickened out? Say something.'

To talk would be to continue; for the moment I am silenced. I am a potted plant and still that is not good enough for her.

'He is paralyzed,' the maid says.

'He is not paralyzed, I am his wife, I am a doctor. I would know if there was something really wrong.'

About the Contributors

'The Ceiling'
By Kevin Brockmeier
Issue # 7
Copyright 2002
Kevin Brockmeier is the author of *City of Names*, *The Truth About Celia*, and *Things that Fall from the Sky*. He is the recipient of numerous literary awards, including an Italo Calvino short fiction award, two O'Henry Awards, and an NEA grant.

'Civilization'
By Ryan Boudinot
Issue # 14
Copyright 2004
Ryan Boudinot's stories have appeared in the *Best American Nonrequired Reading* and many journals. He lives in Seattle, Washington.

'The Kauders Case'
By Aleksandar Hemon
Issue # 8
Copyright 2002
Aleksandar Hemon is the author of the short story collection *The Question of Bruno* and the novel *Nowhere Man*. His

work has appeared in *Esquire*, *Granta*, *Ploughshares*, and *The New Yorker*.

'Notes From a Bunker Along Highway 8'
By Gabe Hudson
Issue # 9
Copyright 2002
Gabe Hudson is a PEN/Hemingway award finalist and was awarded the Sue Kaufman Prize for First Fiction by the American Academy of Arts and Letters. His *Dear Mr President* was selected as a *New York Times* New and Noteworthy paperback and one of *GQ*'s Ten Best Books of the Year.

'The Tears of Squonk, and What Happened Thereafter'
By Glen David Gold
Issue # 10
Copyright 2002
Glen David Gold is the author of *Carter Beats the Devil*.

'No Justice, No Foul'
By Jim Stallard
Issue # 2
Copyright 1999
Jim Stallard is a frequent contributor to McSweeney's Internet Tendency.

'Flush'
By Judy Budnitz
Issue # 5
Copyright 2000

Judy Budnitz is the author of *If I Told You Once*, *Flying Leap*, and *Nice Big American Baby*. She is the recipient of an O. Henry Award; and her work has appeared in *The New Yorker*, *Harper's*, *Story*, *The Paris Review*, and *The Oxford American*.

'Saint Chola'
By K. Kvashay-Boyle
Issue # 9
Copyright 2002
K. Kvashay-Boyle's work has been included in *Best American Nonrequired Reading* 2003. She is a graduate of the Writers' Workshop at the University of Iowa.

'God Lives in St Petersburg'
By Tom Bissell
Issue # 11
Copyright 2003
Tom Bissell is the author of *God Lives in St Petersburg*, a story collection; *Chasing the Sea*, a travelogue; and *Speak, Commentary*, a book of DVD commentaries. He has written for *The Believer*, *Esquire*, *GQ*, *Granta*, and *Harper's*.

'The Woman Who Sold Communion'
By Kate Braverman
Issue # 14
Copyright 2004
Kate Braverman is the author of *Lithium for Medea*, a novel, as well as several collections of stories.

'Red Ant House'
By Ann Cummins

Issue # 7

Copyright 2002

Ann Cummins's stories have been published in *The New Yorker*, *Quarterly West*, and the *Best American Short Stories* collection. 'Red Ant House' is the title story of her collection, published in 2003.

'The Nista Affair'

By Jonathan Ames

Issue # 8

Copyright 2002

Jonathan Ames's books include *I Pass Like Night*, *The Extra Man*, *What's Not to Love?*, *My Less Than Secret Life*, and *Wake Up, Sir!*

'K is for Fake'

By Jonathan Lethem

Issue # 4

Copyright 2000

Jonathan Lethem is the author of *The Fortress of Solitude* and *Motherless Brooklyn*, winner of the National Book Critics Circle Award.

'Banvard's Folly'

By Paul Collins

Issue # 3

Copyright 1999

Paul Collins is the founder and editor of *The Collins Library*, a series of reprints of unusual forgotten classics. He is the author of *Sixpence House*, *Banvard's Folly: Thirteen Tales of People Who Didn't Change the World*, and *Not Even Wrong: Adventures in Autism*.

Penguin and Timothy McSweeney's
are pleased to bring you our favourite works of
literary excellence and adventure

The Best of McSweeney's Volume 1

Edited by Dave Eggers

Writing from the head and the heart and shooting from the hip. Our first-ever best-ever includes David Foster Wallace, Zadie Smith, Rick Moody, Jim Shepard, Arthur Bradford and many more.

£7.99   0141014407

The Best of McSweeney's Volume 2

Edited by Dave Eggers

Featuring some of the best writing to be published anywhere and including the work of Glen David Gold, Judy Budnitz, Ann Cummins, Jonathan Ames, Jonathan Lethem, A. M. Homes and others.

£7.99   0141014989

McSweeney's 13, The Comics Issue

Edited by Chris Ware

The spectacular, beautiful, delicious, nobody-had-a-bad-word-to-say-about-it work of graphic brilliance.

£20   0241142695

McSweeney's Mammoth Treasury of Thrilling Tales

Edited by Michael Chabon

Ghost stories, detective stories, horror stories, fantasy and science-fiction stories by such celebrated writers as Nick Hornby, Neil Gaiman, Michael Moorcock, Elmore Leonard and many more.

£8.99   0141014040

Penguin and Timothy McSweeney's – Anglo-American friends bringing literature to the masses